Designing Enterprise Applications

with the Java™ 2 Platform, Enterprise Edition

The Java™ Series

Lisa Friendly, Series Editor
Tim Lindholm, Technical Editor
Ken Arnold, Technical Editor of The Jini™ Technology Series
Jim Inscore, Technical Editor of The Java™ Series, Enterprise Edition

---

Ken Arnold, James Gosling, David Holmes
The Java™ Programming Language, Third Edition

Greg Bollella, James Gosling, Ben Brosgol, Peter Dibble,
Steve Furr, David Hardin, Mark Turnbull
The Real-Time Specification for Java™

Mary Campione, Kathy Walrath, Alison Huml
The Java™ Tutorial, Third Edition:
A Short Course on the Basics

Mary Campione, Kathy Walrath, Alison Huml,
Tutorial Team
The Java™ Tutorial Continued: The Rest of the JDK™

Patrick Chan
The Java™ Developers Almanac 2000

Patrick Chan, Rosanna Lee
The Java™ Class Libraries, Second Edition, Volume 2:
java.applet, java.awt, java.beans

Patrick Chan, Rosanna Lee
The Java™ Class Libraries Poster, Fifth Edition: Covering
the Java™ 2 Platform, Standard Edition, v1.3

Patrick Chan, Rosanna Lee, Douglas Kramer
The Java™ Class Libraries, Second Edition, Volume 1:
java.io, java.lang, java.math, java.net, java.text, java.util

Patrick Chan, Rosanna Lee, Douglas Kramer
The Java™ Class Libraries, Second Edition, Volume 1:
Supplement for the Java™ 2 Platform,
Standard Edition, v1.2

Zhiqun Chen
Java Card™ Technology for Smart Cards:
Architecture and Programmer's Guide

Li Gong
Inside Java™ 2 Platform Security:
Architecture, API Design, and Implementation

James Gosling, Bill Joy, Guy Steele, Gilad Bracha
The Java™ Language Specification, Second Edition

Jonni Kanerva
The Java™ FAQ

Doug Lea
Concurrent Programming in Java™, Second Edition:
Design Principles and Patterns

Rosanna Lee, Scott Seligman
JNDI API Tutorial and Reference:
Building Directory-Enabled Java™ Applications

Sheng Liang
The Java™ Native Interface:
Programmer's Guide and Specification

Tim Lindholm, Frank Yellin
The Java™ Virtual Machine Specification, Second Edition

Henry Sowizral, Kevin Rushforth, Michael Deering
The Java 3D™ API Specification, Second Edition

Kathy Walrath, Mary Campione
The JFC Swing Tutorial: A Guide to Constructing GUIs

Seth White, Maydene Fisher, Rick Cattell,
Graham Hamilton, Mark Hapner
JDBC™ API Tutorial and Reference, Second Edition:
Universal Data Access for the Java™ 2 Platform

Steve Wilson, Jeff Kesselman
Java™ Platform Performance: Strategies and Tactics

The Jini™ Technology Series

Ken Arnold, Bryan O'Sullivan, Robert W. Scheifler,
Jim Waldo, Ann Wollrath
The Jini™ Specification

Eric Freeman, Susanne Hupfer, Ken Arnold
JavaSpaces™ Principles, Patterns, and Practice

The Java™ Series, Enterprise Edition

Patrick Chan, Rosanna Lee
The Java™ Class Libraries Poster, Enterprise Edition,
version 1.2

Nicholas Kassem, Enterprise Team
Designing Enterprise Applications with the Java™ 2
Platform, Enterprise Edition

Bill Shannon, Mark Hapner, Vlada Matena, James
Davidson, Eduardo Pelegri-Llopart, Larry Cable,
Enterprise Team
Java™ 2 Platform, Enterprise Edition:
Platform and Component Specifications

http://www.javaseries.com

Designing Enterprise Applications

with the Java™ 2 Platform, Enterprise Edition

Nicholas Kassem and the Enterprise Team

ADDISON-WESLEY

Boston • San Francisco • New York • Toronto • Montreal
London • Munich • Paris • Madrid
Capetown • Sydney • Tokyo • Singapore • Mexico City

Library of Congress Cataloging-in-Publication Data is available.

The publisher offers discounts on this book when ordered in quantity for special sales. For more information, please contact:

> Pearson Education Corporate Sales Division
> One Lake Street
> Upper Saddle River, NJ 07458
> (800) 382-3419
> corpsales@pearsontechgroup.com

Visit Addison-Wesley on the Web at www.awl.com/cseng/

Text printed on recycled and acid-free paper.
ISBN 0201702770
3 4 5 6 7 8   MA   03 02 01 00
3rd Printing   October 2000

Contents

Foreword

THE Java™ platform was conceived to connect door knobs to light switches—smart door knobs to smart light switches, certainly, but door knobs to light switches nonetheless. And yet it is now widely used for building large server-side applications which run on some of the largest computers in the world. It is the fate of great inventions to be used in ways unimagined by their creators even when the creators—like James Gosling, creator of the Java programming language—see a horizon the rest of us do not glimpse. This is part of what makes an invention great.

In retrospect, the phenomenal success of the Java platform on servers might seem inevitable. After all, the platform provides exactly what is needed to transform the Internet from a publishing medium to a transactional one. The Java platform is available on all of the many different servers where Internet applications run. "Write Once, Run Anywhere™" works so the programs can be quickly tested and deployed. Engineers are several times more productive when they write to the Java platform. But being the right thing at the right time isn't the whole story. Two more elements were needed: Technical leaders who were looking in a different direction than most of us were, and business leaders who were eager to work together in new ways so the ideas could become reality. The result was the development of consistent products across the computer industry in a surprisingly short period of time.

I joined the JavaSoft Division of Sun Microsystems in late 1995, recruited by Eric Schmidt and Bill Joy, to lead the then tiny band of engineers and marketers. We grew as fast as we could, barely keeping up with the early success of the Java platform and the industry alliances we'd made around it. Even then, when the focus was on applets running in browsers, when version 1.0 had not yet shipped, there were two brilliant engineers with a different idea—Rick Cattell and Graham Hamilton. They were thinking about the Java runtime environment on servers, and even mainframes. Because of them, the now ubiquitous JDBC™ technology was the first significant addition to the Java platform. Many excellent engineers have followed Rick and Graham. But they started it. I'm pleased that I was clever enough to listen to them as we expanded the group and the vision for the platform.

Until recently, "rocket scientists" have been needed to build the applications the industry clamored for—applications that create new ways to do business over the Internet while drawing on the resources already in place, such as databases, transaction systems, inventory systems, invoicing systems, and credit systems. These applications need to scale to thousands, even millions, of users. They must interact with a wide array of legacy technologies that can't be replaced, and they have to be built in a hurry. The engineers who can build them are few—the rocket scientists of our industry. But Rick and Graham saw a way to make the process a lot easier by building the rocket science into the Java platform, bringing portability and consistency through industry standardization, enabling quick adoption by adapting to the systems already in place, and making development much easier by automating most of the complicated details of server programming. These ideas became the underpinnings of the Java 2 Platform, Enterprise Edition.

JDBC was a huge hit. As soon as the Java community released it, drivers for all the important databases materialized in the market. Applications using JDBC rapidly appeared in large numbers. The success of JDBC lead to a parade of other middleware and database adapter projects—the Java Naming and Directory Interface™ API for uniform access to naming and directory services, the Java Message Service for asynchronous exchange of data and events, the Java Transaction API and Java Transaction Service for transactions, JavaServer Pages™ technology for building dynamic Web pages, Java XML for developing XML-oriented applications, and the Enterprise JavaBeans™ architecture, a component model for server applications. All of these were developed in collaboration with industry partners in a process created by Rick and Graham and later refined and formalized as the Java Community Process.

The seminal offering of JDBC in 1996 soon grew into an amazing array of facilities, each with its own acronym and release plan. For those who didn't live with the various "J*'s" (and for some of us who did) it could be confusing. When vendors announced support for Enterprise JavaBeans™ 1.0 before the specification had been completed, we realized it was time to make this now very successful portfolio a little easier to understand and manage.

The Java 2 Platform, Enterprise Edition (J2EE™ platform) brings all of these pieces together. The J2EE platform is defined by four key pieces: the specification, the reference implementation, the compatibility test suite, and the J2EE Blueprints design guidelines. The specification defines how the J2EE platform works, whether it is included in an application server, a database, or anywhere else. The reference implementation is useful for experimenting with the J2EE platform and it offers a working standard for comparison. The compatibility test suite ensures that J2EE vendors implement fully compliant versions of the platform to ensure "Write Once, Run Anywhere" portability, and these design guidelines show developers how the pieces fit together to make up complete applications. The key J2EE specifications are published in *Java 2 Platform, Enterprise Edition : Platform and Components Specifications* (also from Addison-Wesley), while supplemental specifications are available at `http://java.sun.com/j2ee`. The reference implementation used to create the examples in this book is available on the Sun Microsystems Java Software Web site at `http://java.sun.com/j2ee/download.html`.

Many people contributed to the Java 2 Platform, Enterprise Edition. Mala Chandra joined the group to lead the server efforts and quickly became the chief crusader. Her passion and determination carried the project around, over, or through many obstacles. Jeff Jackson, Connie Weiss, Karen Tegan, and Tom Kincaid provided exceptional engineering management. Technical leadership came from many, including Mark Hapner, Vlada Matena, Bill Shannon, Shel Finkelstein, Eduardo Pelegri-Llopart, Larry Cable, and Nick Kassem. Bill Roth, Gina Centoni, George Paolini, and Kathy Knutsen kept the Sun crew connected to the industry.

A staggering list of companies helped build this new server platform—a "Who's Who" of the industry; big, small, old and new. BEA Systems, IBM, Oracle and Sun Microsystems stand out as the companies who worked on nearly every piece, but they were never alone. Many companies sent their most senior architects and engineers and their most experienced managers to quickly build a common platform that set a new standard for ease of development, scalability, and applicability. They put these new Java platform technologies in their products, both old and new. The most widely deployed databases and the newest development tools from Silicon Valley startups now share the same interfaces. We are all the beneficiaries of their foresight and commitment.

In many ways, this book represents the culmination of these collective efforts. *Designing Enterprise Applications with the Java 2 Platform, Enterprise Edition* effectively demonstrates how this new platform simplifies and streamlines the design, development, and deployment of a new generation of enterprise applications.

Jon Kannegaard
Vice President and Deputy Director
Sun Microsystems Laboratories
Mountain View, California
March 20, 2000

Preface

THIS book describes a standard approach to designing multitier enterprise applications with the Java™ 2 Platform, Enterprise Edition. The book does not contain information on how to use individual J2EE™ technologies to develop applications, but rather focuses on guidelines for distributing application functionality across tiers and choosing among design options within each tier.

The book describes the principles and technologies employed in building J2EE applications and the specific approach adopted by a sample application. Striking a balance between specificity on the one hand, and articulating broader principles on the other, is never easy. The hope is that the principles presented are both consistent with and complement the sample application documented in the book.

This book is most relevant to IT managers, system architects, and enterprise application developers considering a transition to or intending to use the J2EE platform or vendors providing J2EE products.

How This Book Is Organized

This book contains the following chapters:

- **Chapter 1, "Introduction,"** discusses challenges in building enterprise applications and describes how the J2EE platform addresses those challenges. The chapter also discusses application scenarios that the J2EE platform supports.

- **Chapter 2, "J2EE Platform Technologies,"** provides an overview of the component, service, and communication technologies supported by the J2EE platform.

- **Chapter 3, "The Client Tier,"** presents implementation options for J2EE clients and provides guidelines for choosing among these options.

- **Chapter 4, "The Web Tier,"** describes technologies available for supporting development in the Web tier. It includes guidelines and techniques for using J2EE Web components and describes several Web application architectures.

- **Chapter 5, "The Enterprise JavaBeans Tier,"** describes the capabilities of the EJB tier of the J2EE platform and discusses design choices for implementing business logic.

- **Chapter 6, "The Enterprise Information System Tier,"** describes recommended approaches for accessing enterprise information systems and how J2EE components must be configured to access them.

- **Chapter 7, "Packaging and Deployment,"** describes the capabilities provided by the J2EE platform for packaging and deploying J2EE applications, provides heuristics and practical tips on how to use these capabilities, and provides recommendations to the vendors who provide deployment tools.

- **Chapter 8, "Transaction Management,"** describes the transaction services provided by the J2EE platform and provides recommendations on how to best use those services.

- **Chapter 9, "Security,"** describes the mapping of the J2EE security model to enterprise computing environments and infrastructures.

- **Chapter 10, "The Sample Application,"** illustrates the J2EE programming model in the context of an in-depth description of a multitier J2EE application.

- **"Glossary,"** is a list of words and phrases found in this book and their definitions.

Obtaining the Sample Application

You can download the sample application described in this book from:

```
http://java.sun.com/j2ee/download.html
```

The sample application requires a J2EE v1.2 compliant platform on which to run. From the sample application download page you can also download Sun's J2EE SDK, a freely available implementation of the J2EE v1.2 platform.

Related Information

Pointers to J2EE documentation can be found at:

```
http://java.sun.com/j2ee/docs.html
```

For information on how to use the J2EE SDK to construct multitier enterprise applications refer to the *J2EE Developer's Guide*, available at:

`http://java.sun.com/j2ee/j2sdkee/techdocs/index.html`

The J2EE technologies cited in this book are described in their specifications:

- *Java™ 2 Platform, Enterprise Edition Specification, Version 1.2* (J2EE specification). Copyright 1999, Sun Microsystems, Inc. Available at `http://java.sun.com/j2ee/download.html`.

- *Java™ 2 Platform, Standard Edition, Version 1.2.2* (J2SE specification). Copyright 1993-99, Sun Microsystems, Inc. Available at `http://java.sun.com/products/jdk/1.2/docs/api/index.html`.

- *Java™ Servlet Specification, Version 2.2* (Servlet specification). Copyright 1998, 1999, Sun Microsystems, Inc. Available at `http://java.sun.com/products/servlet`.

- *JavaServer Pages™ Specification, Version 1.1* (JSP specification). Copyright 1998, 1999, Sun Microsystems, Inc. Available at `http://java.sun.com/products/jsp`.

- *Enterprise JavaBeans™ Specification, Version 1.1* (EJB specification). Copyright 1998, 1999, Sun Microsystems, Inc. Available at `http://java.sun.com/products/ejb`.

- *JDBC™ 2.0 API* (JDBC specification). Copyright 1998, 1999, Sun Microsystems, Inc. Available at `http://java.sun.com/products/jdbc`.

- *JDBC™ 2.0 Standard Extension API* (JDBC extension specification). Copyright 1998, 1999, Sun Microsystems, Inc. Available at `http://java.sun.com/products/jdbc`.

- *Java™ Transaction API, Version 1.0.1* (JTA specification). Copyright 1998, 1999, Sun Microsystems, Inc. Available at `http://java.sun.com/products/jta`.

- *Java™ Transaction Service, Version 0.95* (JTS specification). Copyright 1997-1999, Sun Microsystems, Inc. Available at `http://java.sun.com/products/jts`.

- *Java Naming and Directory Interface™, Version 1.2* (JNDI specification).

Copyright 1998, 1999, Sun Microsystems, Inc. Available at `http://java.sun.com/products/jndi`.

- *Java IDL.* Copyright 1993-99, Sun Microsystems, Inc. Available at `http://java.sun.com/products/jdk/1.2/docs/guide/idl/index.html`.

- *RMI over IIOP 1.0.1.* Available at `http://java.sun.com/products/rmi-iiop`.

- *Java™ Message Service, Version 1.0.2* (JMS specification). Copyright 1998, Sun Microsystems, Inc. Available at `http://java.sun.com/products/jms`.

- *JavaMail™ API Design Specification, Version 1.1* (JavaMail specification). Copyright 1998, Sun Microsystems, Inc. Available at `http://java.sun.com/products/javamail`.

- *JavaBeans™ Activation Framework Specification, Version 1.0.1* (JAF specification). Copyright 1998, Sun Microsystems, Inc. Available at `http://java.sun.com/beans/glasgow/jaf.html`.

Typographic Conventions

Table 1 describes the typographic conventions used in this book.

Table 1   Typographic Conventions

Typeface or Symbol	Meaning	Example
AaBbCc123	The names of commands, files, and directories; interface, class, method, and deployment descriptor element names; programming language keywords	Edit the file `Main.jsp`. How to retrieve a `UserTransaction` object. Specify the `resource-ref` element.
AaBbCc123	Variable name	The files are named *XYZ*`file`.
AaBbCc123	Book titles, new words or terms, or words to be emphasized	Read Chapter 6 in *User's Guide*. These are called *class* options. You *must* be root to do this.

Acknowledgments

This book is the result of many people's efforts.

Each Enterprise Team member had primary responsibility for one chapter and made significant contributions to other chapters. In addition, Danny Coward wrote the initial draft of the deployment chapter.

The authors of the J2EE specifications and the developers of the reference implementation provided useful input at various points during the development of the J2EE programming model.

We are indebted to Rick Cattell, Bill Shannon, Mark Hapner, John Crupi, Sean Brydon, and many other reviewers who provided feedback on early versions of the manuscript.

Jim Inscore and Stephanie Bodoff provided editorial oversight of this project.

About the Author

NICHOLAS KASSEM is a Senior Staff Engineer with Sun Microsystems and has influenced and had responsibility for a number of technologies and initiatives within Java Software including the Java Web Server, Java Embedded Server, the Servlet API, JavaServer Pages, Java Message Queuing, and the J2EE programming model. He is currently leading the XML Messaging initiative.

Nicholas has over twenty years industry experience and has held senior engineering and management positions at Philips (Data Systems) and the Santa Cruz Operation. He has had direct responsibility for a wide variety of engineering projects including the development of Data Communications Gateway Hardware (DISOSS), Novell and Lan Manager protocol stacks, and an implementation of OSF DCE on SCO UNIX. He is an Engineering Graduate of Birmingham University in the UK.

CHAPTER 1

Introduction

by Nicholas Kassem

THE Internet and World Wide Web represent a foundation on which enterprises are working to build an information economy. In this economy, information takes on as much value as goods and services, and becomes a vital part of the market. The information economy challenges today's enterprises to radically re-think the way they do business.

Predictions about the future of this economy range from glowing scenarios of dynamic new business, industrial, and financial environments capable of unlimited expansion, to gloom and doom prophecies of overinflated expectations and unsustainable hypergrowth. Whatever the predictions, the reality is that enterprises have always tried to gain a competitive advantage by any reasonable means at their disposal, including the latest technologies. This is a natural survival instinct: all viable enterprises, including for-profit, non-profit, and government institutions, continuously look for ways to keep pace by adopting such changes. Complacent organizations routinely fall by the wayside, while the innovators work to transform new challenges into business success.

In the information economy, information assets take on far-reaching strategic value to an organization. The ability to capitalize on this value is key to success. Organizations that succeed will do so by increasing their productivity in moving information into the marketplace.

While these may appear to be new challenges, in many ways the Internet and World Wide Web only intensify a challenge that has long faced information technology professionals: the demand for responsive management of information assets. The initial response to this demand was to ensure that all critical business functions were effectively managed by computerized systems. More recently, the response has been to strive for greater integration among these systems, and increased ability to correlate data from disparate sources into information that serves specific strategic needs. Corporate mergers, acquisitions, and partnerships have provided additional incentive for organizations to integrate such information.

Distributed custom applications are the packages in which an organization delivers information as a commodity. Custom applications add value to and extract value from the information assets of an organization. They allow IT organizations to target specific functionality to specific user needs. By making information available within an organization, they add strategic value to the management and planning processes. By selectively projecting information assets outside the organization, they enable exchanges that are mutually valuable to customers, suppliers, and the organization itself.

In the competitive environment of the information economy, response time is key to the value of custom applications to the enterprise. Organizations need to quickly develop and deploy custom applications, and to easily refine and enhance them to improve their value. They need ways to simply and efficiently integrate these applications with existing enterprise information systems, and to scale them effortlessly to meet changing demands. All these factors affect an organization's ability to respond quickly to changes in the competitive environment.

The goal of the Java™ 2 Platform, Enterprise Edition (J2EE™ platform) is to define a standard of functionality that helps meet these challenges and thus increases the competitiveness of enterprises in the information economy. The J2EE platform supports distributed applications that take advantage of a wide range of new and evolving technologies, while simplifying development through a component-based application model. The J2EE model supports applications ranging from traditional client-server applications delivered over corporate intranets to e-commerce Web sites on the Internet.

In presenting the J2EE™ Blueprints programming model, this book hopes to provide enterprise application developers with a strategic perspective on the challenges of the information economy, and a methodical exploration of ways the J2EE platform supports custom applications to meet a reasonably broad range of application requirements. The underlying theme of this discussion is that the J2EE platform provides a single, unified standard that enhances the opportunity for enterprises to project their business information systems beyond their historical borders, while avoiding risks inherent in the task.

This book approaches the J2EE Blueprints programming model by taking a logical view of enterprise platforms and suggesting ways to partition application functionality to use the technologies provided by the J2EE platform most effectively. The intent is to divide the problem of architecting and developing multitier applications with J2EE into manageable portions, then apply appropriate technologies to the portions, leading to more maintainable and scalable solutions. In the process, certain simplifying assumptions are made, not to trivialize certain factors, but to focus on the essential J2EE theme. Note that none of the statements in this book should be interpreted as mandates or requirements, but rather as advice, suggestions, and simple recommendations.

1.1   Challenges of Enterprise Application Development

While timing has always been a critical factor to adopting new technologies, the accelerated pace inherent in a virtual, information-driven business model has put even greater emphasis on response times. To leverage Internet economics, it's imperative not only to project enterprise systems into various client channels, but to do so repeatedly and in a timely manner, with frequent updates to both information and services. The principal challenge is therefore one of keeping up with the Internet's hyper-competitive pace while maintaining and leveraging the value of existing business systems. In this environment, timeliness is absolutely critical in gaining and maintaining a competitive edge. A number of factors can enhance or impede an organization's ability to deliver custom enterprise applications quickly, and to maximize their value over their lifetime.

1.1.1   Programming Productivity

The ability to develop and deploy applications is key to success in the information economy. Applications need to go quickly from prototype to production, and to continue evolving even after they are deployed.

Productivity is thus vital to responsive application development. Providing application development teams with standard means to access the services required by multitier applications, and standard ways to support a variety of clients, can contribute to both responsiveness and flexibility.

One destabilizing factor in Internet and other distributed computing applications is the current divergence of technologies and programming models. Historically (in Web terms), technologies such as HTML and CGI have provided a mechanism for distributing dynamic content, while backend systems such as transaction processors and database management systems have provided controlled access to the data to be presented and manipulated. These technologies present a diversity of programming models, some based on well-defined standards, others on more ad-hoc standards, and others still on proprietary architectures.

With no single application model, it can be difficult for teams to communicate application requirements effectively and productively. As a result, the process of architecting applications becomes more complex. What's more, the skill sets required to integrate these technologies aren't well organized for effective division of labor. For example, CGI development requires coders to define both content and layout to appear on a dynamic Web page.

Another complicating factor in application development time is the choice of clients. While many applications can be distributed to Web browser clients through static or dynamically generated HTML, others may need to support a specific type of client, or to support several types of clients simultaneously. The programming model needs to support a variety of client configurations, with minimum effect on basic application architecture or the core business logic of the application.

1.1.2   Response to Demand

Imagine a brick-and-mortar business trying to increase its customer base by a scale of 10. How much time and effort would they expend on remodelling storefronts, building new warehouses, and so on, to keep up? The fact is, the constant rework would drastically impact their ability to serve the customers they're trying to attract.

This holds for businesses in the information economy as well. The ability for applications to scale easily and automatically to accommodate anticipated—or unexpected—growth is key to achieving the goals. Systems that require any restructuring or redeployment to scale will impede growth and diminish the company's expected performance.

In order to scale effectively, systems need to be designed to handle multiple client interactions with ease. They need mechanisms for efficient management of system resources and services such as database connections and transactions. They need to have access to features such as automatic load balancing without any effort on the part of the application developer. Applications should be able to run on any server appropriate to anticipated client volumes, and to easily switch server configurations when the need arises.

1.1.3   Integration with Existing Systems

Much of the data of value to organizations has been collected over the years by existing information systems. Much of the programming investment resides in applications on those same systems. The challenge for developers of enterprise applications is how to reuse and commoditize this value.

To achieve this goal, application developers needs standard ways to access middle-tier and backend services such as database management systems and transaction monitors. They also need systems that provide these services consistently, so that new programming models or styles aren't required as integration expands to encompass various systems within an enterprise.

1.1.4   Freedom to Choose

Application development responsiveness requires the ability to mix and match solutions to come up with the optimum configuration for the task at hand. Freedom of choice in enterprise application development should extend from servers to tools to components.

Choices among server products gives an organization the ability to select configurations tailored to their application requirements. It also provides the ability to move quickly and easily from one configuration to another as internal and external demand requires.

Access to the appropriate tools for the job is another important choice. Development teams should be able to adopt new tools as new needs arise, including tools from server vendors and third-party tool developers. What's more, each member of a development team should have access to tools most appropriate to their skill set and contribution.

Finally, developers should be able to choose from a ready market of off-the-shelf application components to take advantage of external expertise and to enhance development productivity.

1.1.5   Maintaining Security

Somewhat ironically, projecting information assets to extract their value can jeopardize that very value. Traditionally, IT departments have been able to maintain a relatively high level of control over the environment of both servers and clients. When information assets are projected into less-protected environments, it becomes increasingly important to maintain tight security over the most sensitive assets, while allowing seemingly unencumbered access to others.

One of the difficulties in integrating disparate systems is providing a unified security model. Single signon across internal application and asset boundaries is important to creating a positive user experience with the applications. Security needs to be compatible with existing mechanisms. In cases where customers need to access secure information, the mechanisms need to maintain high security (and user confidence) while remaining as unobtrusive and transparent as possible.

1.2   The Platform for Enterprise Solutions

The J2EE platform represents a single standard for implementing and deploying enterprise applications. The J2EE platform has been designed through an open process, engaging a range of enterprise computing vendors, to ensure that it meets the widest possible range of enterprise application requirements. As a result, the J2EE platform addresses the core issues that impede organizations' efforts to maintain a competitive pace in the information economy.

1.2.1   J2EE Platform Overview

The J2EE platform is designed to provide server-side and client-side support for developing enterprise, multitier applications. Such applications are typically configured as a client tier to provide the user interface, one or more middle-tier modules that provide client services and business logic for an application, and backend enterprise information systems providing data management. Figure 1.1 illustrates the various components and services that make up a typical J2EE environment.

1.2.1.1 Multitier Model

As illustrated, the J2EE platform provides a multitier distributed application model. This means that the various parts of an application can run on different devices. The J2EE architecture defines a *client tier*, a *middle tier* (consisting of one or more subtiers), and a backend tier providing services of existing information systems. The client tier supports a variety of client types, both outside and inside of corporate firewalls. The middle tier supports client services through Web containers in the *Web tier* and supports business logic component services through Enterprise JavaBeans™ (EJB™) containers in the *EJB tier*. The *enterprise information system (EIS) tier* supports access to existing information systems by means of standard APIs.

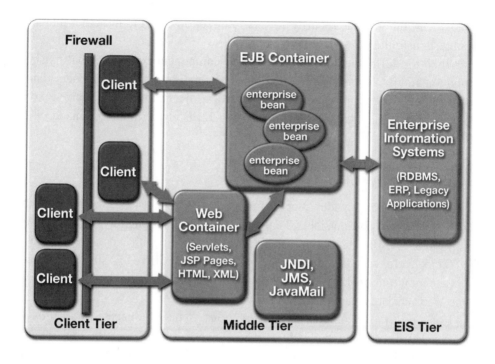

Figure 1.1   J2EE Environment

1.2.1.2 Container-Based Component Management

Central to the J2EE component-based development model is the notion of containers. Containers are standardized runtime environments that provide specific component services. Components can expect these services to be available on any J2EE platform from any vendor. For example, all J2EE Web containers provide runtime support for responding to client requests, performing request time processing (such as invoking JSP or servlet behavior), and returning results to the client. All EJB containers provide automated support for transaction and life cycle management of EJB components, as well as bean lookup and other services. Containers also provide standardized access to enterprise information systems; for example, providing RDBMS access through the JDBC API.

In addition, containers provide a mechanism for selecting application behaviors at assembly or deployment time. Through the use of deployment descriptors (text files that specify component behavior in terms of well-defined XML tags), components can be configured to a specific container's environment when deployed, rather than in component code. Features that can be configured at deployment time include security checks, transaction control, and other management responsibilities.

While the J2EE specification defines the component containers that must be supported, it doesn't specify or restrict the configuration of these containers. Thus, both container types can run on a single platform, Web containers can live on one platform and EJB containers on another, or a J2EE platform can be made up of multiple containers on multiple platforms.

1.2.1.3 Support for Client Components

The J2EE client tier provides support for a variety of client types, both within the enterprise firewall and outside. Clients can be offered through Web browsers by using plain HTML pages, dynamic HTML generated with JavaServer Pages™ (JSP™) technology, or Java applets. Clients can also be offered as stand-alone Java language applications. J2EE clients are assumed to access the middle tier primarily using Web standards, namely HTTP, HTML, and XML.

To support more complex user interactions, it may be necessary to provide functionality directly in the client tier. This functionality is typically implemented as JavaBeans™ components that interact with the service in the middle tier via servlets. Client-tier JavaBeans components would typically be provided by the service as an applet that is downloaded automatically into a user's browser. To eliminate problems caused by old or non-standard versions of the Java virtual machine in a user's browser, the J2EE application model provides special support for automatically downloading and installing the Java Plug-in.

Client-tier beans can also be contained in a stand-alone application client written in the Java programming language. In this case, the enterprise would typically make operating system specific installation programs for the client available for users to download via their browsers. Users execute the installation file and are then ready to access the service. Since Java technology programs are portable across all environments, the service need only maintain a single version of the client program. Although the client program itself is portable, installation of the Java technology client typically requires OS-specific code. There are several commercial tools that automate the generation of these OS-specific installation programs.

If desired, non-Java clients such as Visual Basic programs can present J2EE services to users. Since the service is presented by servlets in the middle tier to first-tier clients using the standard HTTP protocol, it is easy to access it from practically any program running on any operating system.

1.2.1.4 Support for Business Logic Components

In the J2EE platform, middle-tier business logic is implemented in the middle tier as Enterprise JavaBeans components (also referred to as enterprise beans). Enterprise beans allow the component or application developer to concentrate on the business logic while the complexities of delivering a reliable, scalable service are handled by the EJB server.

The J2EE platform and EJB architecture have complementary goals. The EJB component model is the backbone of the J2EE programming model. The J2EE platform complements the EJB specification by:

- Fully specifying the APIs that an enterprise bean developer can use to implement enterprise beans.

- Defining the larger, distributed programming environment in which enterprise beans are used as business logic components.

1.2.1.5 Support for the J2EE Standard

The J2EE standard is defined through a set of related specifications, key among these the J2EE specification, the EJB specification, the Servlet specification, and the JSP specification. Together, these specifications define the architecture described in this discussion. In addition to the specifications, several other offerings are available to support the J2EE standard, including the J2EE Compatibility Test Suite and the J2EE SDK.

The J2EE Compatibility Test Suite (CTS) helps maximize the portability of applications by validating the specification compliance of a J2EE platform product. This test suite begins where the basic Java Conformance Kit (JCK) leaves off. The CTS tests conformance to the Java standard extension API's not covered by the JCK. In addition, it tests a J2EE platform's ability to run standard end-to-end applications.

The J2EE SDK is intended to achieve several goals. First, it provides an operational definition of the J2EE platform, used by vendors as the "gold standard" to determine what their product must do under a particular set of application circumstances. It can be used by developers to verify the portability of an application. And it is used as the standard platform for running the J2EE Compatibility Test Suite.

Another important role for the J2EE SDK is to provide the developer community with a freely available implementation of the J2EE platform to help expedite adoption of the J2EE standard. Although it is not a commercial product and its licensing terms prohibit its commercial use, the J2EE SDK is freely available in binary form to use in developing application demos and prototypes. The J2EE SDK is also available in source form.

One more word on J2EE standards and portability. The J2EE specifications have, by design, set the platform-compatibility-bar at a level that's relatively easy to clear. Owing to the collaborative way in which the platform specifications have been developed, it was deemed important to give platform vendors plenty of opportunity to supply implementations of the J2EE platform. Obvious and unreasonable implementation hurdles were avoided. For example, there are no restrictions on vendors adding value to J2EE products by supporting services not defined in the specifications.

It should therefore not be surprising that J2EE component portability is primarily a function of the dependency a component has on the underlying container. Components using a vendor-specific feature, that falls outside of the J2EE requirements, may have limitations in the area of portability. The J2EE specifications do however spell out a base set of capabilities that a component can count on. Hence, there is a minimum cross-container portability that an application should be able to achieve. Needless to say, an application developer expecting to deploy on a specific vendor implementation of the J2EE platform, should be able to do so across a wide range of operating systems and hardware architectures.

1.2.2   J2EE Platform Benefits

With a set of features designed specifically to expedite the process of distributed application development, the J2EE platform offers several benefits:

- Simplified architecture and development

- Scalability to meet demand variations

- Integration with existing information systems

- Choices of servers, tools, components

- Flexible security model

1.2.2.1 Simplified Architecture and Development

The J2EE platform supports a simplified, component-based development model. Because it's based on the Java programming language and the Java 2 Platform, Standard Edition (J2SE™ platform), this model offers Write Once, Run Anywhere portability, supported by any server product that conforms to the J2EE standard.

The component-based J2EE development model can enhance application development productivity in a number of ways.

Maps easily to application functionality: Component-based application models map easily and flexibly to the functionality desired from an application. As the examples presented throughout this book illustrate, the J2EE platform provides a variety of ways to configure the architecture of an application, depending on such things as client types required, level of access required to data sources, and other considerations. Component-based design also simplifies application maintenance, since components can be updated and replaced independently—new functionality can be shimmed into existing applications simply by updating selected components.

Enables assembly- and deploy-time behaviors: Components can expect the availability of standard services in the runtime environment, and can be dynamically connected to other components providing well-defined interfaces. As a result, many application behaviors can be configured at the time of application assembly or deployment, without any recoding required. Component developers can communicate their requirements to application deployers through specific settings. Tools can automate this process to further expedite development.

Supports division of labor: Components help divide the labor of application development among specific skill sets, enabling each member of a development team to focus on his or her ability. Thus, JSP templates can be created by graphic designers, their behavior by Java programming language coders, business logic by domain experts, and application assembly and deployment by the appropriate team members. This division of labor also helps expedite application maintenance. For example, the user interface is the most dynamic part of many applications, particularly on the Web. With the J2EE platform, graphic designers can tweak the look and feel of JSP-based user interface components without the need for programmer intervention.

A number of generic roles are discussed in the J2EE specifications, including Application Component Provider, Application Assembler, and Application Deployer. On some development teams, one or two people may perform all these roles, while on others, these tasks may be further subdivided into more specific skill sets (such as user interface designers, programmers, and so on).

1.2.2.2 Scales Easily

J2EE containers provide a mechanism that supports simplified scaling of distributed applications, without requiring any effort on the part of the application development team.

Because J2EE containers provide components with transaction support, database connections, life cycle management, and other features that influence performance, they can be designed to provide scalability in these areas. For example, by providing database connection pooling, containers can ensure that clients will have access to data quickly.

Because the J2EE specifications allow server providers freedom to configure containers to run on multiple systems, Web containers can be implemented to perform automatic load balancing as the demand for a particular application fluctuates.

1.2.2.3 Integrating Existing Enterprise Information Systems

The J2EE platform, together with the J2SE platform, includes a number of industry standard APIs for access to existing enterprise information systems. Basic access to these systems is provided by the following APIs:

- JDBC™ is the API for accessing relational data from Java.

- The Java Transaction API (JTA) is the API for managing and coordinating transactions across heterogeneous enterprise information systems.

- The Java Naming and Directory Interface™ (JNDI) is the API for accessing information in enterprise name and directory services.

- The Java Message Service (JMS) is the API for sending and receiving messages via enterprise messaging systems like IBM MQ Series and TIBCO Rendezvous.

- JavaMail™ is the API for sending and receiving email.

- Java IDL is the API for calling CORBA services.

In addition, specialized access to enterprise resource planning and mainframe systems such as IBM's CICS and IMS will be provided in future versions of J2EE through the Connector architecture. Since each of these systems is highly complex and specialized, they each require unique tools and support to ensure utmost simplicity to application developers. As J2EE evolves, enterprise beans will be able to combine the use of connector access objects and service APIs with middle-tier business logic to accomplish their business functions.

1.2.2.4 Choice of Servers, Tools, and Components

The J2EE standard and J2EE brand are central to creating a marketplace for servers, tools, and components. The J2EE brand on a server product ensures the kind of ubiquity that's fundamental to the goals of the J2EE platform. In addition, J2EE standards ensure a lively marketplace for tools and components.

A range of server choices: Application development organizations can expect J2EE branded platforms from a variety of vendors, providing a range of choices in hardware platforms, operating systems, and server configurations. This ensures that businesses get a choice of servers appropriate to the strategic purpose of the applications they need.

Designed for tool support: Both EJB and JSP components are designed to be manipulated by graphical development tools, and to allow automating many of the application development tasks traditionally requiring the ability to write and debug code. Both J2EE server providers and third-party tool developers can develop tools that conform to J2EE standards and support various application development tasks and styles. Application developers get a choice of tools to manipulate and assemble components, and individual team members may choose tools that suit their specific requirements best.

A marketplace for components: Component-based design ensures that many types of behavior can be standardized, packaged, and reused by any J2EE application. Component vendors will provide a variety of off-the-shelf component solutions, including accounting beans, user interface templates, and even vertical market functionality of interest in specific industries. Application architects get a choice of standardized components to handle common or specialized tasks.

The J2EE standard and associated branding programming ensure that solutions are compatible. By setting the stage for freedom of choice, J2EE makes it possible to develop with confidence that the value of your investment will be protected.

1.2.2.5 Simplified, Unified Security Model

The J2EE security model is designed to support single signon access to application services. Component developers can specify the security requirements of a component at the method level, to ensure that only users with appropriate permissions can access specific data operations. While the EJB and Java Servlet APIs both provide mechanisms for building security checks into code, the basic mechanism for matching users with roles (groups of users having specific permissions) is performed entirely at application deployment time. This provides both greater flexibility and better security control.

1.3   J2EE Application Scenarios

The following sections present a number of application scenarios, setting the stage for a detailed discussion of the sample application. In reviewing the J2EE specifications, a large number of application scenarios could be considered. Indeed, the specifications tend to embrace and encourage diversity. The J2EE specifications and technologies, can by definition, make few assumptions about how precisely the APIs are going to be used to deliver application-level functionality. The application-level decisions and choices are ultimately a trade-off, between functional richness and complexity.

The J2EE programming model needs to embrace application scenarios that treat the Web container, and the EJB container as optional logical entities. Figure 1.2 reflects some key scenarios, including those where either the Web container or the EJB container, and potentially both, are bypassed.

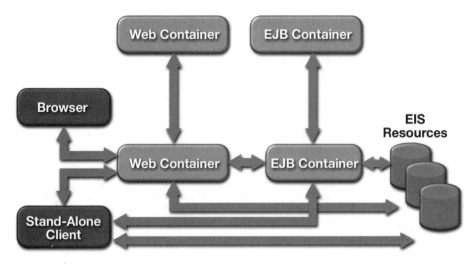

Figure 1.2   J2EE Application Scenarios

The sample application reflects a multitier application model. This decision assumes the presence of both a Web container and an EJB container. The following enterprise requirements heavily influenced the choices made:

- The need to make rapid and frequent changes to the "look" of the application.

- The need to partition the application along the lines of presentation and business logic so as to increase modularity.

- The need to simplify the process of assigning suitably trained human resources to accomplish the development task such that work can proceed along relatively independent but cooperating tracks.

- The need to have developers familiar with back-office applications unburdened from GUI and graphic design work, for which they may not be ideally qualified.

- The need to have the necessary vocabulary to communicate the business logic to teams concerned with human factors and the aesthetics of the application.

- The ability to assemble back-office applications using components from a variety of sources, including off-the-shelf business logic components.

- The ability to deploy transactional components across multiple hardware and software platforms independently of the underlying database technology.

- The ability to externalize internal data without having to make many assumptions about the consumer of the data and to accomplish this in a loosely coupled manner.

Clearly relaxing any or all of these requirements would influence some of the application-level decisions and choices that a designer would make. The J2EE programming model takes the approach that it is highly desirable to engineer a 3-tier application such that the migration to a future multitier architecture is simplified through component reusability. Although it is reasonable to speak of "throw-away" presentation logic (that is, applications with a look and feel that ages rapidly), there is still significant inertia associated with business logic. This is even more true in the case of database schemas and data in general. It is fair to say that as one moves further away from the EIS resources the volatility of the application code increases dramatically; that is, the application "shelf-life" drops significantly.

In summary, the J2EE programming model promotes a model that anticipates growth, encourages component-oriented code reusability, and leverages the strengths of inter-tier communication. It is the tier integration that lies at the heart of the J2EE programming model.

Figure 1.2 illustrates a number of application scenarios that a J2EE product should be capable of supporting. From a J2EE perspective, there is no implicit bias favoring one application scenario over another. However, a J2EE product should not preclude supporting any and all of these scenarios. It is worth considering the scenarios individually and elaborating on the technologies and protocols relevant to an application developer.

1.3.1   Multitier Application Scenario

Figure 1.3 illustrates an application scenario in which the Web container hosts Web components that are almost exclusively dedicated to handling a given application's presentation logic. The delivery of dynamic Web content to the client is the responsibility of JSP pages (supported by servlets). The EJB container hosts application components that, on the one hand, respond to requests from the Web tier, and on the other hand, access the EIS resources. The ability to decouple the accessing of data from issues surrounding end-user interactions is a strength of this particular scenario. For one, the application is implicitly scalable. But more importantly, the application back-office functionality is relatively isolated from the end-user look and feel.

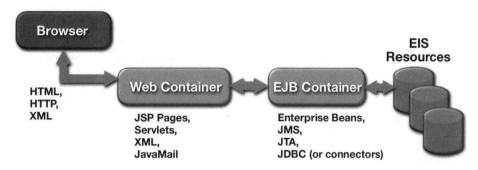

Figure 1.3   Multitier Application

It is worth noting that XML is included as an integral part of this scenario. The role of XML data messaging will be expanded on in subsequent chapters, but the ability to both produce and consume XML data messages in the Web container is viewed as an extremely flexible way of embracing a diverse set of client platforms. These platforms may range from general purpose XML-enabled browsers to specialized XML rendering engines targeting vertical solutions. Irrespective of the specific application area, it is assumed that XML data messages will utilize HTTP as their communication transport. The term XML data messaging is being used to denote a programming model where XML is being used to exchange information as opposed to promoting an object model orthogonal to the Java object model. The relationship of XML to Java is therefore viewed as highly complementary.

At the Web tier, the question of whether to use JSP pages or servlets comes up repeatedly. The J2EE programming model promotes JSP technology as the preferred programming facility within the Web container. JSP pages rely on the servlet functionality but the J2EE programming model takes the position that JSP pages are a more natural fit for Web engineers. The Web container is therefore optimized for the creation of dynamic content destined for Web clients and that use of JSP technology should be viewed as the norm while the use of servlets will most likely be the exception.

1.3.2   Stand-Alone Client Scenario

Figure 1.4 illustrates a stand-alone client scenario.

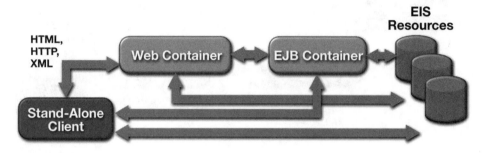

Figure 1.4   Stand-Alone Clients

From a J2EE programming model perspective, we need to consider three types of stand-alone clients:

- EJB clients interacting directly with an EJB server, that is enterprise beans hosted on an EJB container. Such a scenario is illustrated in Figure 1.5. It is assumed that RMI-IIOP will be used in this scenario and that the EJB server will access the EIS resources using JDBC (connectors in the future).

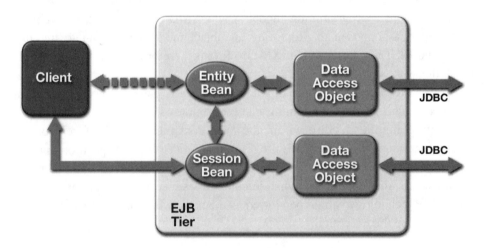

Figure 1.5   EJB-Centric Java Client

- Stand-alone Java application clients accessing enterprise information system resources directly using JDBC and potentially even connectors in the future. In this scenario, presentation and business logic are by definition co-located on the client platform and may in fact be tightly integrated into a single application. This scenario collapses the middle tier into the client platform, and is essentially a client-server application scenario with the associated application distribution, maintenance, and scalability issues.

- Visual Basic clients consuming dynamic Web content, most likely in the form of XML data messages. In this scenario, the Web container is essentially handling XML transformations and providing Web connectivity to clients. Presentation logic is assumed to be handled on the client tier. The Web tier can be designated to handle business logic and directly access the enterprise information system resources. Ideally, the business logic is pushed back onto the EJB server, where the rich component model can be fully leveraged.

1.3.3   Web-Centric Application Scenario

Figure 1.6 illustrates a 3-tier Web-centric application scenario.

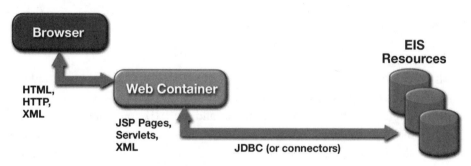

Figure 1.6   Web-Centric Application Scenario

There are numerous examples that one could concoct where an EJB server (at least initially) could be deemed to be an overkill given the problem being tackled. This is the sledge-hammer-to-crack-a-nut problem. In essence, the J2EE specification does not mandate a 2, 3, or multitier application model, nor realistically could it do so. The point is that it is important to use appropriate tools for a given problem space.

The 3-tier Web-centric application scenario is currently in widespread use. The Web container is essentially hosting both presentation and business logic, and it is assumed that JDBC (and connectors in the future) will be used to access the EIS resources.

Figure 1.7 provides a closer look at the Web container in a Web application scenario.

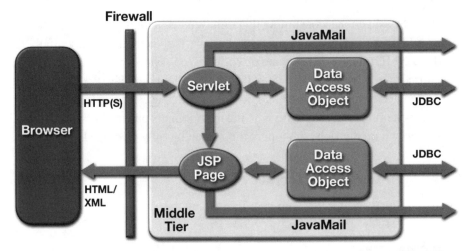

Figure 1.7   Web Container in a 3-Tier Scenario

It is important to keep in mind that the term Web container is being used here in a very precise way. For example, if a given J2EE product chooses to implement, a J2EE server, such that the Web container and the EJB container are co-located (this assumes that the inter-container communication is optimized in some fashion and that the implementation details are private), then the J2EE programming model treats the application deployed on such a platform as essentially a multitier scenario.

1.3.4   Business-to-Business Scenario

Figure 1.8 illustrates a business-to-business scenario.

This scenario focuses on peer-level interactions between both Web and EJB containers. The J2EE programming model promotes the use of XML data messaging over HTTP as the primary means of establishing loosely coupled communications between Web containers. This is a natural fit for the development and deployment of Web-based commerce solutions.

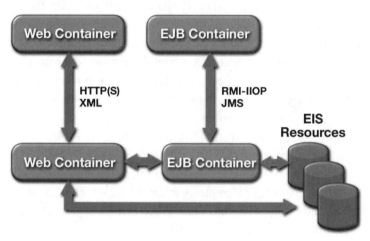

Figure 1.8 Business-to-Business Scenario

The peer-level communications between EJB containers is currently a more tightly coupled solution most suitable for intranet environments. With the imminent integration of JMS into the J2EE platform, the development of loosely-coupled intranet solutions will become increasingly practical.

1.3.5 A Note on the MVC Architecture

A brief aside here regarding the subsequent discussions of application scenarios. Throughout the remainder of this book, the Model-View-Controller (MVC) application architecture is used to analyze features of distributed applications. This abstraction helps in the process of breaking an application up into logical components that can be architected more easily. This section explores the general features of MVC.

The MVC architecture is a way to divide functionality among objects involved in maintaining and presenting data so as to minimize the degree of coupling between the objects. The MVC architecture was originally developed to map the traditional input, processing, and output tasks to the graphical user interaction model. However, it is straightforward to map these concepts into the domain of multitier Web-based enterprise applications.

In the MVC architecture, the Model represents application data and the business rules that govern access and modification of this data. Often the model serves as a software approximation to a real world process and simple real world modeling techniques apply when defining the model.

The model notifies views when it changes and provides the ability for the view to query the model about its state. It also provides the ability for the controller to access application functionality encapsulated by the model.

A View renders the contents of a model. It accesses data from the model and specifies how that data should be presented. When the model changes, it is the view's responsibility to maintain consistency in its presentation. The view forwards user gestures to the controller.

A Controller defines application behavior; it interprets user gestures and maps them into actions to be performed by the model. In a stand-alone GUI client, these user gestures could be button clicks or menu selections. In a Web application, they appear as GET and POST HTTP requests to the Web tier. The actions performed by the model include activating business processes or changing the state of the model. Based on the user gesture and the outcome of the model commands, the controller selects a view to be rendered as part of the response to this user request.

There is usually one controller for each set of related functionality. For example, human resources applications typically have a controller for managing employee interactions and a controller for human resources personnel.

Figure 1.9 depicts the relationships between the model, view, and controller portions of an MVC application.

1.4   Summary

The challenge to IT professionals today is to efficiently develop and deploy distributed applications for use on both corporate intranets and over the Internet. Companies that can do this effectively will gain strategic advantage in the information economy.

The Java 2 Platform, Enterprise Edition is a standard set of Java technologies that streamline the development, deployment, and management of enterprise applications. The J2EE platform is functionally complete in the sense that it is possible to develop a large class of enterprise applications using only the J2EE technologies. Applications written for the J2EE platform will run on any J2EE-compatible server. The J2EE platform provides a number of benefits for organizations developing such applications, including a simplified development model, industrial-strength scalability, support for existing information systems, choices in servers, tools, and components, and a simple, flexible security model.

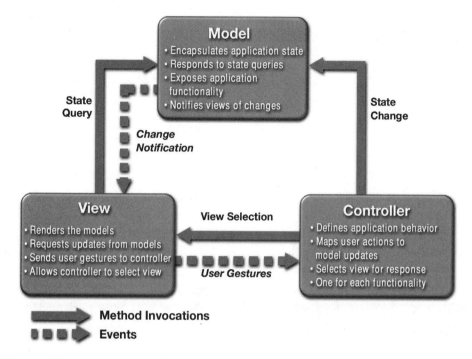

Figure 1.9   Relationships Between MVC Participants

By providing the ability to deploy component-oriented enterprise applications across multiple computing tiers in a platform-neutral manner, J2EE can give fast-moving enterprises a significant and measurable competitive edge.

About the Author

STEPHANIE BODOFF is a staff writer at Sun Microsystems. She has been involved with object-oriented enterprise software since graduating from Columbia University with an M.S. in electrical engineering. For several years she worked as a software engineer on distributed computing and telecommunications systems and object-oriented software development methods. During that period she co-authored *Object-Oriented Software Development: The Fusion Method*, Prentice Hall. For the past 4 years Stephanie has concentrated on technical writing, documenting object-oriented databases, application servers, and enterprise application development methods.

CHAPTER 2

J2EE Platform Technologies

by Stephanie Bodoff

THE J2EE platform specifies technologies to support multitier enterprise applications. These technologies fall into three categories: component, service, and communication.

The component technologies are those used by developers to create the essential parts of the enterprise application, namely the user interface and the business logic. The component technologies allow the development of modules that can be reused by multiple enterprise applications. The component technologies are supported by J2EE platform system-level services which simplify application programming and allow components to be customized to use resources available in the environment in which they are deployed.

Since most enterprise applications require access to existing enterprise information systems, the J2EE platform supports APIs that provide access to database, transaction, naming and directory, and messaging services. Finally, the J2EE platform provides technologies that enable communication between clients and servers and between collaborating objects hosted by different servers.

This chapter will provide an overview of the J2EE platform technologies.

2.1   Component Technologies

A *component* is an application-level software unit. In addition to JavaBeans components, which are part of the J2SE platform, the J2EE platform supports the following types of components: applets, application clients, Enterprise JavaBeans™ components, and Web components. Applets and application clients run on a client platform and EJB and Web components run on a server platform.

All J2EE components depend on the runtime support of a system-level entity called a *container*. Containers provide components with services such as life cycle management, security, deployment, and threading. Because containers manage these services, many component behaviors can be declaratively customized when the component is deployed in the container. For example, an Application Component Provider can specify an abstract name for a database that an Enterprise Java-Beans component needs to access and a Deployer will link that name with the information (such as a user name and password) needed to access the database in a given environment.

The following sections provide overviews of the different types of J2EE components and containers.

2.1.1   Applets and Application Clients

Applets and *application clients* are client components that execute in their own Java virtual machine. An applet container includes support for the applet programming model. A J2EE client may make use of the Java Plug-in to provide the required applet execution environment. An application client container provides access to the J2EE service (see Section 2.3 on page 33) and communication (see Section 2.5 on page 41) APIs. Applets and application clients are covered in Chapter 3.

2.1.2   Web Components

A *Web component* is a software entity that provides a response to a request. A Web component typically generates the user interface for a Web-based application. The J2EE platform specifies two types of Web components: servlets and JavaServer Pages™ (JSP) pages. The following sections give an overview of Web components. Web components are discussed in detail in Chapter 4.

2.1.2.1 Servlets

A *servlet* is a program that extends the functionality of a Web server. Servlets receive a request from a client, dynamically generate the response (possibly querying databases to fulfill the request), and then send the response containing an HTML or XML document to the client.

A servlet developer uses the servlet API to:

- Initialize and finalize a servlet

- Access a servlet's environment

- Receive requests and send responses

- Maintain session information on behalf of a client

- Interact with other servlets and other components

2.1.2.2 JavaServer Pages Technology

The JavaServer Pages (JSP) technology provides an extensible way to generate dynamic content for a Web client. A JSP page is a text-based document that describes how to process a request to create a response. A JSP page contains:

- Template data to format the Web document. Typically the template data uses HTML or XML elements. Document designers can edit and work with these elements on the JSP page without affecting the dynamic content. This approach simplifies development because it separates presentation from dynamic content generation.

- JSP elements and scriptlets to generate the dynamic content in the Web document. Most JSP pages use JavaBeans and/or Enterprise JavaBeans components to perform the more complex processing required of the application. Standard JSP actions can access and instantiate beans, set or retrieve bean attributes, and download applets. JSP is extensible through the development of custom actions, which are encapsulated in tag libraries.

2.1.2.3 Web Component Containers

Web components are hosted by servlet containers, JSP containers, and Web containers. In addition to standard container services, a *servlet container* provides network services (by which requests and responses are sent), decodes requests, and formats responses. All servlet containers must support HTTP as a protocol for requests and responses, but may also support additional request-response protocols such as HTTPS. A *JSP container* provides the same services as a servlet container and an engine that interprets and processes a JSP page into a servlet. A *Web con-*

tainer provides the same services as a JSP container and access to the J2EE service and communication APIs.

2.1.3   Enterprise JavaBeans Components

The Enterprise JavaBeans (EJB) architecture is a server-side technology for developing and deploying components containing the business logic of an enterprise application. Enterprise JavaBeans components, termed *enterprise beans*, are scalable, transactional, and multi-user secure. There are two types of enterprise beans: session beans and entity beans. The following sections give an overview of enterprise beans. Enterprise beans are discussed in detail in Chapter 5.

2.1.3.1 Session Beans

A *session bean* is created to provide some service on behalf of a client and usually exists only for the duration of a single client-server session. A session bean performs operations such as calculations or accessing a database for the client. While a session bean may be transactional, it is not recoverable should its container crash.

Session beans can be stateless or can maintain conversational state across methods and transactions. If they do maintain state, the EJB container manages this state if the object must be removed from memory. However, the session bean object itself must manage its own persistent data.

2.1.3.2 Entity Beans

An *entity bean* is a persistent object that represents data maintained in a data store; its focus is data-centric. An entity bean can manage its own persistence or it can delegate this function to its container. An entity bean can live as long as the data it represents.

An entity bean is identified by a primary key. If the container in which an entity bean is hosted crashes, the entity bean, its primary key, and any remote references survive the crash.

2.1.3.3 EJB Component Containers

Enterprise beans are hosted by an *EJB container*. In addition to standard container services, an EJB container provides a range of transaction and persistence services and access to the J2EE service and communication APIs.

2.1.4   Components, Containers, and Services

The J2EE component types and their containers are illustrated in Figure 2.1.

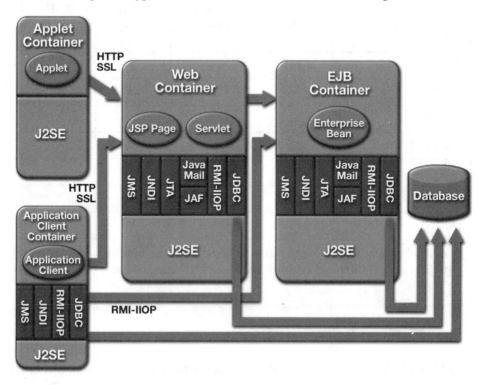

Figure 2.1   J2EE Components and Containers

Containers provide all application components with the J2SE platform APIs, which include the Java IDL and JDBC 2.0 core enterprise APIs. Table 2.1 lists the Standard Extension APIs that are available in each type of container. The J2EE platform APIs are described in Section 2.4 on page 39 and Section 2.5 on page 41.

Table 2.1   J2EE Required Standard Extension APIs

API	Applet	Application Client	Web	EJB
JDBC 2.0 Extension	N	Y	Y	Y
JTA 1.0	N	N	Y	Y

Table 2.1   J2EE Required Standard Extension APIs (continued)

API	Applet	Application Client	Web	EJB
JNDI 1.2	N	Y	Y	Y
Servlet 2.2	N	N	Y	N
JSP 1.1	N	N	Y	N
EJB 1.1	N	Y[a]	Y[b]	Y
RMI-IIOP 1.0	N	Y	Y	Y
JMS 1.0	N	Y	Y	Y
JavaMail 1.1	N	N	Y	Y
JAF 1.0	N	N	Y	Y

a   Application clients can only make use of the enterprise bean client APIs.
b   Servlets and JSP pages can only make use of the enterprise bean client APIs.

2.2   Platform Roles

The J2EE platform defines several distinct roles in the application development and deployment life cycle: J2EE Product Provider, Application Component Provider, Application Assembler, Deployer, System Administrator, Tool Provider. In general, the roles are defined to aid in identifying the tasks performed by various parties during the development, deployment, and running of a J2EE application. However, while some of these roles, such as System Administrator and Tool Provider, perform tasks that are common to non-J2EE platforms, other roles have a meaning specific to the J2EE platform, because the tasks those roles perform are specific to J2EE technology. In particular, Application Component Providers, Application Assemblers, and Deployers must configure J2EE components and applications to use J2EE platform services (described in Section 2.3 on page 33).

The roles can be fulfilled by whatever personnel match an organization's actual application development and deployment workflow. Thus, each J2EE role may be performed by a different party or a single party may perform several roles. For example, a programmer may perform the roles of Application Component Provider and Application Assembler.

The following sections define the J2EE platform roles. Subsets of some of these roles are defined in the EJB (Enterprise Bean Provider, EJB Container Provider, EJB Server Provider), JSP (JSP Container Provider), and Servlet (Application Developer, Servlet Container Provider, Web Container Provider, Web Server Provider) specifications.

2.2.1   J2EE Product Provider

A J2EE Product Provider, typically an operating system vendor, database system vendor, application server vendor, or a Web server vendor, implements a J2EE product providing the component containers, J2EE platform APIs, and other features defined in the J2EE specification. A J2EE product is free to implement the interfaces that are not specified by the J2EE specification in an implementation-specific way.

A J2EE Product Provider provides application deployment and management tools. Deployment tools enable a Deployer (described in Section 2.2.4 on page 32) to deploy components on the J2EE product. Management tools allow a System Administrator (described in Section 2.2.5 on page 32) to manage the J2EE product and the applications deployed on the J2EE product. The form of these tools is not prescribed by the J2EE specification.

2.2.2   Application Component Provider

Application Component Providers produce the building blocks of a J2EE application. They typically have expertise in developing reusable components as well as sufficient business domain knowledge. Application Component Providers need not know anything about the operational environment in which their components will be used. There are multiple roles for Application Component Providers, including HTML document designers, document programmers, enterprise bean developers, and so on. These roles use tools provided by a Tool Provider (described in Section 2.2.6 on page 32) to produce J2EE components and applications.

2.2.3   Application Assembler

An Application Assembler takes a set of components developed by Application Component Providers and assembles them into a complete J2EE application. Their expertise lies in providing solutions for a specific problem domain, for example, the financial industry. Application Assemblers may not be familiar with the source code of the components that they use, but they use declarative descriptors for the components in order to know how to build applications from them. Like Application Component Providers, they need not know anything about the operational environment in which their applications will be used. An Application Assembler will generally use GUI tools provided by either a Product Provider or Tool Provider. An Application Assembler is responsible for providing assembly instructions describing external dependencies of the application that the Deployer must resolve in the deployment process.

2.2.4   Deployer

A Deployer, an expert in a specific operational environment, is responsible for deploying J2EE components and applications into that environment. A Deployer uses tools supplied by the J2EE Product Provider to perform deployment tasks. A Deployer installs components and applications into a J2EE server and configures components and applications so as to resolve all the external dependencies declared by the Application Component Provider and Application Assembler.

2.2.5   System Administrator

A System Administrator is responsible for the configuration and administration of an enterprise's computing and networking infrastructure. A System Administrator is also responsible for overseeing the runtime well-being of the deployed J2EE applications. The System Administrator typically uses runtime monitoring and management tools provided by the J2EE Product Provider to accomplish these tasks.

2.2.6   Tool Provider

A Tool Provider provides tools used for the development and packaging of application components. A variety of tools are anticipated, corresponding to the many component types supported by the J2EE platform. Platform independent tools can be used for all phases of development up to the deployment of an application. Platform dependent tools are used for deployment, management, and monitoring of applications. Future versions of the J2EE specification may define more interfaces that allow such tools to be platform independent.

2.3   Platform Services

J2EE platform services simplify application programming and allow components and applications to be customized at deployment time to use resources available in the deployment environment. This section gives a brief overview of the J2EE platform naming, deployment, transaction, and security services.

2.3.1   Naming Services

J2EE naming services provide application clients, enterprise beans, and Web components with access to a JNDI (described in Section 2.4.3 on page 40) naming environment. A *naming environment* allows a component to be customized without the need to access or change the component's source code. A container implements the component's environment, and provides it to the component as a JNDI *naming context*.

A J2EE component locates its environment naming context using JNDI interfaces. A component creates a `javax.naming.InitialContext` object and looks up the environment naming context in `InitialContext` under the name `java:comp/env`. A component's naming environment is stored directly in the environment naming context, or in any of its direct or indirect *subcontexts*.

A J2EE component can access named system-provided and user-defined objects. The names of system-provided objects, such as JTA `UserTransaction` objects, are stored in the environment naming context, `java:comp/env`. The J2EE platform allows a component to name user-defined objects, such as enterprise beans, environment entries, JDBC `DataSource` objects, and message connections. An object should be named within a subcontext of the naming environment according to the type of the object. For example, enterprise beans are named within the subcontext `java:comp/env/ejb` and JDBC `DataSource` references in the subcontext `java:comp/env/jdbc`.

2.3.2   Deployment Services

J2EE deployment services allow components and applications to be customized at the time they are packaged and deployed.

J2EE applications are deployed as a set of nested units. Each unit contains a *deployment descriptor,* an XML-based text file whose elements declaratively describe how to assemble and deploy the unit into a specific environment. Deployment descriptors contain many elements related to customizing J2EE platform services such as transactions and security.

The following sections give an overview of J2EE platform deployment services. Deployment services are discussed in detail in Chapter 7.

2.3.2.1 Deployment Units

A *J2EE application* consists of one or more J2EE modules and one J2EE application deployment descriptor. An application deployment descriptor contains a list of the applications's modules and information on how to customize the application. A J2EE application is packaged as a Java Archive (JAR) file with an .ear (Enterprise ARchive) extension.

A *J2EE module* consists of one or more J2EE components for the same container type and one component deployment descriptor of that type. A component deployment descriptor contains declarative data to customize the components in the module. A J2EE module without an application deployment descriptor can be deployed as a stand-alone J2EE module.

The three types of J2EE modules are:

- Enterprise JavaBeans modules contain class files for enterprise beans and an EJB deployment descriptor. EJB modules are packaged as JAR files with a .jar extension.

- Web modules contain JSP files, class files for servlets, GIF and HTML files, and a Web deployment descriptor. Web modules are packaged as JAR files with a .war (Web ARchive) extension.

- Application client modules contain class files and an application client deployment descriptor. Application client modules are packaged as JAR files with a .jar extension.

2.3.2.2 Platform Roles in the Deployment Process

Each J2EE platform role performs specific activities related to deployment. An Application Component Provider specifies component deployment descriptor elements and packages components into modules. An Application Assembler resolves references between modules and assembles modules into a single deployment unit. A Deployer creates links between entities referred to by the application and entities in the deployment environment.

2.3.3   Transaction Services

Transactions divide an application into a series of indivisible or "atomic" units of work. A system that supports transactions ensures that each unit fully completes without interference from other processes. If the unit can be completed in its entirety, it is committed. Otherwise, the system completely undoes (rolls back) whatever work the unit had performed. Transactions simplify application development because they free the Application Component Provider from the complex issues of failure recovery and multi-user programming.

Transactions, as provided by the J2EE platform, have the following characteristics:

- J2EE transactions are flat. A flat transaction cannot have any child (nested) transactions.

- The J2EE platform implicitly handles many transaction details, such as propagating information specific to a particular transaction instance, and coordinating among multiple transaction managers.

The following sections give an overview of J2EE platform transaction services. Transaction services are discussed in detail in Chapter 8.

2.3.3.1 Accessing Transactions

A *JTA transaction* is a transaction that can span multiple components and resource managers. A *resource manager local transaction* is a transaction that is specific to a particular enterprise information system connection.

JTA transactions are created and managed using the `javax.transaction.UserTransaction` interface. Different types of components access `UserTransaction` objects in different ways:

- Enterprise beans provide a mechanism for JTA transactions to be started automatically by their containers. Enterprise beans that use bean-managed transactions (described in Section 2.3.3.3 on page 36) use the method `EJBContext.getUserTransaction` to look up the `UserTransaction` object.

- Applets and application clients may or may not be able to directly access a `UserTransaction` object depending on the capabilities provided by the container. However, they can always invoke enterprise beans that use a `UserTransaction` object.

- Web components use JNDI to look up the UserTransaction object.

A resource manager local transaction is created and managed in a manner specific to a particular connection. For example, each SQL statement executed on a JDBC connection has its own transaction.

2.3.3.2 Web Component Transactions

Web components (JSP pages and servlets) are not designed to be transactional. Because of this, Application Component Providers should only perform transactional work directly in Web components on a very limited basis. Preferably, an Application Component Provider should delegate transactional work to the appropriate enterprise beans. When an enterprise bean is used to perform transactional work, the enterprise bean or container takes care of properly setting up the transaction.

Nevertheless, there are times when a Web component may need to directly demarcate transactions. It can do so using the javax.transaction.UserTransaction interface. You should however, be aware of limitations in transaction propagation and state isolation, as described in the following discussions.

Transaction Propagation

Transactions are propagated from a Web component to an enterprise bean only when the Web component starts the transaction using the UserTransaction interface. Since Web components are server-side components, Web browsers and other clients don't have direct access to transactions and so a transaction initiated by a Web component *cannot* be propagated from the client of the component or between Web components and transactional resources such as JDBC connections.

State Isolation

A Web component can keep state for the lifetime of a client session or component. However, because Web components are not transactional components, their state cannot be isolated based on transactions. For example, separate servlets will see the same state of a client session even if they each start their own transaction.

2.3.3.3 Enterprise Bean Transactions

The J2EE platform provides two styles of transaction demarcation for enterprise beans: bean-managed and container-managed.

With *bean-managed transaction demarcation*, the enterprise bean is required to manage all aspects of a transaction. This entails operations such as:

- Creating the transaction object

- Explicitly starting the transaction

- Completing the transaction. There are two basic ways of completing a transaction:

  - Committing the transaction when all updates are completed.

  - Rolling back the transaction if an error occurred.

With *container-managed transaction demarcation*, the EJB container handles transaction management. The container performs the transaction demarcation based on the Application Assembler's deployment instructions; it handles starting and ending the transaction, plus it maintains the transaction context throughout the life of the transaction object. This greatly simplifies an Application Component Provider's responsibilities and tasks, especially for transactions in distributed environments.

Session beans, both stateful and stateless varieties, can use either container- or bean-managed transactions. However, a bean cannot use both types of transaction at the same time. The Application Component Provider decides the type of transaction demarcation that a session bean will use and must declare the transaction style via attributes in the enterprise bean's deployment descriptor. The attributes indicate whether the bean or container will manage the bean's transactions and, if the latter, how the container will manage the transactions. Entity beans can only use container-managed transaction demarcation.

2.3.4 Security Services

The J2EE platform security services are designed to ensure that resources are accessed only by users authorized to use them. Access control involves two steps:

1. Authentication—An entity must establish its identity through *authentication*. It typically does so by providing *authentication data* (such as a name and password). An entity that can be authenticated is called a *principal*. A principal can be a user or another program. Users are typically authenticated by logging in.

2. Authorization—When an authenticated principal tries to access a resource, the

system determines whether the principal is authorized to do so based on the security policies in force in the application's *security policy domain*.

The following sections give an overview of J2EE platform security services. Security services are discussed in detail in Chapter 9.

2.3.4.1 Security Methodologies

Containers provide two security methodologies: declarative and programmatic. *Declarative security* refers to the means of specifying an application's security structure in a form external to the application. An Application Component Provider specifies declarative security in a component's deployment descriptor. *Programmatic security* refers to security mechanisms accessed within a program. An Application Component Provider accesses programmatic security for EJB and Web components with J2EE platform security APIs.

2.3.4.2 Authentication

The J2EE platform allows an Application Component Provider to choose how a principal is authenticated. A Web client can provide authentication data to a Web container using HTTP basic authentication, digest authentication, form-based authentication, or certificate authentication.

With *basic authentication,* the Web server authenticates a principal using the user name and password obtained from the Web client. Like basic authentication, *digest authentication* authenticates a user based on a user name and a password. However, the authentication is performed by transmitting the password in an encrypted form, which is much more secure than the simple base64 encoding used by basic authentication. With *form-based authentication*, the Web container can provide an application-specific form for logging in. With *certificate authentication*, the client uses a public key certificate to establish its identity and maintains its own security context.

There is no way to authenticate to an EJB container. However, authentication data is also often required when an enterprise bean accesses an external resource. An enterprise bean can provide authentication data to a resource directly, or it can request the container to perform this service for it. If the Application Component Provider specifies that the container should propagate authentication data, the Deployer specifies the authentication data for each resource factory reference declared by the enterprise bean, and the container uses the authentication data when obtaining a connection to the resource.

2.3.4.3 Authorization

J2EE platform authorization is based on the concept of security roles. A *security role* is a logical grouping of users that is defined by an Application Component Provider or Application Assembler. Each security role is mapped by a Deployer to principals in the deployment environment. A security role can be used with declarative security and/or programmatic security.

An Application Component Provider or Application Assembler can control access to an enterprise bean's methods by specifying the `method-permission` element in the enterprise bean's deployment descriptor. The `method-permission` element contains a list of methods that can be accessed by a given security role. If a principal is in a security role allowed access to a method, the principal may execute the method. Similarly, a principal is allowed access to a Web component only if the principal is in the appropriate security role. An Application Component Provider controls access programmatically by using the `EJBContext.isCallerIn-Role` or `HttpServletRequest.isRemoteUserInRole` methods.

For example, suppose a payroll application specifies two security roles: `employee` and `administrator`. Salary update operations are executable only by a principal acting in the role of `administrator`, but salary read operations are executable by both roles. When the payroll application is deployed, the Deployer provides a mapping between the set of administrator and employee principals (or groups) and their respective roles. When the salary update method is executed, the enterprise bean's container can check whether the principal or group propagated from the Web server is in a role that can execute that method. Alternatively, the method itself could use one of the security APIs to perform the check.

2.4   Service Technologies

The J2EE platform service technologies allow applications to access a wide range of services in a uniform manner. This section describes technologies that provide access to databases, transactions, naming and directory services, and enterprise information systems.

2.4.1   JDBC API

The JDBC™ API provides database-independent connectivity between the J2EE platform and a wide range of tabular data sources. JDBC technology allows an Application Component Provider to:

- Perform connection and authentication to a database server

- Manage transactions

- Move SQL statements to a database engine for preprocessing and execution

- Execute stored procedures

- Inspect and modify the results from `Select` statements

The J2EE platform requires both the JDBC 2.0 Core API (included in the J2SE platform), and the JDBC 2.0 Extension API, which provides row sets, connection naming via JNDI, connection pooling, and distributed transaction support. The connection pooling and distributed transaction features are intended for use by JDBC drivers to coordinate with a J2EE server. Access to databases and enterprise information systems is covered in detail in Chapter 6.

2.4.2   Java Transaction API and Service

The Java Transaction API (JTA) allows applications to access transactions in a manner that is independent of specific implementations. JTA specifies standard Java interfaces between a transaction manager and the parties involved in a distributed transaction system: the transactional application, the J2EE server, and the manager that controls access to the shared resources affected by the transactions.

The Java Transaction Service (JTS) specifies the implementation of a transaction manager that supports JTA and implements the Java mapping of the Object Management Group Object Transaction Service 1.1 specification. A JTS transaction manager provides the services and management functions required to support transaction demarcation, transactional resource management, synchronization, and propagation of information that is specific to a particular transaction instance.

2.4.3   Java Naming and Directory Interface

The Java Naming and Directory Interface™ (JNDI) API provides naming and directory functionality. It provides applications with methods for performing standard directory operations, such as associating attributes with objects and searching for objects using their attributes. Using JNDI, an application can store and retrieve any type of named Java object.

Because JNDI is independent of any specific implementations, applications can use JNDI to access multiple naming and directory services, including existing naming and directory services such as LDAP, NDS, DNS, and NIS. This allows applications to coexist with legacy applications and systems.

2.4.4   Connector Architecture

A future version of the J2EE platform will support the Connector architecture, a standard API for connecting the J2EE platform to enterprise information systems, such as enterprise resource planning, mainframe transaction processing, and database systems. The architecture defines a set of scalable, secure, and transactional mechanisms that describe the integration of enterprise information systems with an EJB server and enterprise applications.

To use the Connector architecture, an enterprise information system vendor provides a standard connector for its enterprise information system. The connector has the capability to plug in to any EJB server that supports the Connector architecture. Similarly, an EJB server vendor extends its system once to support this Connector architecture and is then assured of a seamless connectivity to multiple enterprise information systems.

2.5   Communication Technologies

Communication technologies provide mechanisms for communication between clients and servers and between collaborating objects hosted by different servers. The J2EE specification requires support for the following types of communication technologies:

- Internet protocols

- Remote method invocation protocols

- Object Management Group protocols

- Messaging technologies

- Data formats

The following sections give an overview of J2EE platform communication technologies. How these communication technologies are used by clients is discussed in Chapter 3.

2.5.1   Internet Protocols

Internet protocols define the standards by which the different pieces of the J2EE platform communicate with each other and with remote entities. The J2EE platform supports the following Internet protocols:

- TCP/IP—Transport Control Protocol over Internet Protocol. These two protocols provide for the reliable delivery of streams of data from one host to another. Internet Protocol (IP), the basic protocol of the Internet, enables the unreliable delivery of individual packets from one host to another. IP makes no guarantees about whether or not the packet will be delivered, how long it will take, or if multiple packets will arrive in the order they were sent. The Transport Control Protocol (TCP) adds the notions of connection and reliability.

- HTTP 1.0—Hypertext Transfer Protocol. The Internet protocol used to fetch hypertext objects from remote hosts. HTTP messages consist of requests from client to server and responses from server to client.

- SSL 3.0—Secure Socket Layer. A security protocol that provides privacy over the Internet. The protocol allows client-server applications to communicate in a way that cannot be eavesdropped or tampered with. Servers are always authenticated and clients are optionally authenticated.

2.5.2   Remote Method Invocation Protocols

Remote Method Invocation (RMI) is a set of APIs that allow developers to build distributed applications in the Java programming language. RMI uses Java language interfaces to define remote objects and a combination of Java serialization technology and the Java Remote Method Protocol (JRMP) to turn local method invocations into remote method invocations. The J2EE platform supports the JRMP protocol, the transport mechanism for communication between objects in the Java language in different address spaces.

2.5.3 Object Management Group Protocols

Object Management Group (OMG) protocols allow objects hosted by the J2EE platform to access remote objects developed using the OMG's Common Object Request Broker Architecture (CORBA) technologies and vice versa. CORBA objects are defined using the Interface Definition Language (IDL). An Application Component Provider defines the interface of a remote object in IDL and then uses an IDL compiler to generate client and server stubs that connect object implementations to an Object Request Broker (ORB), a library that enables CORBA objects to locate and communicate with one another. ORBs communicate with each other using the Internet Inter-ORB Protocol (IIOP). The OMG technologies required by the J2EE platform are: Java IDL and RMI-IIOP.

2.5.3.1 Java IDL

Java IDL allows Java clients to invoke operations on CORBA objects that have been defined using IDL and implemented in any language with a CORBA mapping. Java IDL is part of the J2SE platform. It consists of a CORBA API and ORB. An Application Component Provider uses the `idlj` IDL compiler to generate a Java client stub for a CORBA object defined in IDL. The Java client is linked with the stub and uses the CORBA API to access the CORBA object.

2.5.3.2 RMI-IIOP

RMI-IIOP is an implementation of the RMI API over IIOP. RMI-IIOP allows Application Component Providers to write remote interfaces in the Java programming language. The remote interface can be converted to IDL and implemented in any other language that is supported by an OMG mapping and an ORB for that language. Clients and servers can be written in any language using IDL derived from the RMI interfaces. When remote interfaces are defined as Java RMI interfaces, RMI over IIOP provides interoperability with CORBA objects implemented in any language. RMI-IIOP contains:

- The `rmic` compiler, which generates:
  - Client and server stubs that work with any ORB.
  - An IDL file compatible with the RMI interface. To create a C++ server object, an Application Component Provider would use an IDL compiler to produce the server stub and skeleton for the server object.

- A CORBA API and ORB

Application clients must use RMI-IIOP to communicate with enterprise beans.

2.5.4   Messaging Technologies

Messaging technologies provide a way to asynchronously send and receive messages. The Java Message Service provides an interface for handling asynchronous requests, reports, or events that are consumed by enterprise applications. JMS messages are used to coordinate these applications. The JavaMail API provides an interface for sending and receiving messages intended for users. Although either API can be used for asynchronous notification, JMS is preferred when speed and reliability are a primary requirement.

2.5.4.1 Java Message Service

The Java Message Service (JMS) is an API for using enterprise messaging systems such as IBM MQ Series and TIBCO Rendezvous. JMS messages contain well-defined information that describe specific business actions. Through the exchange of these messages, applications track the progress of the enterprise. The JMS supports both point-to-point and publish-subscribe styles of messaging.

In *point-to-point messaging*, a client sends a message to the message queue of another client. Often a client will have all its messages delivered to a single queue. Most queues are created administratively and are treated as static resources by their clients.

In *publish-subscribe messaging*, clients publish messages to, and subscribe to messages from, well-known nodes in a content-based hierarchy called topics. A topic can be thought of as a message broker that gathers and distributes messages addressed to it. By relying on the topic as an intermediary, message publishers are independent of subscribers and vice versa. The topic automatically adapts as both publishers and subscribers come and go. Publishers and subscribers are *active* when the objects that represent them exist. JMS also supports the optional *durability* of subscribers that "remember" the existence of the subscribers while they are inactive.

The JMS API definitions must be included in a J2EE product, but a product is not required to include an implementation of the JMS `ConnectionFactory` and `Destination` objects. These are the objects used by an application to access a JMS service provider. A future version of the J2EE platform will require that a J2EE product provide support for both JMS point-to-point and publish-subscribe messaging, and thus must make those facilities available using the `ConnectionFactory` and `Destination` APIs.

2.5.4.2 JavaMail

The JavaMail™ API provides a set of abstract classes and interfaces that comprise an electronic mail system. The abstract classes and interfaces support many different implementations of message stores, formats, and transports. Many simple applications will only need to interact with the messaging system through these base classes and interfaces.

The abstract classes in JavaMail can be subclassed to provide new protocols and add functionality when necessary. In addition, JavaMail includes concrete subclasses that implement widely used Internet mail protocols and conform to specifications RFC822 and RFC2045. They are ready to be used in application development. Developers can subclass JavaMail classes to provide the implementations of particular messaging systems, such as IMAP4, POP3, and SMTP.

JavaBeans Activation Framework

The JavaBeans Activation Framework (JAF) integrates support for MIME data types into the Java platform. JavaBeans components can be specified for operating on MIME data, such as viewing or editing the data. The JAF also provides a mechanism to map filename extensions to MIME types.

The JAF is used by JavaMail to handle the data included in email messages; typical applications will not need to use the JAF directly, although applications making sophisticated use of email may need it.

2.5.5 Data Formats

Data formats define the types of data that can be exchanged between components. The J2EE platform requires support for the following data formats:

- HTML 3.2: The markup language used to define hypertext documents accessible over the Internet. HTML enables the embedding of images, sounds, video streams, form fields, references to other HTML documents and basic text formatting. HTML documents have a globally unique location and can link to one another.

- Image files: The J2EE platform supports two formats for image files: GIF (Graphics Interchange Format), a protocol for the online transmission and interchange of raster graphic data, and JPEG (Joint Photographic Experts Group), a standard for compressing gray-scale or color still images.

- JAR file: A platform-independent file format that permits many files to be aggregated into one file.

- Class file: The format of a compiled Java file as specified in the Java Virtual Machine specification. Each class file contains one Java language type—either a class or an interface—and consists of a stream of 8-bit bytes.

- XML: A text-based markup language that allows you to define the markup needed to identify the data and text in XML documents. XML will be supported in a future version of the J2EE specification. As with HTML, you identify data using tags. But unlike HTML, XML tags describe the data, rather than the format for displaying it. In the same way that you define the field names for a data structure, you are free to use any XML tags that make sense for a given application. When multiple applications use the same XML data, they have to agree on the tag names they intend to use.

2.6   Summary

The primary focus of the Java 2 Platform, Enterprise Edition is a set of component technologies (Enterprise JavaBeans™, JavaServer Pages™, and servlets) that simplify the process of developing enterprise applications. The J2EE platform provides a number of system-level services that simplify application programming and allow components to be customized to use resources available in the environment in which they are deployed. In conjunction with the component technologies, the J2EE platform provides APIs that enable components to access a variety of remote services, and mechanisms for communication between clients and servers and between collaborating objects hosted by different servers.

About the Author

ABHISHEK CHAUHAN has been working on the design of scalable network services and distributed programs. At Sun Microsystems, Abhishek was involved in the evolution of the J2EE programming model from its inception. He pioneered work on Web access optimization techniques and implementation of the Java Web Server. He worked on the JavaServer Pages specification and Sun's JavaServer Pages implementations.

Abhishek was one of the founders and a lead architect at Vxtreme, where he worked on the design of its streaming server. Vxtreme was acquired by Microsoft in 1997. In a former life, Abhishek worked at Microsoft on the Office Visual Basic scripting engine. He has an M.S. from the University of Wisconsin, Madison and a Bachelor's degree from the Indian Institute of Technology at Delhi.

CHAPTER 3

The Client Tier

by Abhishek Chauhan

$\mathbf{A}$ user's perception of an enterprise application is often closely tied to the behavior of the application's client tier. A client makes requests to the server on behalf of the user, and presents the outcomes of those requests to the user. Therefore, it's important to choose a client configuration that best addresses the requirements of the application and empowers the user with a rich interface.

The J2EE platform supports many types of clients. A J2EE client can connect across the World Wide Web, or inside an enterprise's intranet. Clients can run on hardware ranging from powerful desktop machines to tiny wearable assistants. They can provide a browser-based or stand-alone interface. A client can communicate with, and use the services provided by, one or more tiers of the enterprise application. Clients can also be written in a number of languages and use a variety of development environments.

Since client software executes on user systems, it can be hard to control aspects of the client environment such as hardware, operating system platform, and browser version. In any distributed application, there are trade-offs to be made in partitioning application responsibility between server and client. The more functionality you keep on the client (closer to the user), the better *perceived* quality of service the user gets. The more you provide on the server, the easier it is to distribute, deploy, and manage the application.

This chapter presents considerations for J2EE client design and provides guidelines for choosing among the available options. First, it discusses the requirements to consider before deciding on a client type. Then it presents a classification of clients based on the differences in the implementation model, and provide rules for translating client requirements into a choice of a client implementation.

3.1   Requirements and Constraints

For every application, there are requirements and expectations that the client must meet, constrained by the environment in which the client needs to operate. Some of the considerations guiding our choice of client are: Is the client intended to be used over the Internet, or within a company intranet? Will it present its user interface through a Web browser or a stand-alone application? What host platforms must the client work on? This section identifies the constraints to consider when choosing a client. For each specific enterprise application, some constraints are more important than others. There are also a number of choices rather than constraints the developer needs to keep in mind. This section considers the effect of various operating environment, deployment, and implementation constraints.

3.1.1   Operating Environment

Whether the client will be deployed inside a company intranet or in the Internet determines many aspects of the client.

Intranets are usually managed environments, with higher quality network service and less variance than the Internet. Virtual private networks (VPNs) and extranets have characteristics that are a hybrid of Internet and intranet characteristics. A VPN is comparable to an intranet in terms of confidentiality and firewall concerns, but it is like the Internet when it comes to quality of network service.

Applications designed for the Internet typically take a lowest-common-denominator approach to the client. In other words, the client must work acceptably over the slowest link and assume only a minimal set of platform capabilities. Clients intended to be deployed on a company intranet may differ significantly from those destined for the Internet. Within an intranet, it is possible to force standardization to some extent. This means less variance and possibly a higher common denominator.

This section considers the effect of operating environment on the level of network service, and security requirements and constraints.

3.1.1.1 Network Service

Clients working across local area networks in a company's intranet typically enjoy a high level of network service. Bandwidths of the order of multiple megabits/sec. are available, and latency is negligible, often less than 25 milliseconds. On the other hand, clients on the Internet can expect lower levels of service. Moreover, there is a wide variance in network quality of service across Internet clients. While some clients are connected across dialup telephone lines, others could be connected over cable modems, DSL, or better services.

Network service plays an important role in the design of any distributed application. Let's look at two key network characteristics—bandwidth and latency—and see how they affect the choice of what type of client to use.

Highly interactive applications place greater demands on network bandwidth and well as latency. Low bandwidth requires settling for a less interactive interface. Or, it may be necessary to move portions of the presentation responsibilities to the client; this, coupled with some form of caching of the data, could yield acceptable response times. Clients such as applets and application clients that can take over presentation responsibilities, may be better adapted to work in low bandwidth situations.

Consider a browser-based client that displays a hierarchy of information as a tree, for example, a navigational menu or a list of mail folders. If the network is fast, it may be acceptable to make a request to the server every time the user selects a node to see a list of the node's children. The server then dynamically generates a new screen reflecting the expanded node. However, if the network is slow, a better approach might be to have the client cache the node hierarchy.

3.1.1.2 Security and Firewalls

The Internet and intranets have different security constraints.

Clients that work within the intranet usually do not have to worry about firewalls between the client and the server. However, clients that need to connect over the Internet must be designed to be able to talk to servers that are often behind firewalls. The presence of a firewall limits the possible choices for protocols that the client can use. With the prevalence of the World Wide Web, most firewalls are configured to allow HTTP and HTTPS protocols to pass across. Firewalls configured to allow IIOP communications are not widespread. And even when a corporation allows IIOP to pass through, the details of configuring firewalls for this purpose may not be widely understood.[1]

Within an intranet, the client and server may be in the same security domain, and can integrate with the environment better in terms of security. For instance, it may be possible to have single signon clients within an enterprise. Over the Internet, clients and the server are typically in different security domains. Another aspect of security is confidentiality. While confidentiality is not a concern for a

---

[1] It is possible to configure most firewalls to pass IIOP. However, because this is an exception rather than the rule, most firewall administrators may be wary of doing so.

large category of enterprise information within the corporate intranet, confidentiality must be ensured if the communication occurs over the Internet. In this case, its necessary to use a protocol that can ensure confidentiality, such as HTTPS.[2]

3.1.2   Deployment

The deployment mechanisms available affect the choice of client type. A developer needs to consider:

- The delivery vehicle for the client software

- The roll-out and upgrade strategy

- How often the client needs to be upgraded

The bandwidth available to the client plays a role in deciding the client deployment model. For example, some clients such as applets must be downloaded every time the user establishes a session with the server. In this case, the download must complete in an acceptable amount of time. Thus, when applets are used as part of the client framework, keeping the size of the client small is important unless the network can be expected to support a large bandwidth.

Web-based clients usually have very little that requires explicit deployment. They therefore work well when the client is changed or upgraded often. By keeping most of the functionality on the server, an application can also use older versions of supporting software on the client.

3.1.3   Implementation

This section considers constraints on the client based on the platform and programming language.

3.1.3.1   Platform

The first constraint to consider is whether the client presents its interface in a specific platform, a browser or as a stand-alone Java application, or does the client need to run on multiple hardware and/or software platforms. In the latter case, an enterprise application developer could take one of two approaches: choose a browser-

---

[2] IIOP can be made to work over SSL connections, although such configurations are not in widespread use.

based client, where the browser software handles platform differences,[3] or a Java technology-based solution, where the Java runtime environment insulates the client software from the platform.

The computation that can be done on the clients limits some client options. For example, if the client executes in a cell-phone or pager, the server should perform as much computation and data processing as possible and the client should only display the results. Conversely, powerful client platforms may be leveraged for distributed problem-solving. For example, when a financial analysis system runs on a powerful desktop platform, it might make sense to off-load complex financial-projection computation to the client.

3.1.3.2 Programming Language

The choice of implementation language is usually governed by non-technical factors such as the availability of expertise and the desire to integrate with other legacy application clients. If you already have a client that integrates services from several enterprise applications that you are extending to add this new service you might use a language, such as Visual Basic, C++, or another language, that does not integrate with the J2EE platform as seamlessly as Java.

3.2 Overview of Client Options

Choices such as which tier or tiers of the application that clients interact with, the protocols used for this communication, and the implementation language used for the client are dependent on several factors. Different tiers expose different levels of detail and complexity.

The Web tier presents a simplified functional facade to the application. It takes care of presentation issues for the client. The EJB tier presents an interface to access and manipulate the business objects according to the business rules set in the application, leaving presentation issues to the client connecting to it. The enterprise information system tier presents a raw view of the data, delegating the responsibility of enforcing the business rules, as well as presenting the data to the client.

The protocols used for communication have different strengths and limitations. The Web tier typically uses HTTP-based protocols. HTML over HTTP is

---

[3] Recently, browsers act much like platforms. In such cases, the application will still have to deal with differences in browser "platforms."

suitable for handling the presentation needs of the client, while XML over HTTP is better suited for interchange of data to be presented by the client. The EJB tier uses the RMI-IIOP protocol. As a full-scale distributed computing protocol, it gives the client direct access to the services of the EJB tier. A client can use business objects hosted by the EJB server and can participate in transactions.

For clients of the J2EE platform, the Java programming language is the implementation language of choice because Java technology-based implementations can take advantage of services provided by the platform. Other languages, such as C++ and Visual Basic, can be used, albeit with some limitations.

Many aspects of the client are determined by the tier of the enterprise application the client connects to. This discussion classifies clients into three broad categories based on the tiers that they interact with:

- Web clients connect to the Web tier. They execute on a desktop or other browser host usually inside a Web browser or a browser plug-in. The presentation logic as well as the business logic of the application can run on the server or the client.

- EJB clients connect to the EJB tier. These are typically GUI programs that execute on a desktop computer. EJB clients have access to all of the facilities of the J2EE EJB tier. The presentation logic of the application runs on the EJB client, while the business logic runs on the server.

- Enterprise information system clients interface directly to an enterprise information system resource. Typically these programs serve administrative and management functions for the back-end system. Both presentation and business logic are contained in the client.

3.3   Web Clients

Web clients usually run inside a browser and use the services of the browser to render content provided by the Web tier. In these clients, the user interface is generated on the server side by the Web tier and communicated via HTML. Applets and JavaScript can be used to enhance the browsing interface. On the client side, a browser or equivalent program renders this user interface and carries out interactions with the user. Data interchange is facilitated through XML.

3.3.1   Protocols

Web clients use HTTP or HTTPS as the transport protocol. These protocols have several advantages:

- They are widely deployed. Almost every computer now has a browser that can communicate over HTTP. Thus the deployment of the application is simplified.

- They are robust and simple. The protocol is simple and well understood. Good implementations of HTTP servers and clients are widely available.

- They go through firewalls. Due to the extensive use of HTTP, firewalls are typically set up to pass HTTP through. This makes it the protocol of choice on the Internet where the server and the client are separated by a firewall.

At the same time, the simplicity of the protocols presents a couple of minor disadvantages that can largely be overcome:

- They are sessionless. HTTP is a request-response protocol, with no built-in concept of a session. Therefore, individual requests are treated independently. Moreover, there are simple ways to provide session semantics, so in practice this is not an issue.

- They are non-transactional. HTTP is a networking protocol, not designed for general purpose distributed computing. As a result, it has no concept of transaction or security contexts. However, this is not a problem in practice because transactions and security are commonly handled on the server.

3.3.2   Content Format

The content served over the HTTP protocol is typically the result of an action performed on the server in response to a client request. This result can be formatted using HTML or XML.

3.3.2.1 HTML

HTML content is widely supported by browsers and operating systems. Along with HTML, a server may also provide JavaScript code in the response to enrich the user interface.

This content type is best suited when presentation of the response is generated on the server side and communicated to the browser for display. It should be used as a markup language that instructs the browser how to present the results.

HTML is a good means of encoding static documents. However, presenting complex documents consistently is difficult using HTML. Style sheets and dynamic HTML (DHTML) allow more complex documents to be displayed. However, the various commonly used browsers do not handle style sheets and DHTML consistently, so it is necessary to design different versions of each page or to include browser-specific markup in the pages.

HTML's strength is its wide support in many applications on many platforms. HTML documents that do not rely on browser-specific tags should be similar in appearance on the most commonly used browsers. The combination of HTTP and HTML ensures that a document can be widely viewed on many platforms.

3.3.2.2 XML

The XML (eXtensible Markup Language) standard provides a mechanism for structuring content and data. XML allows applications to transfer both page content and information on how the content is structured.

The structure of the data contained within an XML document is described in a Data Type Definition (DTD). Applications that support XML can communicate and exchange data without any prior knowledge of each other, as long as they share or are capable of interpreting the DTD. For example, the interoperability portion of the sample application sends a list of orders to a Microsoft Excel spreadsheet using XML over HTTP. J2EE servers may also transfer information to other J2EE servers or applications using XML over HTTP. This is not possible with HTML, because of the limited number of tags it provides to identify data.

While DTDs are useful to validate XML documents, they suffer from a number of shortcomings, many of which stem from the fact that a DTD specification is not hierarchical. This affects the ability to name elements relative to one another and the ability to scope comments to sections of a document. Finally, DTDs do not allow you to formally specify field-validation criteria, such as a limitation on the size and content of a zip code field. To remedy these shortcomings, a number of proposals have been made for future versions of XML to provide database-like hierarchical schemas that specify data validation criteria.

XML also allows dynamic data presentation. That is, the same data can be presented differently depending on the style sheet used. Fortunately, the XSL (eXtensible Style Sheet) standard, which provides a standard approach to XML presentation, will be completed and accepted in the near future. Most of the commonly used Web browsers support now, or will soon support, XML. However, since XML is evolving, support by browsers is not as uniform as HTML. This means that an applet, plug-in, or other application component, that handles XML responses might be necessary. In the case of Java applets, this can happen automatically at request time.

Use XML for your responses when:

- The client needs to get data from the server and process it before displaying it to the user.

- The client needs to show multiple views of the same data. When the client downloads XML data from the server, it can generate views on the client side depending on local settings. This saves a round-trip to the server and reduces load on the server by reducing the number of client requests.

  For example, consider a stock quote system, where the client wants to see a chart of the last hour's trades, as well as a table of the same data. The client could download the quote data from the server just once, then render that data as either a chart or a table (or both), at the user's requests without resending a request to the server.

- The client can pass XML in requests. The HTTP protocol allows for POST data, in any content type, in a request. An XML-aware application component running on the client could use POST requests with XML data to exchange objects with the server.

3.3.3   Types of Web Clients

Most Web clients run inside of or in conjunction with a Web browser. The browser can handle details of HTTP communication and HTML rendering, while an application component can focus on interactions that cannot be expressed in HTML. In fact, a Web browser without any other application component is the simplest, most widespread J2EE Web client. Additional application components such as Java applets, browser plug-ins, or ActiveX components can make the client user interface richer and more featureful. Finally, Web clients can be implemented as stand-alone programs.

3.3.3.1 Web Browsers

The Web browser is the simplest J2EE client. It serves to render HTML content delivered by the Web tier. With more and more browsers supporting JavaScript and DHTML, powerful user interfaces can be created using just a Web browser.

A stand-alone Web browser is the Web client of choice on the Internet. It is widely available, users are familiar with using it, and there are no issues with deployment. Additionally, since Web browsers can be used wherever an Internet connection is available, support for roaming users is possible.

3.3.3.2 Java Applets

Applets are GUI components that typically execute in a Web browser, although they can execute in a variety of other applications or devices that support the applet programming model. Applets can be used to provide a powerful user interface for J2EE applications.

Since applets are Java-based components, they have access to all the features and advantages of the Java platform technology. In a heterogeneous Web environment, it is especially important that client-side components be portable. For the protection of the client machine, it is important to be able to place security restriction on these components and detect security violations. Java applets serve both these needs.

Browser-based applet clients communicate over HTTP. Applets can also communicate over a network using serialized objects or some other type of proprietary protocol.

One advantage of applets is that they provide application with rich GUIs that can be managed at a single location. The main disadvantage with browser-based applets is that they can be difficult to deploy, particularly when the client browsers run a diverse set of embedded Java virtual machines. For this reason, applets may be more successfully deployed where the browser environment is controlled (such as an intranet).

Deployment

Applets are delivered through applet tags embedded in HTML. The Web browser downloads the code for the applet at request time and executes it in a Java virtual machine on the client machine.

When JSP pages are used to generate HTML, an Application Component Provider can use the `jsp:plugin` tag to ensure the availability of a specific JVM on the client.

Security

The Java applet programming model protects the user from security violations. All downloaded code is considered untrusted and strict limitations are placed on it. For users to be more comfortable with executing application code downloaded from another computer, vendors should use signed applets. Signed applets provide a secure way to identify the applet's distributor. A signed applet can also request additional permissions from the client machine if it needs access to additional functionality.

Session Management

When applets communicate with servlets or JSP pages over HTTP they need to manage some details of the HTTP protocol to participate in a session. Sessions over HTTP are managed using HTTP cookies. The server sets the cookie at the beginning of the session; the client then sends the cookie back to the server each time it makes another request. When the applet makes a request, it needs to explicitly make sure that it sends the cookie as part of the request.

3.3.3.3 Browser Plug-ins

In addition to applets, Web browsers often support other embedded components, such as plug-ins in the Netscape browser and ActiveX components in Microsoft's Internet Explorer. These can be used just like applets to enhance the user experience. There are some things to keep in mind when planning to use these component types in a J2EE client:

- Plug-ins are usually written for a particular architecture and operating system. On the Internet, multiple versions of these plug-ins need to be implemented for each kind of client. If the clients run on a homogeneous intranet environment, this is less of an issue.

- Since plug-ins run natively on the browser's platform, security is harder to enforce, which could expose your clients to an unacceptable risk.

3.3.3.4 Stand-Alone Web Clients

The discussion so far has considered Web clients with the application component embedded in a browser. Sometimes, though, it might be desirable to invert this model by embedding the browser in an application client. This type of client is referred to as a stand-alone Web client.

In this configuration, the application client creates a top level window and user interface, then uses a browser-like component to render HTML responses from the server.

This is desirable where the client needs to look like a native application, and provide a more interactive and customized GUI to the user. These clients often use XML over HTTP to communicate with JSP pages or servlets and render the data interchanged in their customized GUI.

A stand-alone Web client suffers from the same drawbacks as other stand-alone applications:

- The client must be explicitly deployed on each user desktop. Client upgrades are also harder for the same reason.

- Implementing the client is more work since the client must be coded to create the bulk of the user interface.

With the availability of tools, some of this work can be automated. However, deploying a stand-alone client remains a complex process.

Java Clients and the Swing API

The user interface of a stand-alone Web client is typically written using the Swing API from the J2SE platform. The Swing API provides a comprehensive set of GUI components (tables, trees, and so on) that can be used to provide a more interactive experience than the typical HTML page. Additionally, Swing supports HTML text components that can be used to display responses from a server. Swing APIs can be used for both applets and stand-alone Java applications.

Non-Java Clients

Stand-alone Web clients can also be written in C++ or in automation languages such as Visual Basic.[4] These clients can use their own HTML renderers or third-party browser components to present responses from the server.

Non-Java clients may be desirable where specialized services are made available by the development environment. For example, a chart plotting application might find it useful to take advantage of this fact. If Microsoft Excel is available on the client desktops throughout an enterprise, it might be desirable to use it for rendering charts. A Visual Basic client embedded in Microsoft Excel could communicate with a JSP page and download the chart data using XML. The client could then use specialized services in Excel to render this chart.

3.4 EJB Clients

EJB clients are application clients that interact with the J2EE EJB tier. EJB clients are GUI programs that typically execute on a desktop computer; they manage their own GUI and offer a user experience similar to that of native applications. Here we discuss how to develop and deploy EJB clients.

3.4.1 Protocols and Facilities

EJB clients interact with the J2EE EJB tier using the RMI-IIOP protocol. A variety of middle-tier services are available to an application client:[5] JNDI for directory lookups, JMS for messaging, and JDBC for relational database access.

An EJB client depends on a client container to provide some system services. Such a container is typically very lightweight compared to other J2EE containers and usually provides security and deployment services.

3.4.1.1 The Client Container

A client container is usually a library that is distributed along with the client. It is specific to the J2EE EJB container,[6] and is often provided by the same vendor. The container manages details of RMI-IIOP communication. It also handles security,

---

[4] Using the scripting engine on a Windows platform, a developer could use other scripting languages such as JavaScript or Perl. The component model remains COM.

[5] These services are only available if the application client is implemented using Java.

[6] The IIOP protocol does not completely specify details of the security and transaction contexts, thus different implementations of the protocol may not be compatible.

transaction, and deployment issues. The following discussion assumes a Java client container. The J2EE specification doesn't define service requirements for applications implemented in other languages. However, a similar set of services should be provided by containers for such clients.

3.4.1.2 Deployment

EJB application clients are packaged in JAR files that include a deployment descriptor similar to other J2EE application components. The deployment descriptor describes the enterprise beans and external resources referenced by the application. As with other J2EE application components, access to resources is configured at deployment time, names are assigned for enterprise beans and resources, and so on.

The J2EE platform does not specify tools to deploy an application client, or mechanisms to install it. Very sophisticated J2EE products might allow the application client to be deployed on a J2EE server and automatically made available to some set of (usually intranet) clients. Other J2EE products might require the J2EE application bundle containing the application client to be manually deployed and installed on each client machine. Another approach would be for the deployment tool on the J2EE server to produce an installation package that could be taken to each host to install the application client.

3.4.1.3 Transactions

Since client containers aren't required to provide direct access to transaction facilities, EJB clients should use enterprise beans to start transactions. They can also use transaction facilities of JDBC. However, doing so may be risky since the J2EE platform doesn't define a mechanism for propagating the transaction context to the EJB server.

3.4.1.4 Security

The client application must be authenticated to access the J2EE middle tier. Techniques for authentication are provided by the client container, and are not under the control of the application client. The container can integrate with the platform's authentication system, authenticate when the application is started, or use some other lazy authentication policy. The container takes responsibility for gathering authentication data from the user, by presenting a login window to the user.

EJB clients in the Java programming language execute in an environment with a security manager installed. They have similar security permission requirements as servlets.

3.4.2   Strengths and Weaknesses

EJB clients have a number of strengths, including:

- Provide a more flexible user interface

   Application clients can be made to look and feel more like native applications on the client machine. Since these clients implement their own user interface, they can provide a richer, more natural interface to the application tasks.

- Distribute the workload

   An application client can share some of the computational expense by doing the task on the client desktop, and thereby reducing load on the server. In particular, the work of generating the user interface is performed by each client. This is useful for applications with specific graphical display capabilities.

- Handle complex data models

   Sometimes the data associated with an application is sufficiently complex and the manipulation interface rich enough, that a Web-based interface to manage the interaction is not enough. In such cases, you want direct access to the underlying object model on the client and to manipulate it directly.

   For example, in a financial analysis system, it might make sense to offload some of the complex financial-projection number crunching to the client. Or consider an application that allows manipulation of CAD schemas such as a design of a circuit board (PCB). An application client, with direct access to the objects of the CAD system, can redraw views of the layout more easily than a Web-based interface, and with better performance. The server should be delegated to background tasks such as converting a PCB layout to a plot of the PCB traces.

- Are transaction-capable

   Since EJB clients communicate using RMI-IIOP, they are capable of participating in client-demarcated transactions through JTA APIs.

- Provide integrated security

    Application client containers can integrate with the security of the under-
lying operating system where the client is executed, thereby providing a more
transparent and manageable security infrastructure.

    For example, in an enterprise intranet, where the client and the server
belong to the same security domain, an application client container might
simply forward the credentials of the user already logged into the client desktop operating system, thereby effecting single signon. A Web client, on the
other hand, would require explicit sign on and security management.

The disadvantages of EJB clients are that they:

- Require explicit deployment

    EJB clients need to be distributed and installed on the client desktops. In
an intranet, where desktops can be standardized, this is less of an issue. However, on the Internet, distribution becomes a serious consideration. Furthermore, upgrades and fixes to the client need to be distributed as well, and the
server has to deal with multiple versions of the client programs.

- Require firewall reconfiguration

    The RMI-IIOP protocol does not usually go through firewalls without
additional setup on the firewall host. This makes use of EJB clients on the
Internet very limited.

- Tend to be more complex

    Since the application client needs to manage its own user interface, its
implementation is more complex. Furthermore, it communicates with the
J2EE server at a much lower level than browser-based Web clients and needs
to handle the complexity introduced as a result.

3.4.3   Types of EJB Clients

EJB clients can be implemented using either the Java programming language, or
languages such as Visual Basic or C++. When a language other than Java is used,
depending on the implementation on the client container, some of the facilities of
the J2EE platform may not be available.

3.4.3.1 Java Technology Clients

Java clients execute in their own Java virtual machine. Following the model for Java applications, they are invoked at their main method and run until the virtual machine is terminated. Security and deployment services are provided through the use of a client container.

The Java programming language should be used for implementation of EJB clients. Since the EJB server communicates using RMI-IIOP, the client needs to support RMI-IIOP. This is most naturally done using services provided by the standard Java platform.

Some facilities cannot be easily implemented in other languages as a result, client containers for these languages may not provide the full set of features.

Multitier Clients

Java technology clients are usually stand-alone Java applications. However, when appropriately signed and trusted, Java applets can also be used as EJB clients. Applets and applications have essentially the same set of platform service available to them. Additionally, a Java applet can communicate with the Web tier as well as the application tier to get its job done. In this sense it is a multitier client.

3.4.3.2 Non-Java Clients

EJB clients can be implemented in programming languages other than Java. Since the EJB server uses RMI-IIOP, this requires some form of RMI-IIOP support available to the client.

Accessing Enterprise Beans as COM Objects

Scripting COM objects together into an application is a common client implementation approach. It is possible for a client container to make enterprise beans appear as COM objects on the client machine.

When enterprise beans are exposed as COM objects, any scripting languages supported by the Active Scripting Engine can be used to automate the components to develop the application client. While Visual Basic is most often used for this purpose, languages such as JavaScript or Perl can also be used.

The specific approach to developing such clients will be largely dependent on the J2EE product used and the platform. Client containers will be provided by the J2EE server.

Here's an example of how such clients might work:

- Create an RMI-IIOP proxy in the client. This proxy runs in a Java virtual machine. The client uses RMI-IIOP to communicate with the EJB tier.

- The client container exposes each enterprise bean that is part of the application as a COM object by generating and a registering type library for each enterprise bean. Note that the type libraries must be installed on every client desktop. The COM objects that are registered act as enterprise bean proxies.

- When the COM IDispatch interface of the enterprise bean proxy object is used to make a method invocation, it communicates with the RMI-IIOP proxy using Java Native Interface, or some other proprietary mechanism. The RMI-IIOP proxy communicates with the EJB tier just like a Java application client and forwards the invocation.

Limitations

Translating between one distributed computing architecture and another is not straightforward. There are some limitations when using Visual Basic clients that access the EJB tier:

- Security: It is hard to propagate security contexts between the J2EE platform and Visual Basic clients. The RMI-IIOP proxy to the EJB server appears to be the application client. The proxy thus needs to somehow authenticate the user on behalf of the Visual Basic client. Integration with the native security system is harder.

- Transactions: Transaction contexts cannot be propagated from a non-Java client to the EJB tier. Although availability of JTA or propagation of contexts is not required by the J2EE platform, it is often available in Java client containers. However, this is not possible when using the COM.

- Deployment: The type libraries that need to be generated for each enterprise bean are application-specific and need to be distributed and installed for each Visual Basic application client.

When to Use COM Clients

The decision to use Visual Basic clients is largely non-technical. It depends on the expertise available, as well as the desire to integrate with existing EJB clients. When legacy issues are not a concern, EJB clients should be developed using Java technology.

Active Server Pages

There is one interesting case where a COM-based scripting client might interact with an EJB server. This is the scripting present in Microsoft IIS Active Server Pages (ASP). ASPs are server-side scripting components that use Visual Basic script to produce dynamic content. An ASP developer that wishes to use the J2EE platform for its middle tier needs, can do so using the techniques outlined above.

3.5   Enterprise Information System Clients

Enterprise information system clients access enterprise information system resources directly and assume responsibility for enforcing the business rules of the application.

Enterprise information system clients can use the JDBC API to access relational databases. A future release of the J2EE specification will describe standard ways to implement enterprise information system clients with connectors to non-relational resources, such as mainframe or enterprise resource planning systems.

These programs should be implemented with caution, since they access the database directly. Widely distributing such programs can also cause security problems.

Enterprise information system clients must both manage their user interface and enforce business rules. Fully functional applications designed this way tend to be complex. These programs should be limited to administration or management tasks, where the user interface is small or nonexistent and the task is simple and well understood.

For example, a stand-alone enterprise information system client could perform maintenance on database tables, and be invoked every night through an external mechanism.

The J2EE programming models doesn't recommend techniques for implementing these programs.

3.6   Designing for Multiple Types of Client

We have discussed several approaches to building clients for enterprise applications and how the choice of a client influences service implementation. Often, an enterprise application will have more than one type of client accessing its services.

A banking application might expose a simple Web interface for account-holders to view account balances, as well as provide a richer interface through a stand-alone client that customers can install on their desktop computers. In this example both clients have similar functionality although they use different mechanisms to present their interface to the user. A banking application might also provide a stand-alone client administration interface.

When designing an enterprise application, you should pay attention to handling multiple types of client interactions. The overall application design should support each new type of client with minimal additional effort. It should also avoid duplicating code either by sharing the application objects among multiple clients, or by reusing them through encapsulation, delegation, or inheritance.

This section discusses approaches to designing enterprise applications that can support multiple types of clients.

Application data and business rules are independent of the clients that access the application, making it desirable to design these objects to be shared across all the different clients of the application. When different types of clients present the same functionality through different interfaces, it is useful to share objects that encapsulate this functionality or client behavior.

The distinction between objects that can be shared or reused, and objects that need to be implemented separately for each type of client can be discussed in terms of the MVC architecture. The follow sections consider the issues that arise when designing the model, view, and controller to support multiple types of clients.

3.6.1   Model

The model is a software abstraction of the application data and the business rules that apply for changing this data. The model can be shared across all clients of the application. It should be consistent regardless of the type of client accessing the data. If the model faithfully captures all possible ways that data can be changed, there is no need to implement different model classes, or develop specific model objects for each client type.

When each type of client represents a different level of authorization to the system, it is sometimes desirable to wrap the access to the underlying model into security mediator objects. This allows the model to be shared across all clients, while access control restrictions can be enforced more flexibly. Security mediator objects are described in Section 9.3.6 on page 229.

In situations where the models that two clients of the application work with are independent of one another, the application can be thought of as being comprised of multiple subapplications. In this case the programming model would be applied to each of these subapplications independently.

3.6.2 View

A view renders the contents of a model. It accesses data from the model and specifies how that data should be presented. The view changes most significantly across clients. This makes it hard to share entire view implementations. However, some code sharing can still be effected at a finer grained level. This is especially true when clients use the same medium for presentation, but provide different functionality.

For example, the sample application could provide a Web-based shopping interface and a Web-based administration interface. Although very different in functionality, they both are Web based. If a showOrder custom JSP tag were used to render details of a particular order to HTML, the same tag could be used by both the shopping and the administration clients.

3.6.3 Controller

A controller defines application behavior; it interprets user gestures and maps them into actions to be performed by the model. Each client that exposes different functionality requires a separate controller. For example, the sample application would need separate controllers for shopping and administration clients. There is always some opportunity to reuse code that is part of the application controller framework; however, this is independent of the type of clients accessing the application.

However, multiple clients that expose similar or identical functionality should be able to share the controller responsible for the functionality. If the clients provide only slightly different functionality, it should still be possible to reuse the controller implementation by using a single class to implement the common behavior and using subclasses to implement the custom behavior. For example, the banking application described earlier has a Web-based interface as well as a stand-alone desktop client. The difference between the clients is how they present the interface—the view. Therefore they can share the same controller.

Because the controller interacts directly with the view it is not completely insulated from changes in the view implementation. For example, strongly typed references to view objects in the controller make it difficult to redeploy. In order to design the controller to allow a large portion of its implementation to be shared, we need to examine the interactions between the view and the controller and find ways to minimize the effect of those interactions on the controller. The interactions are:

- Interpreting user gestures generated through the view

- Selecting the view

3.6.3.1 Interpreting User Gestures

The controller accepts user gestures from the view. These depend on the medium that the view uses to present the user interface. For example, in a JFC application, the user gestures could be "button pressed" events or "mouse moved" events, and so on. In a Web interface, the user gestures appear as GET or POST requests for URLs of the application. In a messaging environment, the user gestures take the form of asynchronous messages.

To keep the controller as reusable as possible, the controller must *translate* these user gestures as soon as possible and turn them into *business events*—uniform, view-neutral representations of the actions requested by the user.

The sample application uses RequestToEventTranslator for this purpose. This object takes an HttpServletRequest from the view—a browser in this case—and translates it into an EStoreEvent business event. RequestToEvent-Translator is discussed in Section 10.6.3 on page 285. The rest of the controller implementation deals only with EStoreEvent and can be reused for different implementations of the view. If we wanted to implement a JFC-based client for the sample application, we could just add another translator that translates JFC events into business events.

Code Example 3.1 shows how RequestToEventTranslator takes a request and translates it into a business event. An object that implements ShoppingClientControllerInterface, which provides the core of the controller responsibilities, invoked using an EStoreEvent, does not need to change when the client changes.

```
public class RequestProcessor {
    ShoppingClientControllerInterface scc;
    RequestToEventTranslator eventTranslator;

    public void processRequest(HttpServletRequest req) {
        ...
        // translate view specific event into EStoreEvent
        EStoreEvent event = eventTranslator.processRequest(req);
        if (event != null) {
            // invoke the controller with EStoreEvent, instead of
            // using the view specific HttpServletRequest
            Collection updatedModelList = scc.handleEvent(event);
            mm.notifyListeners(updatedModelList);
        }
        ...
    }
}
```

Code Example 3.1   Translating View-Dependent Gestures into View-Neutral
Business Events

3.6.3.2 Selecting the View

The controller selects which view to display. These depend on the medium that the
view uses to present the user interface. For example, in a JFC application, the user
views are composed of Swing components such as panels, lists, tables, and so on. In
a Web interface, the views are HTML pages that are rendered by a browser.

To keep the controller as reusable as possible the controller needs to express
views in a technology-neutral fashion and translate them to technology-specific ren-
ditions as late as possible. This would require a layered view selection component
that uses objects to represent views (analogous to the business events in the previous
section) which are forwarded to specific types of view generators. For example, a
product list view would contain all the data needed to represent a list of products.
This object could be passed to a view generator, which would render the data in a
specific user interface medium. Note that depending on the medium, the view generator may reside on the server (HTML) or on the client (JFC).

3.6.3.3 Example: The Sample Application Controller

The sample applications controller is in two parts: the EJB controller, which interacts with enterprise beans and a controller proxy, which interacts with views. In the current release, the proxy is monolithic and specific to Web clients.

If another type of shopping client interface were required, the EJB controller could be shared without modification. However, the proxy portion of the controller would have to be rearchitected to support more than one type of view technology. For example, a JFC-based view selection component would need to register event listeners when the view is created. These listeners would then post or propagate the events to the client portion of the controller.

3.7   Summary

This chapter has discussed various types of J2EE clients, as illustrated in Figure 3.1.

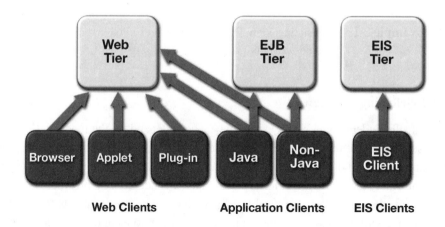

Figure 3.1   Client Options

In general, J2EE applications should use Web clients when possible. With the help of technologies such as DHTML and JavaScript, Web browsers can support reasonably powerful and fast user interfaces. Additional capabilities can be provided by using applets. Java applets can be used in conjunction with the browser using HTML or XML over HTTP for additional enhancements. A Java applet can also communicate with the middle tier for further control and flexibility. The Web browser is a truly universal Web client, so for simple user interfaces, and for Internet applications, it is the client of choice.

Application clients should be used when the data model is complex and cannot be expressed through the Web interaction model. Application clients are well-suited for intranet enterprise distribution. They can provide a richer user experience and blend well with the desktop windowing environment. However due to the increased complexity of such clients, there are reasons to avoid them in favor of Web-based applications. What's more, ongoing enhancements to the Web client speed and functionality will continue to erode the need to deploy stand-alone clients for all but a handful of cases.

The use of application clients on the open Internet is not straightforward because of distribution, deployment, security, and firewall issues. These clients are best suited for the intranets, where they can provide a more featureful user interface to the user and provide integrated security. Implementation of stand-alone clients requires more effort.

Special purpose application clients can be used for administrative and management tasks. These clients are not intended to be distributed to every user, and often have a minimal user interface. They perform specific tasks, perhaps invoked automatically by the system, through means external to the J2EE specification.

Use of enterprise information system clients should be limited to simple, well-understood management or administrative tasks.

The Java programming language is preferred for stand-alone clients, although similar capabilities may be possible with languages other than Java.

About the Author

GREG MURRAY is an engineer in the J2EE programming model team at Sun Microsystems. He assisted in the design and implemented much of the Web tier of the portions of Java Pet Store sample application. Prior to joining the J2EE programming model team Greg was a member of Global Products Engineering at Sun. Greg graduated with a B.A. in International Relations with a minor in Japanese from Brigham Young University.

CHAPTER 4

The Web Tier

by Greg Murray

Users have benefited significantly from the increasing ability of Web-based applications to generate dynamic content customized to their needs. JavaServer Pages (JSP) and servlets are J2EE technologies that support dynamic content generation in a portable, cross-platform manner. Web-based J2EE applications that use these technologies can be architected in a number of ways. Simple Web-based J2EE applications can use basic JSP pages and servlets or JSP pages with modular components. More complex transactional J2EE applications use JSP pages and modular components in conjunction with enterprise beans.

This chapter begins with a description of Web applications and Web containers. It discusses the use of the Common Gateway Interface, servlets, and JSP technology for providing dynamic and interactive content. It describes what situations require the use of servlets and when to use JSP technology and how to design the interface of a Web-based application with internationalization and localization in mind. Review of various design patterns for Web application will follow. Finally we will discuss migration strategies from Web-centric to EJB-centric applications.

4.1 Web Applications and Web Containers

In the J2EE lexicon, a Web application is a collection of HTML/XML documents, Web components (servlets and JSP pages), and other resources in either a directory structure or archived format known as a Web ARchive (WAR) file. A Web application is located on a central server and provides service to a variety of clients.

Web applications provide dynamic and interactive content to browser-based clients. Browser-based Web applications can be used for any type of application: from secure business-to-business applications to electronic commerce Web sites.

A Web container is a runtime environment for a Web application; a Web application runs within a Web container of a Web server. A Web container provides Web components with a naming context and life cycle management. Some Web servers may also provide more services, such as security, concurrency, transactions, and swapping to secondary storage. A Web server may work with an EJB server to provide such services. A Web server need not be located on the same machine as the EJB server. In some cases, a Web container may communicate with other Web containers.

4.2   Dynamic Content Creation

In the Internet world, the need to deliver dynamically generated content in a maintainable fashion is extremely important. This content may be personalized to an individual. Great care must be taken when designing the user experience of an application because it will distinguish one application from another and potentially make or break a company.

The sample application is an example of a Web application that delivers dynamically generated content. The underlying data that is used to generate the content for the sample application can be changed without modifying the sample application code. This would allow the administrator of the application to add new products or services which would immediately be available in the application. The sample application was designed to be general enough to not be tied to any product or service. With little effort, the sample application could be tailored to offer different products or services.

In this section we will discuss the technologies used to design a personalized Web application in which the logic that drives the application is separate from the content. We will begin by examining the conventional technology used to generate dynamic content, namely Common Gateway Interface (CGI) scripts. Following the discussion of CGI we will review the features of Java servlets and JavaServer Pages technology.

4.2.1   Common Gateway Interface

While the Internet was originally designed to provide static content, the need to present dynamic content, customized to a user's needs, has quickly come to drive the development of Web technology. The earliest response to this need was the Common Gateway Interface (CGI). This interface allows Web servers to call scripts to obtain data from (or send data to) databases, documents, and other programs, and present that data to viewers via the Web. However, CGI technology has a number of limitations.

One limitation is that the code within a CGI script that accesses resources, such as a file system or database, must be specific to the server's platform. Therefore most CGI applications will not run on another server platform without modification. This limits their utility in a distributed environments where Web applications may need to run on multiple platforms.

Second, because a new process must be created each time a CGI script is invoked, CGI scripts are often resource intensive and slow and thus tend not to scale well. Increasing the amount of hardware will allow a CGI application to scale to a point. However, the extent to which the application will scale is limited to the hardware and the operating system.

Finally, CGI applications are difficult to maintain because they combine content and display logic in one code base. As a consequence, two types of expertise are needed to maintain and update CGI scripts.

Many Web server vendors have enhanced CGI for their specific products and have developed better ways of handling CGI-like functions by providing extensions to their products. These have enabled the development of sophisticated Web applications based on CGI. However, the root problems still exist: CGI applications are platform-specific, do not scale well, and are difficult to maintain.

The J2EE platform supports two technologies, servlets and JavaServer Pages, that provide alternate solutions that overcome these problems.

4.2.2   Servlets

Java servlets are a means of extending the functionality of a Web server. Servlets can be viewed as applets that run on the server. Servlets are a portable platform- and Web server-independent means of delivering dynamic content. A browser-based application that calls servlets need not support the Java programming language because a servlet's output can be HTML, XML, or any other content type.

Servlets are written in the Java programming language. This allows servlets to be supported on any platform that has a Java virtual machine and a Web server that supports servlets. Servlets can be used on different platforms without recompiling. They can use generic APIs such as JDBC to communicate directly with existing enterprise resources. This simplifies application development, allowing Web applications to be developed more rapidly.

Servlets are extensible because they are based on the Java programming language. This allows developers to extend the functionalities of a Web application just as they would a Java application. A good example of this would be a controller servlet that is extended to be a secure controller. All of the functionalities of the original controller would be provided along with new security features.

Servlets perform better than CGI scripts. A servlet can be loaded into memory once and then called as many times as needed and scale well without requiring additional hardware. Once a servlet is loaded into memory it can run on a single lightweight thread while CGI scripts must be loaded in a different process for every request. Another benefit of servlets is that, unlike a CGI script, a servlet can maintain and/or pool connections to databases or other necessary Java objects which saves time in processing requests.

Servlets eliminate much of the complexity of getting parameters from an HTTP request; components have direct access to parameters because they are presented as objects. With CGI-based applications, parameters posted from a form are converted to environment properties which must then read into a program.

One of their greatest benefits is that servlets provide uniform APIs for maintaining session data throughout a Web application and for interacting with the user requests. Session data can be used to overcome the limitations of Web applications due to the stateless nature of HTTP.

4.2.3 JavaServer Pages Technology

JavaServer Pages (JSP) technology was designed to provide a declarative, presentation-centric method of developing servlets. Along with all the benefits servlets offer, JSP technology offers the ability to rapidly develop servlets where content and display logic are separated, and to reuse code through a component-based architecture.

Both servlets and JSP pages describe how to process a request (from an HTTP client) to create a response. While servlets are expressed in the Java programming language, JSP pages are text-based documents that include a combination of HTML and JSP tags, Java code, and other information. Although both servlets and JSP pages can be used to solve identical problems, each is intended to accomplish specific tasks. Servlet technology was developed as a mechanism to accept requests from browsers, retrieve enterprise data from application tier or databases, perform application logic on the data (especially in the case where the servlet accessed the database directly), and format that data for presentation in the browser (usually in HTML). A servlet uses print statements to post HTML data, both hard-coded tags and dynamic content based on the enterprise data retrieved from the back-end tiers, back to the user's browser.

Embedding HTML in print statements causes two problems. First, when HTML is embedded in the print statements of a servlet, Web designers cannot preview the look and feel of an HTML page until runtime. Second, when data or its display format changes, locating the appropriate sections of code in the servlet is very difficult. In addition, when presentation logic and content are intermixed, changes in the content require that a servlet be recompiled and reloaded into the Web server.

JSP pages provide a mechanism to specify the mapping from a JavaBeans component to the HTML (or XML) presentation format. Since JSP pages are text-based, a Web designer uses graphical development tools to create and view their content. The same tools can be used to specify where data from the EJB or enterprise information system tiers is displayed. JSP pages use the Java programming language for scripting complex formatting, such as the creation of dynamically-sized tables for master-detail forms. Some JSP editing tools may provide advanced features so that a Web designer can specify the formatting of complex data without using Java code. Alternatively, Java programmers can provide their Web designers with a set of JavaBeans components and/or custom tags that handle complex dynamic formatting of HTML, so that the Web designers do not need to understand how to code in the Java programming language in order to create a complex JSP page.

When a Web designer changes a JSP page, the page is automatically recompiled and reloaded into the Web server. In addition, all the JSP pages in a Web application can be compiled prior to deploying the application for greater efficiency.

Thus JSP technology allows content developers and Web application designers to clearly define what is application logic and what is content. Content providers don't need to know Java technology to update or maintain content. Instead they can design interfaces using the JavaBeans components and custom tags provided by the Web application developer. Web application developers need not be experts in user interface design to build Web applications. At the same time, a Web application development and content can easily be performed by a single person.

Like servlets, JSP technology is an efficient means of providing dynamic content in a portable platform- or application-independent means. JSP technology also supports a reusable component model through the inclusion of JavaBeans technology and custom tag extensions. Note that the JavaBeans components used by JSP pages are not the same AWT or JFC JavaBeans components. These Java-Beans components simply expose properties using get and set methods. custom tags can be viewed as intelligent JavaBeans components with the exception that the actions can better interact with the JSP page (see Section 4.4.2 on page 86).

In summary, JSP technology provides an easy way to develop servlet-based dynamic content, with the additional benefit of separating content and display logic. In a properly designed JSP page, content and application logic can be independently updated by developers with specific expertise in each area.

Currently CGI scripts are widely used to provide dynamic content. Technologies such as servlets and the JSP technology that are scalable and easy to write and maintain should be used instead of CGI scripts. This is driven by the need to provide dynamic content in a platform-independent, scalable way.

4.3   Servlets and JSP Pages

In an environment where only servlet technology is available, servlets can handle complex logic processing, navigation paths between screens, access to enterprise data, and formatting the data into an HTML response. In an environment where both servlet and JSP technology is available, JSP pages should be used to handle almost all of these tasks.

The Java code used within JSP pages should remain relatively simple. Therefore, a developer should encapsulate complex tasks within custom tags and Java-Beans components. A sophisticated Web application can consist solely of JSP pages, custom tags, and JavaBeans components; servlets are rarely necessary.

In this section we will review the roles that Web components can play, when to use servlets, when to use JSP pages, and when either technology may be used.

4.3.1   Web Component Roles

Although a common view is that Web components are mainly used to provide an application's presentation, in the J2EE application programming model Web components can serve two roles: as presentation components and as front components. *Presentation components* generate the HTML/XML response that when rendered determines the user interface. A JSP page acting as a presentation component may contain reusable custom tags or presentation logic. A presentation component could also be a servlet that produces binary data, such as an image. *Front components* don't do any presentation, but rather manage other components and handle HTTP requests or convert the requests into a form that an application can understand. Front components are useful because they provide a single entry point to an application, thus making security, application state, and presentation uniform and easier to maintain.

Figure 4.1 illustrates the basic mechanism. The front component accepts a request, then determines the appropriate presentation component to forward it to. The presentation component then processes the request and returns the response to the front component, which forwards it to the server for presentation to the user.

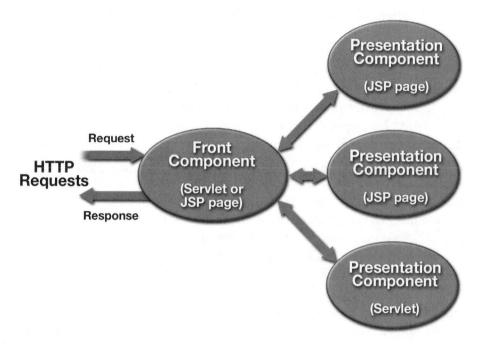

Figure 4.1   Web Component Roles

4.3.1.1 Front Components

While the sample application uses a JSP page as its front component, you could also use a servlet. The JSP page simplifies the initialization of the Web-tier JavaBeans components used by the sample application. However, a servlet could also perform this initialization.

The sample application front component parses all form data posted to the page and generates the events that result from the posted data. The events generated by the front component are forwarded to a template presentation component.

Front components perform the function of a controller when used in an MVC architecture (see Section 4.6.3 on page 103).

4.3.1.2 Presentation Components

Many Web applications have a shopping cart that contains the products that a user has selected for purchase. In most applications the content of the shopping cart needs to be displayed repeatedly. JSP technology can be used to iterate through the list of items maintained in a shopping cart (implemented as a JavaBeans component) and display the contents to the user.

The code that generates the shopping cart display should be maintainable by content providers. Since the shopping cart JavaBeans object and JSP page that generates the HTML representation of the shopping cart can also be used in more than one part of an application, the presentation components used to generate the HTML representation of the shopping cart should also be modular and reusable.

Modular design allows separation of roles. Content providers can specialize in how content is displayed, and component developers can focus on the logic that is used in the JavaBeans component to manipulate the shopping cart data, and on the JSP page that generates the HTML representation of the data. Note that the data that is presented to the user may be taken from multiple sources.

Other requirements that presentation components must address are creating a consistent look and feel for an application while providing mechanisms for personalizing the user interface. For example, consider a Web site that has a personalized banner, a navigation menu that displays only information that a user wants to see, and the content a user wants to see. The next section describes how to design a JSP page or set of JSP pages that allow for a consistent look and feel throughout an application.

Presentation Component Templates

Figure 4.2 illustrates an application in which all pages share a common banner, navigation menu, body, and footer. Each item in the example can be seen as a component that is used to generate the final look and feel, can contain dynamic information, and should be customizable. This is the kind of page design that can benefit from the use of JSP templates.

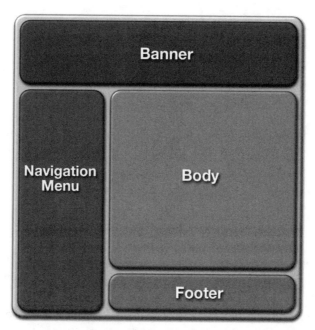

Figure 4.2   Presentation Components

There are two ways of constructing the page shown in Figure 4.2. Depending on the granularity that you want your application to have, you could either build the page using custom tags and JavaBeans components or you could break up each portion into separate JSP pages each containing the necessary custom tags and JavaBeans components needed to generate their portions of the content, then build the whole page from a JSP page that incorporates the others using runtime includes.

Code Example 4.1 contains the template used to provide the screen components depicted in Figure 4.2. The template is constructed of an included JSP page (ScreenDefinitions.jsp), and the custom tag j2ee:insert. The content and pages are described in the ScreenDefinitions.jsp file. The template uses the insert custom tag to do runtime includes of the components needed to build it. See Section 10.3.2.1 on page 259 for more discussion of the sample application's template mechanism.

```
<%@ taglib uri="Web-INF/tlds/taglib.tld" prefix="j2ee" %>
<%@ include file="ScreenDefinitions.jsp" %>
```

```
<html>
  <head>
    <title>
      <j2ee:insert template="template" parameter="HtmlTitle" />
    </title>
  </head>
  <body bgcolor="white">
    <j2ee:insert template="template" parameter="HtmlBanner" />
    <j2ee:insert template="template" parameter="HtmlBody" />
  </body>
</html>
```

Code Example 4.1   JSP Page Templating Mechanism

This example illustrates a clean separation between presentation logic, data, and content. There is no Java code in this page, so it could be managed by a content provider not familiar with the Java programming language.

We recommend using JavaBeans components or custom tags to do data rendering. These can be created by a developer familiar with the Java programming language. If JavaBeans components and custom tags are designed in a general manner, they should be reusable in other portions of the application or in other applications.

4.3.2   Servlets

Although JSP pages can be used for most purposes, there are some circumstances where servlets are more appropriate. The following sections describe common uses of servlets.

4.3.2.1 Generating Binary Data

Servlets are well suited for dynamically generating binary data such as images or a new content type. Requests for content of that type would be mapped to servlets that know how to generate the content, but from the Web client's point of view, it is merely requesting delivery of an ordinary image. The only assumption that need be made about the client is that it supports the image format being generated.

One example of this would be a servlet that generates a graph summarizing stock performance from data retrieved from a database or other source. This image can be kept in memory and updated every minute or so as needed. Using a servlet to generate the data, then keeping the data in memory for ready display, can save time and improve performance in both execution cycles and file access time.

4.3.2.2 Extending a Web Server's Functionality

Servlets are a portable mechanism for extending the functionality of a Web server. For example, if a new data format must be supported, a servlet can be mapped to the file type for the format.

A good example of a servlet that extends a Web server is the servlet that is mapped to JSP files. This servlet parses all files that end with a `jsp` file extension and compiles the JSP pages into servlets. The resulting servlets are then executed by the Web container and the resulting response is sent back to the client.

4.3.3   JSP Pages Versus Servlets

Depending on the composition of your development team, time constraints, and application architecture, your use of JSP pages and servlets will differ. Both technologies have merits and should be used accordingly. In some cases there is not a single correct choice of whether to use a servlet or JSP page.

Servlets are a programmatic tool and are best suited for low-level application functions that don't require frequent modification.

JSP pages are a presentation-centric, declarative means of binding dynamic content and logic. JSP pages should be used to handle the HTML representation that is generated by a page. They are coded in HTML-like pages with structure and content familiar to Web content providers. However, JSP pages provide far more power than ordinary HTML pages. JSP pages can handle application logic through the use of JavaBeans components and custom tags. JSP pages themselves can also be used as modular, reusable presentation components that can be bound together using a templating mechanism.

4.4   JSP Page Design

JSP pages are unique in that they can contain both presentation logic and content. They provide a variety of options for designing applications that are easy to maintain and extend. The options available for binding content to logic include Java-

Beans components, custom tags, and scriptlets. The following sections describe some of these options and recommend when to use each.

4.4.1   JavaBeans Components

JavaBeans technology is useful for building portable and reusable components that can used in conjunction with JSP technology. There are many ways to use Java-Beans components within an application.

One way to use JavaBeans components is as data-centric model objects. If these beans are created specifically to manipulate and return data, they can be used by multiple views of an application and by many different clients at one time.

In conjunction with a front component, a JavaBeans component can be used as a controller. The sample application uses a JavaBeans component to process all requests received from the front component and pass them along to the appropriate page.

Page-specific JavaBeans components provide the logic to process data and generate a result for a particular page. The disadvantage of using these types of beans is that they are more difficult to reuse.

4.4.2   Custom Tags

Custom tags are the mechanism provided by JSP technology for defining customized, declarative, and modular functionality for use by JSP pages. Custom tags are delivered as *tag libraries* and are imported into a JSP page using the `taglib` directive. Once imported, a custom tag can be used in the page using the prefix defined by the directive.

Custom tags provide the same functionality as JavaBeans components. However, unlike JavaBeans components which must first be declared and then accessed using get and set methods, custom tags work with a page by obtaining initialization information through parameters defined when the tag is created. Custom tags have access to the Web container and all the objects available to JSP pages. Custom tags can modify the generated response. Custom tags can also be nested within one another, allowing for complex interactions with a JSP page.

Custom tags are portable and reusable. They are written in the Java programming language which allows them to be used across platforms and Web containers. If you plan on reusing custom tags, you should take care to design tags that are not application-specific.

Custom tags are ideal for iterating through data and generating the HTML code needed to render a page. For example, a custom tag could take the data contained within a shopping cart JavaBeans component and generate the HTML to render the shopping cart. Proper use of custom tags can reduce, if not eliminates, the amount of Java language code used in a JSP page to generate dynamic content. Portions of a page that require logic, such as looping or state display, are also good places to use custom tags.

The template page in Code Example 4.1 provides a familiar interface to a designer or HTML authoring tools. The custom tags in the page appear as HTML tags. In contrast, Java language code can get corrupted by a tool or page designer not familiar with the Java programming language.

In addition to rendering HTML, custom tags can be used to process data. This can reduce the amount of Java language code needed within an application and make portions of an application configurable by a page designer.

Code Example 4.2 shows one such use for custom tags: as a `switch` statement for processing user input. The `CreateTemplate` custom tag creates a `Template` object and places it in the request containing the data necessary to render the current page. The `CreateTemplate` tag has nested tags that correspond to `case` statements in a `switch` statement. These nested tags include `Screen` tags which in turn have `Parameter` tags nested within them. Depending on the current screen ID obtained from the `ScreenManager`, the proper `Template` object will be created and the parameters will be set to reflect the appropriate page components. The `Template` object is processed by the JSP templating mechanism illustrated in Code Example 4.1. Notice that expressions within the tag parameters are used to interact with sample application data.

```
<j2ee:CreateTemplate template="template"
    screen="<%=screenManager.getCurrentScreen(request)%>">
    <j2ee:Screen screen="<%=ScreenNames.MAIN_SCREEN%>">
        <j2ee:Parameter parameter=
            "HtmlTitle" value="Welcome to Java(TM) Pet Store Demo"
                direct="true"/>
        <j2ee:Parameter parameter="HtmlBody"
            value="/index.jsp" direct="false"/>
    </j2ee:Screen>

    <j2ee:Screen screen="<%=ScreenNames.SIGN_IN_SUCCESS_SCREEN%>">
        <j2ee:Parameter parameter="HtmlTitle"
            value="Welcome" direct="true"/>
```

```
        <j2ee:Parameter parameter="HtmlBody"
            value="/signinsuccess.jsp" direct="false"/>
    </j2ee:Screen>
  </j2ee:CreateTemplate>
```

Code Example 4.2   Data-Centric Custom Tags

4.4.3   Using Scriptlets and Expressions

When designing a Web site with interactive and dynamic content, it may be necessary to use small portions of code to generate content. Scriptlets are small fragments of scripting code whose language is defined by the language parameter in the JSP page directive. Expressions are like scriptlets, except that they are played directly in the response.

To make code easier to read and maintain, we recommend that JSP pages be used mainly for presentation. While a major portion of an application could be developed in JSP technology, placing large amounts of code in JSP pages makes them more difficult to update and can be confusing to page designers.

We recommend including Java code only when necessary. JavaBeans components and custom tags provide a means of adding functionality while avoiding scriptlets. A developer can use expressions with JavaBeans components or custom tags to generate dynamic content.

4.5   Internationalization and Localization

Internationalization may sometimes be overlooked when developing a Web application targeted at a particular enterprise or localized market. However, it is becoming increasingly important when developing a Web application that may be used in more than one country or region that you consider internationalization from the outset. This section presents approaches to developing an internationalized Web application.

Internationalization is the process of preparing an application to support various languages, while *localization* is the process of adapting an internationalized application to support a specific language or locale. A *locale* is a language or subset of a language that includes both regional and language-specific information. Internationalization involves identifying and isolating portions of the application that present strings of data to the user so that the strings can be acquired from a single source such as a file. Localization involves translating these strings into a specific language and assembling them in a file that the application can access. Thus internationalizing an application allows it to be easily adapted to new languages and markets while localization provides the adaptation of an internationalized application to a particular country or region. Neither the Web nor EJB container need be running in the same locale as the client's Web browser.

Internationalization should not be an afterthought when developing a Web application. It is easier to design an application that is capable of being internationalized than to retrofit an existing application, which can be both costly and time consuming. A great deal of time and money can be saved by planning for internationalization and localization at the outset of a project.

An application written in the Java programming language is not automatically internationalized and localizable. Though a developer of a Web application can deal with many different character sets by using the J2SE platform, the platform's support for Unicode 2.0 is only as good as the data that is input into the application.

With a Web application, the presentation layer is the focus of internationalization and localization efforts. This includes the JSP pages and supporting helper JavaBeans components.

4.5.1   Internationalization

Data handling is one part of a Web application most affected by internationalization, with impact in three areas: data input, data storage, and locale-independent data presentation.

4.5.1.1 Data Input

Data is typically input to a Web application by posts from a form on an HTML page. We assume that the client's platform will provide a means for inputting the data.

The browser running in the client's native locale is responsible for encoding the form parameter data in the HTTP request so that it reaches a Web application in a readable format. By the time the application receives the data it is in Unicode format and a developer should not have to worry about character set issues. If you need to do any type of word breaking or parsing it is recommended that you look at the `BreakIterator` class in the `java.text` package.

4.5.1.2 Data Storage

Setting your database to a Unicode 2.0 character encoding (such as UTF-8 or UTF-16), allows data to be saved correctly in many different languages. The content you are saving must be entered properly from the Web tier and the JDBC drivers must also support the encoding you choose. Refer to your data storage vendor for the best means of providing data persistence.

4.5.1.3 Enabling Locale-Independent Data Formatting

An application must be designed to present localized data appropriately for a target locale. For example, you must ensure that locale-sensitive text such as dates, times, currency, and numbers are presented in a locale-dependent way. If you design your text-related classes in a locale-independent way, they can be reused throughout an application. The following methods are used to format currency in locale-specific and locale-independent ways.

Code Example 4.3 illustrates how to format currency in a locale-specific manner. The NumberFormat class obtained will be the default NumberFormat for the system. Note that the string pattern contains a "$" character. This method will only display correctly for countries that use dollars. There is not much value with this approach because it is tied to a specific locale.

```java
public static String formatCurrency(double amount){
        NumberFormat nf = NumberFormat.getCurrencyInstance();
        DecimalFormat df = (DecimalFormat)nf;
        df.setMinimumFractionDigits(2);
        df.setMaximumFractionDigits(2);
        df.setDecimalSeparatorAlwaysShown(true);
        String pattern = "$###,###.00";
        df.applyPattern(pattern);
        return df.format(amount);
}
```

Code Example 4.3   Locale-Specific Currency Formatting

Code Example 4.4 shows how to format currency in a locale-independent manner. The user can specify any supported locale and the resulting String will be formatted for that locale. For best results, the string `pattern` should be obtained from a resource bundle.

```
public static String formatCurrency(double amount, Locale locale){
        NumberFormat nf = NumberFormat.getCurrencyInstance(locale);
        DecimalFormat df = (DecimalFormat)nf;
        df.setMinimumFractionDigits(2);
        df.setMaximumFractionDigits(2);
        df.setDecimalSeparatorAlwaysShown(true);
        String pattern = "###,###.00";
        return df.format(amount);
}
```

Code Example 4.4   Locale-Independent Currency Formatting

In a JSP page, the functions described in Code Example 4.3 and Code Example 4.4 for formatting currency can be used by including the following code:

```
<%=JSPUtil.formatCurrency(cart.getTotal(), Locale.JAPAN)%>
```

This expression uses the method `formatCurrency` which is located in a class named `JSPUtil`. The total that is returned from the `cart.getTotal` method is a `double`. Note that when using this code you will need to import the `java.util.Locale` and `com.sun.estore.util.JSPUtil` classes.

4.5.2   Localization

Once an application has been internationalized it can be localized. This section focuses on techniques for delivering localized content to clients. It also reviews techniques for delivering localized content through the use of resource bundles and language-specific JSP files.

4.5.2.1 Delivering Localized Content

Care must be taken to ensure that the application being developed handles data in code sets other than the default ISO 8859-1 (Latin-1). Many Java virtual machines will support code sets other than English. A detailed listing of character sets supported by Sun's Java virtual machine can be found at:

will support code sets other than English. A detailed listing of character sets supported by Sun's Java virtual machine can be found at:

```
http://java.sun.com/products/jdk1.2/docs/guide/
        intl/encoding.doc.html
```

Depending on what content is delivered to the users, localization can be done in a few different ways. Web applications can be designed to deliver localized content based on a user preference or to automatically deliver localized content based on information in the HTTP request.

When an application allows users to select a language, the preferred language can be stored in the session. The selection can occur through a URL selection or a form post that sets an application-level language preference. The posted preference data can be maintained as part of a user profile as a cookie on the client's system using a cookie or in a persistent data store on the server. Giving users the ability to select a language ensures that the user gets the content that they expect.

Applications can also automatically deliver localized content by using Accept-Language attribute in header information of the HTTP request and mapping it to a supported locale. The Accept-Language attribute is set in the user's Web browser and differs slightly between browsers. When using automatic application-level locale selection, it is prudent to also provide a mechanism to let the user override the automatic selection and select a preferred language. Automatic locale selection also depends on application support for different locales. Care needs to be taken to ensure that unsupported languages are handled properly.

4.5.2.2 Localized Messages

The Java programming language provides facilities for localization. This section discusses methods of providing localized data in a Web application.

In some cases an application may need to support multiple languages on the same JSP page. List resource bundles are also useful when using servlets. Code Example 4.5 shows how to deliver content from a user-specified locale using a ListResourceBundle.

```java
public class WebMessages extends java.util.ListResourceBundle{
    public Object [][] getContents(){
        return contents;
    }
    static final Object[][] contents = {
```

```
        //Messages
        {"com.sunw.messages.welcome",
            "Welcome to Java(TM) Pet Store Demo"},
        {"com.sunw.messages.any_message",
            "Untranslated message},
        {"com.sunw.messages.come_back_soon", "Come Back Soon"}
    }
}
```

Code Example 4.5   English Resource Bundle

In this example, localized content for messages in each supported language is contained in separate files. Code Example 4.6 demonstrates a similar resource bundle file that contains Japanese messages.

```
public class WebMessages_ja extends java.util.ListResourceBundle{
    public Object [][] getContents(){
        return contents;
    }

    static final Object[][] contents = {
        //Messages
        {"com.sunw.messages.welcome",
            "Japanese welcome Java(TM) Pet Store Demo"},
        {"com.sunw.messages.come_back_soon",
            "Japanese Come Back Soon"}
    }
}
```

Code Example 4.6   Japanese Resource Bundle

Inside a servlet or JSP page, the messages contained in a resource bundle can be obtained with the code shown in Code Example 4.7.

```
// set the user's desired locale
session.setValue("preferredLocale", Locale.JAPAN);
// load preferred locale
```

```
ResourceBundle messages = ResourceBundle.getResource("WebMessages",
    (Locale)session.getValue("preferredLocale");
```

Code Example 4.7   Getting Messages From a Resource Bundle

Note that the Japanese resource bundle's class file name ends with "_ja". When loading resources, the Japanese version of the resource bundle file will be loaded if `Locale.JAPAN` is specified in the request or the default application is running in a Japanese locale. Also note that this file contains only the messages that you want to appear in translation. All messages not defined in this file will be used from the default file, which has no extension following its name.

This example shows how to specify and store a user's preferred target language and load messages for that language. Once the resource bundle is loaded a message can be obtained by using the command:

```
messages.getString("com.sunw.messages.welcome");
```

In this example, `messages` refers to the name of the resource bundle and `welcome` refers to the message that you would like to load. You need to ensure that the `contentType` of the page is set to an encoding that supports multiple languages (the next section provides details on setting the `contentType`). UTF-8 encoding allows you to display multiple languages on a single Web page. Moreover, UTF-8 encoding is supported by the most commonly used Web browsers.

It may be useful to create a JavaBeans component to assist in loading and managing the messages for an application to save resources. The details of how to create this type of component aren't covered in this document.

Resource bundles are useful for providing localized content as long as the logic for displaying internationalized text is not going to be greatly changed by the target locale. If the logic changes, it is recommended to use separate JSP files for the content, as described in the following section.

Localized Content in JSP Pages

Where you need to provide messages that vary depending on the target locale, or where the content and display logic are drastically different, it is better to use a completely different JSP file.

Since JSP pages are responsible for the presentation of a Web application's user interface, they provide an ideal place to put locale-specific information. It is important that the JSP pages and the supporting JavaBeans components and tag libraries be able to deal with localized content. This section discusses how to design a localized page and how to integrate this page into a Web application.

The encoding of a JSP page must be specified in order for the Web container to process it. An Application Component Provider sets the encoding of a JSP page using the `contentType` attribute of the `page` directive. This attribute sets the encoding for both the JSP page and the subsequent output stream. The value of `contentType` should be "TYPE" or "TYPE;charset=CHARSET" followed by a ";" and a valid IANA registry value. The default value for TYPE is `text/html`; the default value for the character encoding is `ISO-8859-1`. The IANA registry values can be found at:

```
ftp://venera.isi.edu/in-notes/iana/assignments/character-sets
```

If you are using the `contentType` attribute of the `page` directive, the resulting output stream should not be a problem; otherwise, you will need to ensure the output stream is set properly. Keep in mind that when using the `page` directive you can only set the content type once, because a `page` directive is set at page compile time. If it is necessary to change the content type dynamically, you can do so with a servlet.

When using servlets it is important to set the response encoding correctly. The `ServletResponse` interface contains a `setLocale` method which should be used to ensure that data is set to the proper locale. The Servlet specification indicates that the locale should be set before calling the `getWriter` method. For more details, refer to the Servlet specification.

To prepare an application for localization, you should follow these steps:

1. Separate the display logic from the content in the presentation layer (JSP) of the Web application. This makes localizing content easier and prevents integration errors which could occur if portions of the display logic were localized by accident.

    The J2EE programming model recommends that you deliver locale-specific files that follow the naming convention used by resource bundles. This naming convention is the base file name followed by an underscore (_) and the language variant. A country and a variant can also be used:
   a. Language

    ```
    jsp + _ + language
    ```

b. Language and country

```
jsp + _ + language + _ + country
```

c. Language with country and a variant

```
jsp + _ + language + _ + country + _ + variant
```

2. Ensure that the character encoding of the localized files is supported by the Java virtural machine of the system running the Web application. Also, be sure that the correct encoding is listed in the contentType tag included in the page directive of the JSP page.

A properly internationalized application can be quickly localized for any number of languages without any modifications to the code of the Web application. It is much easier to internationalize an application the beginning of a development cycle when application design is first specified.

4.6   Application Designs

There are many ways to design a Web application. The complexity of an application depends on various needs and requirements such as limitations on application development, capabilities of the development team, longevity of an application, and dynamism of the content in an application. Even if the original application is not intended for widespread use, it is always benefical to design an application in such a way that it can be migrated to a scalable, multitier design as a project's scope changes.

Four general types of Web applications can be implemented with the J2EE platform: basic HTML, HTML with basic JSP pages, JSP pages with JavaBeans components, and highly-structured applications that use modular components and enterprise beans. The first three types of applications are considered to be *Web-centric*, whereas the last type is *EJB-centric*. The spectrum of application designs is presented in Figure 4.3.

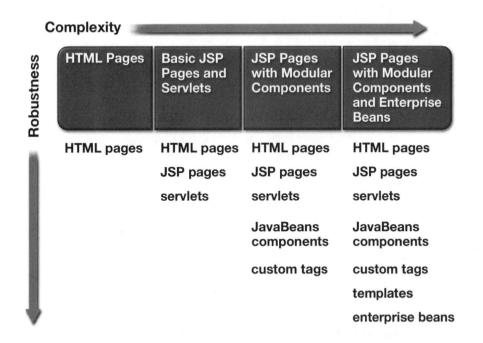

Figure 4.3   Application Designs

4.6.1   Applications with Basic JSP Pages and Servlets

Web applications with basic JSP pages and servlets are similar in complexity to conventional HTML and CGI-based applications widely deployed on the Web, except that the dynamic portions of the pages and user interaction are handled by JSP or servlets in place of CGI scripts.

HTML applications with basic JSP pages are entry-level Web applications with much of their logic in servlets or JSP pages. These applications can be developed quickly, but are more difficult to extend and maintain.

In these simple applications, some pages display static HTML content. Where necessary to display dynamic content, (for example, content generated using data from a database), a JSP page or servlet should contain code to connect to the database and retrieve the data.

In these simplest applications, the layout will not change frequently. The content used for the page layout of the application will be tied to the application.

This means that changes to dynamic pages can only be made by an engineer or page designer familiar with the Java programming language.

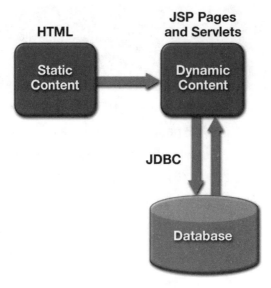

Figure 4.4   Applications with Basic JSP Pages and Servlets

Including much of the logic in JSP pages or servlets is good for prototyping an application or for controlled environments, such as intranet sites, where the application is not expected to be used by a large number of users.

As the complexity of the application increases, a model that allows for more modularization of components would be useful. The next section describes how to handle more complex user interaction or dynamic data processing.

4.6.2   Applications with Modular Components

When developing Web applications with dynamic content and a large degree of user interaction, you should use JSP pages with JavaBeans components, custom tags, and included JSP pages. These three types of components can be used to generate content, process requests, and handle the display of personalized content.

Figure 4.5 shows a path that a user might take through a hypothetical, interactive Web application and shows how reusable components can be used at each step in the process.

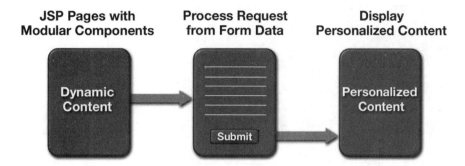

Figure 4.5   Process Flow of JSP Pages with Modular Components

Although this example appears simple, a number of components are needed to take the user through the process. Creating more modular components will allow for more code reuse and make the application more maintainable.

Let's look at each of the steps in more detail.

4.6.2.1 Modular Components in a JSP Page

JSP pages can be created using a variety of components. Used consistently, these components provide a common look and feel throughout an application. This technique is similar to templates, yet each page can be unique if needed. Figure 4.6 shows how to design a JSP page that contains products obtained from a catalog implemented as a JavaBeans component.

In this example the file `banner.jsp` contains a reusable component. Putting the logic to display the banner for the site in one JSP page means that the banner code does not need to appear on each page. Instead, the JSP page containing the banner code is added to each page using a runtime include.

In the center of the page, the body is generated using data from the `Catalog` component (and possibly some custom tags for HTML rendering of the data). A `Catalog` connects with an external data source using a connection obtained from the JDBC connection pool JavaBeans component. A `Catalog` is also responsible for updating the data or holding data that has been previously entered in the application.

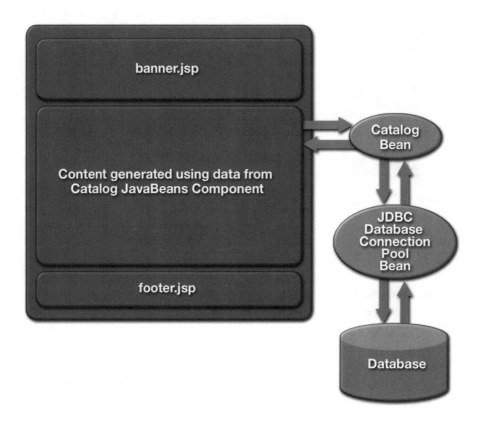

Figure 4.6   Reusable Components in a JSP Page

4.6.2.2 Processing Requests with Modular Components

Processing user requests is another important aspect of Web application behavior that can be effectively implemented using modular components. Applications that use modular components for request processing will be easier to develop and maintain. Figure 4.7 depicts how data from a form can be processed in a Web application.

In this example, a user submits data from a browser. The data is posted to the process request bean, which extracts the user data and converts it into account data maintained by a the account bean JavaBeans component. The account data is stored in a database using a JDBC connection obtained from the JDBC connection pool bean, also a JavaBeans component. If the data was entered correctly, the process request bean forwards the user to the appropriate page confirming the creation of the account.

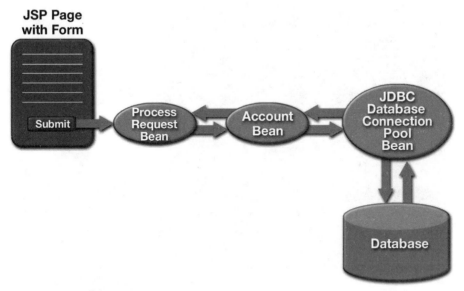

Figure 4.7   Processing a Request with Reusable Components

To avoid confusion, JavaBeans components that interact with users and external data (in this example, the bean that processes requests) should be separate from the components that represent that data (the account JavaBeans component). This separation of content and data enables the components to be reused and the application as a whole to be migrated to a more complex design as its scope changes.

4.6.2.3 Displaying Personalized Content

A JSP page that displays the personalized content is similar to the example shown in Figure 4.6 except that the displayed data is obtained from the account bean.

The data used to generate the content of this page includes data entered by the user. The page can also include other information personalized to the user's needs. After setting up an account, the users can be taken directly to a personalized page each time they log into the application. Data reflecting a user's previous visits can be saved as part of the user account and used to drive the content of the application seen by that user.

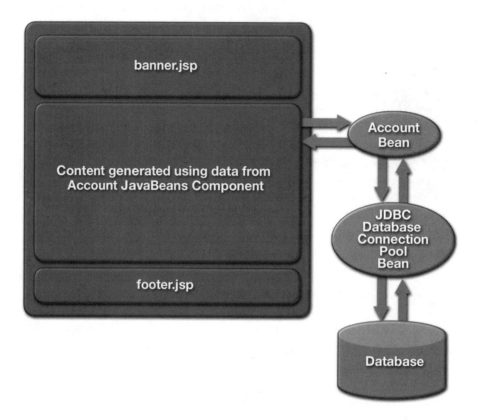

Figure 4.8   Displaying Personalized Content in a JSP Page

This type of application can be used in many types of situations. However, as an application using this design becomes larger, the level of complexity increases. More of the developer's time may be for work on the system-level issues such as managing the connection pool and application state and transaction management. Migrating to an EJB-centric design will allow the developer to stay focused on the application design.

A well-designed application using JSP pages with JavaBeans components and custom tags will have a clean separation of business from display logic. The content will be easier to modify and the components, if designed well, will be reusable. The major weakness of this design is the need for developers to provide connections to legacy applications and transaction support. As an application becomes more complex and the need for more transactional support and external resource integration becomes an issue, a more structured approach is required.

4.6.3   EJB-Centric Applications

An EJB-centric application extends the modular, component-based application described in the previous section, with two main differences. First, this design uses a front component for a controller. Second, data represented by the JavaBeans components is maintained by enterprise beans. This design provides flexibility, manageability, and separation of developer responsibilities.

Flexibility is provided by using a MVC architecture in conjunction with a front component. The MVC architecture allows for a clean separation of business logic, data, and presentation logic. This design also enables content providers and application developers to focus on what they do best. The sample application uses an MVC architecture to separate business from presentation logic.

Figure 4.9 shows how an MVC architecture can be implemented using JSP pages, servlets, and JavaBeans components.

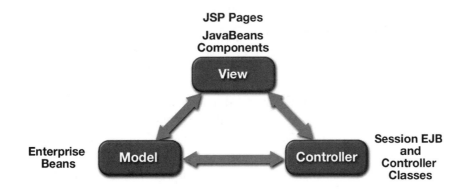

Figure 4.9   Model-View-Controller Architecture

As illustrated in the figure, the logic driving the application is separate from the presentation logic and from data presented to the user. This design is similar to the design in the previous section, except that a central controller receives all requests and updates the JavaBeans components that contain view data.

Now let us explore each part of the MVC architecture and consider how a Web application can benefit from it.

4.6.3.1 Model

The model represents the data on which an application is based. In an EJB-centric application, enterprise beans hold the data needed by the application. All modifications to the data occur thorough events sent to the EJB controller.

4.6.3.2 View

A view presents the data represented by the model in a way that's targeted at a specific type of client. Most enterprise applications will support a number of different views. The same model could have a Visual Basic client view, a Swing view, or a Web view. The view for a Web application consists of JSP files, which have sole responsibility for displaying the model data. The JSP files can contain JavaBeans components, custom tags, or included JSP page components (as described in Section 4.6.2.1 on page 99).

JSP pages should only contain code related to the display of model data. Repetitive HTML rendering, such as banners and navigation bars, should be handled by custom tags or JavaBeans components whenever possible. Miscellaneous tasks such as locale-specific currency formatting should be handled by custom tags or by helper classes.

The view can employ a templating mechanism, as described in "Presentation Component Templates" on page 82, to provide a consistent look and feel for an application.

In the sample application, the model data maintained by enterprise beans is mirrored by JavaBeans components that reside in the Web tier. The components in the Web tier allow the data maintained by the enterprise beans to be easily displayed by a JSP page. The JavaBeans view objects are responsible for updating themselves with the data maintained by the enterprise beans that they mirror. These JavaBeans components register with the Web controller to listen for model update events received from the EJB controller. When an update event is received, JavaBeans components contact the enterprise beans they mirror and refresh the data they contain. These JavaBeans components contain read-only data, since data modification is the responsibility of the controller.

4.6.3.3 Controller

To ensure that a Web application runs smoothly with the Model-View-Controller architecture, a central point of control is necessary. This is provided by using a front component and some helper classes. This controller maintains the data in the model and ensures that the data presented by the view is consistent with the corresponding model.

The controller provides a level of control that isn't possible by using statically-linked Web pages. With static pages, there is no guarantee that all users of a Web site will use the preferred point of entry. Without a single entry point, it is difficult to ensure that a Web application will be properly initialized to handle a user's request. A controller can also provide a way to prevent deep linking to information within a site.

In designing a controller-centric application, a Web application developer can use a front component to receive all requests. A front component works with some JavaBeans components and enterprise beans that act as the controller. The controller components span both the Web tier and the EJB tier. The design of the components to create a controller that spans both the Web and EJB tiers is described in the following section.

Controller Components

The controller is made up of many components responsible for taking data posted in an HTTP request and converting it into an event to update the model data. The components that make up the controller include: front component, request processor, Web controller, and EJB controller.

Figure 4.10 is a diagram of a controller that converts an HTTP request into an event that updates the application model data. This figure shows the flow of an HTTP request from an HTTP client to the controller mechanism. As mentioned before, all requests from HTTP clients go to a front component. The requests are then sent to the request processor, which converts them to events and then sends the events to the Web controller. The Web controller acts as a proxy and sends the event to the EJB controller, which processes the event and updates the model data maintained by the enterprise beans accordingly.

All business logic is handled by the EJB controller and enterprise beans. The EJB controller returns a set of changed models to the Web controller. The Web controller then sends the model update events to the respective views. The views then contact the enterprise beans that they mirror and update their data from the enterprise beans. The JavaBeans components do not change any data; they only read the model data contained by the enterprise beans when they receive the model update notification.

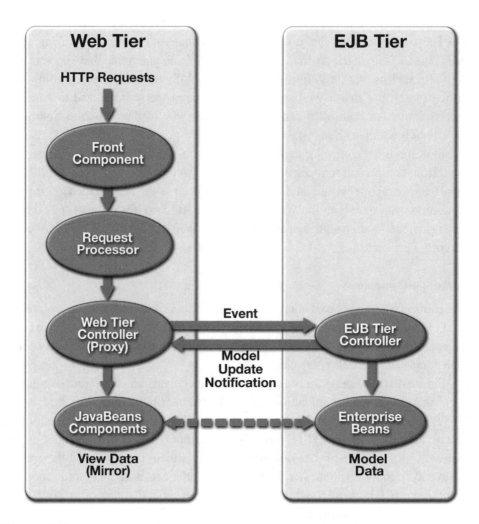

Figure 4.10   Controller Conversion of HTTP Request to Model Change Event

Now that we have described the process of how model data is updated by the controller mechanism we review each component of the controller.

- **Front component**

    The front component is a component to which all requests for application URLs are delivered. The front component ensures that the Web components needed by the application are initialized at the correct time and that all HTTP requests are sent to the request processor.

- **Request processor**

    The request processor is the link between the Web application and an HTTP-based client. The request processor is responsible for converting HTTP requests to events which will be used throughout the application. This component allows the application developer to centralize all HTTP-specific processing in one location. This component also allows the EJB portion of the application to be independent of any single client type.

- **Web controller**

    The Web controller is responsible for forwarding the event(s) generated by the request processor component to the EJB controller. The Web controller ensures that the resulting updated models returned from the EJB controller are propagated to the appropriate Web-tier view JavaBeans components.

- **EJB controller**

    The EJB controller accepts events from the Web controller and makes the calls on the enterprise beans affected by the event. The EJB controller is also responsible for maintaining the state of the user session with the application. After each event is processed, the EJB controller is responsible for returning a set of updated models to the Web controller.

    In general it is best to design the EJB controller so that it is not tied to a single type of client. This makes the application usable by both application and Web-centric clients. The EJB controller is the only part of the Web application allowed to manipulate the model data. Any less restrictive means of data modification would be contrary to the MVC architecture and make it difficult to debug the application.

For more details about controller design, see the discussion of the sample application's controller in Section 10.6 on page 280.

4.7   Application Migration

It's always a good practice to design an application so that it can be extended. If you follow the Web application design path described in this chapter, this migration can be a gradual process. However, if you are working with a preexisting application that does not resemble any of the application types listed in Figure 4.3, migration will be more difficult.

When migrating an application it is best to first determine the type of application you want to implement. Figure 4.3 shows a generalized migration path that may be followed for migrating applications of different levels of complexity. The simpler an application is, the easier it will be to migrate. The sections corresponding to the columns in Figure 4.3 review what can be done to make the components of a Web application more modular.

When migrating applications that use basic JSP pages and servlets to a more complex design, the general theme should be to migrate components into reusable modules. As much as possible, the application and presentation logic should be separated using custom tags and JavaBeans components.

The most difficult migration will be from a modular, component-based application to an EJB-centric application with enterprise beans. The following sections review some strategies for this migration.

4.7.1   Migrating a Web-Centric Application to Use Enterprise Beans

When migrating a Web-centric application to use enterprise beans apply the following steps:

1. Change Web portions of the application to use a front component and MVC architecture.

2. Create enterprise beans representing model objects.

3. Move application logic to enterprise beans.

4. Move external resource communication from JavaBeans components to enterprise beans.

5. Minimize display logic code in JSP pages.

4.7.1.1 Centralize Application Control Using an MVC Architecture

If your Web components do not already use an MVC architecture, you will need to modify the design. For more details on implementing an MVC architecture with Web components and enterprise beans, refer to Section 4.6.3 on page 103.

4.7.1.2 Create Enterprise Beans

You will need to create enterprise beans corresponding to the JavaBeans components used within your application. For an EJB-centric application, you will also need to design a controller enterprise bean. The responsibilities of the controller enterprise bean are described in "Controller Components" on page 105. You may also want to introduce other enterprise beans to handle other tasks, such as sending and receiving messages.

4.7.1.3 Move Application Logic to Enterprise Beans

All application logic provided by JavaBeans components in the Web application will need to be migrated to enterprise beans. This includes code to communicate with external resources.

Application logic for processing events generated by the Web components will need to be moved into the EJB controller. The EJB controller will also need logic for returning model update events to the Web controller.

4.7.1.4 Modify JavaBeans Components

JavaBeans components originally designed to hold the model data will need to be modified to obtain data from the enterprise beans when they receive model update events from the EJB controller. In addition, application logic in JavaBeans components will need to be moved to the enterprise beans representing the model.

After this modification, the JavaBeans components will become part of the view to represent the contract between JSP pages and the model. The only other logic that should remain in the Web container components is that tied to handling HTTP requests and managing the flow of the application.

4.7.1.5 Minimize Display Logic in JSP Pages

JSP pages should be used to render HTML instructions. To make the JSP pages more manageable, display logic code should be moved out of the JSP pages into custom tags and JavaBeans components whenever possible. For more details, refer back to Section 4.4 on page 85 of this chapter.

4.8   Summary

As a medium, the Web requires application developers to create user interfaces that are flexible and easy to maintain. Web applications can be made more flexible and maintainable through the use of J2EE component technologies such as servlets and JavaServer Pages which used to generate dynamic content in a portable and scalable manner.

Enterprise Web applications should be developed using modular components. These components include servlets, JSP pages, JavaBeans components, and tag libraries containing custom tags. Depending on the composition of your development team, time constraints, and application architecture, the use of JSP pages and servlets will differ. Both technologies have merits and should be used accordingly.

Internationalization expands the potential user base of a Web application. A properly internationalized application can be quickly localized for any number of languages without modifications to the code. It is much easier to internationalize an application during the design phase at the beginning of a development cycle. Retrofitting an existing application can be difficult and expensive.

Architectures for Web applications include basic JSP pages and servlets, Web-centric applications that use JSP pages with modular components, and EJB-centric applications that use JSP pages with enterprise beans. A Web-centric application can be migrated to a highly manageable, scalable, modular, EJB-centric application by using the steps described in this chapter. Gradual migration to a more complex design is less risky than making large-scale design changes to an application.

About the Author

VINITA KHANNA is a Member of Technical Staff at Sun Microsystems, where she works as an enterprise bean developer in the J2EE programming model team. Her major contributions include best practices and guidelines when developing business solutions using enterprise beans. Prior to the APM project Vinita was a member of the Enterprise Software Solutions Group where she was involved in the design and development of mission critical business applications for Sun. Vinita holds a B.Tech. degree in Electronics from Kamla Nehru Institute of Technology, India and a M.S. degree in Computer Science from California State University, Hayward.

CHAPTER 5

The Enterprise JavaBeans Tier

by Vinita Khanna

$\mathbf{I}$N a multitier J2EE application, the Enterprise JavaBeans (EJB) tier hosts application-specific business logic and system-level services such as transaction management, concurrency control, and security. Enterprise JavaBeans technology provides a distributed component model that enables developers to focus on solving business problems while relying on the J2EE platform to handle complex system-level issues. This separation of concerns allows rapid development of scalable, accessible, and highly secure applications. In the J2EE programming model, EJB components are a fundamental link between presentation components hosted by the Web tier and business-critical data and systems maintained in the enterprise information system tier.

This chapter examines the nature of business logic and describes the problems a developer needs to resolve when implementing business logic. It then describes the component model that the EJB tier of the J2EE platform provides to address these problems. The chapter then presents recommendations and practices to best utilize the services provided by the J2EE platform.

5.1   Business Logic

Business logic, in a very broad sense, is the set of guidelines to manage a specific business function. Taking the object-oriented approach enables the developer to decompose a business function into a set of components or elements called *business objects*. Like other objects, these business objects will have both characteristics (state or data) and behavior. For example, an employee object will have data such as a name, address, social security number, and so on. It will have methods for assigning it to a new department or changing its salary by a certain percentage. To manage this business problem we must be able to represent how these objects function or interact to provide the desired functionality. The business-specific rules that help us identify the structure and behavior of the business objects, along with the pre- and post-conditions that must be met when an object exposes its behavior to other objects in the system, is known as *business logic*.

The following discussion demonstrates how to define the structure and behavior of a business object from the requirements imposed by the business problem it belongs to. For example, the sample application contains a group of business objects: a catalog object to show available pets, a shopping cart object to temporarily hold client's selection of pets, an account object to keep information about clients, and an order object to keep track of placed orders. We consider the requirements on an account object:

1. Each client must have a unique account.

2. Each account should have contact information for a client such as name, street address, and email address.

3. Clients must be able to create new accounts.

4. Clients must be able to update contact information for their account.

5. Clients must be able to retrieve information for their account.

6. Clients can retrieve and update only their own account information.

7. The account information must be maintained in persistent storage.

8. Multiple clients must be able to access their account information at the same time.

9. Multiple clients cannot update the same account concurrently.

The first two requirements specify the structural attributes of the account object. Following these rules, the account object should have a field to hold account identification and several other fields to hold address, phone, and other contact information.

The behavior of the account object is described in requirements three, four, and five. For example, accounts should have methods to create a new account, update contact information, and to get the account information.

The last four requirements specify general conditions that must be met when realizing the behavior of the account object. For example, when a client updates an account, the client should be authorized to access that particular account, updated account information should be written to persistent storage, and concurrent access to the account information to multiple clients should be prohibited.

Similar analysis and requirement definitions could be performed for other objects. For example, an order object will have a set of general conditions on its behavior that have a significant correlation to the behavior of an account object. That is, a client needs to be authorized before updating or reading the status of an order, order details need to be written to a persistent storage, and so on.

If you examine business objects in similar applications you will see that even though the actual structure and behavior of the object is tied closely to the business problem it is going to solve, many services that these business objects provide follow specific patterns that are quite generic in nature.

5.1.1   Common Requirements of Business Objects

This section describes common requirements of business objects.

5.1.1.1 Maintain State

A business object often needs to maintain the state represented in its instance variables between the method invocations. The state can be either conversational or persistent.

Consider a shopping cart object. The state of the shopping cart object represents the items and quantities of the items purchased by the client. The cart is initially empty and gains meaningful state when a user adds an item to the cart. When a user adds another item to the cart, the cart should have both the items in it. Similarly, when a user deletes an item from the cart, the cart should reflect the change in its state. When a user exits the application, the cart object needs to be reinitialized. When the object gains, maintains, and loses its state as a result of repeated interactions with the same client we say the object maintains conversational state.

To understand persistent state, consider an account object. When a user creates an account, the account information needs to be stored permanently so that when the user exits the application and re-enters the application, the account information can be presented to the user again. The state of an account object needs to be maintained in persistent storage such as a database. Typically, the business objects that operate on session-neutral data exhibit persistent state maintenance.

5.1.1.2 Operate on Shared Data

Another common characteristic of business objects is that they often operate on shared data. In this case, measures must be taken to provide concurrency control and appropriate levels of isolation of the shared data. An example of such a scenario would be multiple users updating the same account information. If two users try to update the same account at the same time, the business object should provide a mechanism to keep the data in a consistent state.

5.1.1.3 Participate in Transactions

A transaction can be described as a set of tasks that need to be completed as a unit. If one of the tasks fail, all the tasks in the unit will be rolled back. If all of them succeed, the transaction is said to be committed.

Business objects often need to participate in transactions. For example, order placement needs to be transactional because of the set of tasks required to complete an order—decrementing the quantity of the purchased item in the item inventory, storing the order details, and sending an order confirmation to the user. For the transaction to be completed, all of these tasks must succeed. If any one of these tasks fail, work done by other tasks needs to be undone.

In many business operations, transactions may span more than one remote data source. Such transactions—called distributed transactions—require special protocols to ensure data integrity. In the sample application, order placement is a distributed transaction because the inventory table and the order table reside in different data sources.

5.1.1.4 Service a Large Number of Clients

A business object should be able to provide its services to a large number of clients at the same time. This translates into a requirement for instance management algorithms that give each client an impression that a dedicated business object is available to service its request. Without such a mechanism, the system will eventually run out of resources and will not be able to service any more clients.

5.1.1.5 Provide Remote Access to Data

A client should be able to remotely access the services offered by a business object. This means that the business object should have some type of infrastructure to support servicing clients over the network. This in turn implies that a business object should be part of a distributed computing environment that takes care of fundamental issues in distributed systems such as location and failure transparency.

5.1.1.6 Control Access

The services offered by business objects often require some type of client authentication and authorization mechanism to allow only a certain set of clients to access protected services. For example, an account business object needs to validate the authenticity of the client before allowing it to update its account information. In many enterprise scenarios, different levels of access control are needed. For example, employees are allowed to view only their own salary objects, while a payroll administrator can view as well as modify all salary objects.

5.1.1.7 Reusable

A common requirement of business objects is that they be reusable by different components of the same application and/or by different applications. For example, an application used by the payroll department to keep track of employees' salary may have two business objects: employee and salary. A salary business object may use the services of an employee business object to get the grade level of an employee. An application that tracks the employee vacation allowances may want to use this employee object to get the name of the employee through the employee number. In order for business objects to be able to be used by inter- and intra-application components, they need to be developed in a standard way and run in an environment that abides by these standards. If these standards are widely adopted by the vendor community, an application can be assembled from off-the-shelf components from different vendors. In addition to enabling rapid application development, this approach helps developers avoid vendor lock-in.

5.2   Enterprise Beans as J2EE Business Objects

As we discussed in the previous section, business objects need to provide some generic services to clients, such as support for transactions, security, and remote access, These common services are very complex in nature and are outside the domain of the business logic required to implement an application. To simplify development, enterprise applications need a standard server-side infrastructure that can provide such services.

The EJB tier of the J2EE platform provides a standard server-side distributed component model that greatly simplifies the task of writing business logic. In the EJB architecture, system experts provide the framework for delivering system-level services and application domain experts provide the components that hold only business-specific knowledge. The J2EE platform enables enterprise developers to concentrate on solving the problems of the enterprise instead of struggling with system-level issues.

To use the services provided by the J2EE platform, business objects are implemented by EJB components, or *enterprise beans*. There are two primary kinds of enterprise beans: entity beans and session beans. Session beans are intended to be private resources used only by the client that created them. For this reason, session beans, from the client's perspective, appear anonymous. In contrast, every entity bean has a unique identity which is exposed as a primary key. Later sections in this chapter discuss each type of enterprise bean in detail.

In addition to components, the EJB architecture defines three other entities: servers, containers, and clients. Enterprise beans live inside EJB containers, which provide life cycle management and a variety of other services. An EJB container is part of an EJB server, which provides naming and directory services, email services, and so on. When a client invokes an operation on an enterprise bean the call is intercepted by its container. By interceding between clients and components at the method call level, containers can manage services that propagate across calls and components, and even across containers running on different servers and different machines. This mechanism simplifies development of both components and clients.

5.2.1   Enterprise Beans and EJB Containers

The EJB architecture endows enterprise beans and EJB containers with a number of unique features that enable portability and reusability:

- Enterprise bean instances are created and managed at runtime by a container. If an enterprise bean uses only the services defined by the EJB specification, the enterprise bean can be deployed in any compliant EJB container. Specialized containers can provide additional services beyond those defined by the

EJB specification. An enterprise bean that depends on such a service can be deployed only in a container that supports that service.

- The behavior of enterprise beans is not wholly contained in its implementation. Service information, including transaction (described in Chapter 8) and security (described in Chapter 9) information, is separate from the enterprise bean implementation. This allows the service information to be customized during application assembly and deployment. The behavior of an enterprise bean is customized at deployment time by editing its deployment descriptor entries (described in Chapter 7). This makes it possible to include an enterprise bean in an assembled application without requiring source code changes or recompilation.

- The Bean Provider defines a client view of an enterprise bean. The client view is unaffected by the container and server in which the bean is deployed. This ensures that both the beans and their clients can be deployed in multiple execution environments without changes or recompilation. The client view of an enterprise bean is provided through two interfaces. These interfaces are implemented by classes constructed by the container when a bean is deployed, based on information provided by the bean. It is by implementing these interfaces that the container can intercede in client operations on a bean and offer the client a simplified view of the component. The following sections describe these interfaces and classes: the home and remote interfaces, and enterprise bean class.

5.2.1.1 Home Interface

The home interface provides methods for creating and removing enterprise beans. This interface must extend `javax.EJB.EJBHome`. The enterprise bean's home interface allows a client to do the following:

- Create new enterprise bean instance

- Remove an enterprise bean instance

- Get the meta-data for the enterprise bean through the `javax.ejb.EJBMetaData` interface. The `javax.ejb.EJBMetaData` interface is provided to allow application assembly tools to discover the meta-data information about the enterprise bean at deployment time.

- Obtain a handle to the home interface, which provides the mechanism for persistent enterprise beans. The home handle can be serialized and written to stable storage. Later, possibly in a different Java virtual machine, the handle can be deserialized from stable storage and used to obtain a reference to the home interface.

In addition, the home interface of an entity bean provides methods for finding existing entity bean instances within the home. A client that knows the primary key of an entity object can obtain a reference to the entity object by invoking the findByPrimaryKey method on the entity bean's home interface.

5.2.1.2 Remote Interface

The remote interface defines the client view of an enterprise bean—the set of business methods available to the clients. This interface must extend javax.ejb.EJBObject. An EJBObject supports:

- The business methods of the object. The EJBObject delegates invocation of a business method to the enterprise bean instance.

The javax.ejb.EJBObject interface defines the methods that allow clients to perform the following operations on a reference to an enterprise bean instance:

- Obtain the home interface

- Remove the enterprise bean instance

- Obtain a handle to the enterprise bean instance

- Obtain an entity bean instance's primary key

5.2.1.3 Enterprise Bean Class

The enterprise bean class is the second part of the mechanism that allows for container-managed services in the EJB architecture. It provides the actual implementation of the business methods of the bean. It is called by the container when the client calls the corresponding methods listed in the remote interface. This class must implement the javax.ejb.EntityBean or javax.ejb.SessionBean interface.

In addition to business methods, the remote interface and enterprise bean class also share responsibility for two specialized categories of methods: create methods and finder methods. The create methods provide ways to customize the bean at the time it is created, and the finder methods provide ways to locate a bean.

For each `create` method listed in the home interface, the bean class implements the corresponding `ejbCreate` method. For each finder method listed in home interface, the bean class provides the corresponding `ejbFindBy...` method. The enterprise bean class must also provide implementations of the methods listed in the interface it extends. A developer can choose to provide empty implementations of any methods in the interface that aren't required for the specific purposes of a bean.

Figure 5.1 illustrates the implementation of the client view of an enterprise bean.

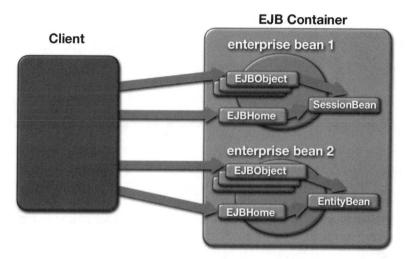

Figure 5.1   Implementation of Client View of Enterprise Beans

The following two sections contain in-depth discussions of the properties and uses of entity and session beans.

5.3   Entity Beans

An entity bean represents an object view of business data stored in persistent storage or an existing application. The bean provides an object wrapper around the data to simplify the task of accessing and manipulating it. This object interface lends itself to software reuse. For example, an entity bean representing user account information can be used by order management, user personalization, and marketing in a uniform way.

An entity bean allows shared access from multiple clients and can live past the duration of client's session with the server. If the state of an entity bean is being updated by a transaction at the time of server crash, the entity bean's state is automatically reset to the state of the last committed transaction.

5.3.1   Guidelines for Using Entity Beans

A Bean Provider can use the following entity bean characteristics as guidelines when deciding whether to model a business object as an entity bean:

- Representing persistent data

    If the state of a business object needs to be stored in a persistent storage and its behavior primarily represents manipulation of data represented in its state, then it should be modeled as entity bean.

    However, it should be noted that every method call to an entity object via the remote and home interface is potentially a remote call. Even if the calling and called enterprise beans are located in the same Java virtual machine, the call must go through the container, which must create copies of all parameters that are passed through the interface by value. The container also checks security and applies declarative transaction attributes on the inter-component calls. Therefore modeling every object representing a row in the database as an entity bean is not recommended. An entity bean is better suited to represent a coarse-grained business object that provides more complex behavior than only get and set methods for its fields.

- Providing concurrent access by multiple clients

    When the state and behavior of a business object needs to be shared among multiple clients, they should be modeled as entity beans. This kind of business object needs to maintain state between method calls. However, this state is not specific to a particular client but is representative of persistent state of the business object, typically stored in a database. By modeling such business objects as entity beans, a Bean Provider can rely on an EJB server to ensure appropriate synchronization for entity beans as they are accessed concurrently from multiple transactions.

- Representing a single logical record (row) of data

    The business objects that typically operate on one logical record in the database are excellent candidates to model as entity beans. In fact, entity beans are designed to represent an individual (logical) record in the database. Entity beans provide methods to locate, create, and manipulate one row at a time.

- Providing robust, long-lived persistent data management

    A business object that needs to live after a client's session with the server is over or that needs to be present when the server comes back after a crash, should be modeled as an entity bean. Entity beans live even after a client's session with the server is over and can even survive server crashes. If the state of an entity bean is being updated by a transaction at the time of server crash, the entity bean's state is automatically reset to the state of the last committed transaction.

5.3.1.1 Example: A User Account Bean

The concept of a user account is central to all clients in many e-commerce applications. Multiple clients need to share behavior such as creating an account, verifying an existing account, and updating account information. Updates to the state of an account object need to be written to persistent storage and an account object lives even when the client's session with the server is over. Therefore, in the sample application, an account object is modeled as entity bean.

To avoid expensive remote methods to get the value of account objects fields, the sample application uses a value object (discussed in Section 5.5.2 on page 134) to represent account details. Only one remote call is required to retrieve the value object and then a client's request to query the state of an account object can then be satisfied via local get methods on this details object. Similarly, to avoid fine-grained set methods, the sample application uses a coarse-grained method to update all account information via one remote call. Code Example 5.1 shows the remote interface of the Account enterprise bean and the implementation of AccountDetails.

```
public interface Account extends EJBObject {
    public void changeContactInformation(ContactInformation info)
```

```
            throws RemoteException;
        public AccountDetails getAccountDetails()
            throws RemoteException;
    }


    public class AccountDetails implements java.io.Serializable {
        private String userId;
        private String status;
        private ContactInformation info;

        public String getUserId() {
            return userId;
        }
        ...
    }
```

Code Example 5.1   Account Remote Interface and `AccountDetails` Class

Like most entity beans, the account bean provides an object view of data stored in a database and most of its code revolves around connecting to, accessing, and updating database tables. The next section discusses options for implementing data access logic for entity beans.

5.3.2   Persistence in Entity Beans

The protocol for transferring the state of an entity between the enterprise bean instance and the underlying persistent store is referred to as object persistence. An entity bean can implement persistence in the following ways:

- Directly implementing persistence in the enterprise bean class or in one or more helper objects provided with the enterprise bean class (bean-managed persistence)

- Delegating the handling of its persistence to its container (container-managed persistence)

With bean-managed persistence, the Bean Provider writes database access calls. The data access calls can be coded directly into the enterprise bean class, or can be encapsulated in a data access component that is part of the entity bean. If data access calls are coded directly in the enterprise bean class, it may be more difficult to adapt the entity component to work with a database that has a different schema, or with a different type of database. Encapsulating data access calls in a data access object makes it easier to adapt the enterprise bean's data access to different schemas or different database types. The sample application uses separate data access objects for implementing persistence. Data access objects are discussed in detail in Section 5.5.1 on page 130.

With container-managed persistence, the Bean Provider identifies the fields to be stored to the database and the Container Provider's tools generate database access calls at deployment time. The type and structure of the data source is transparent to the Bean Provider. The container tools can generate classes that use JDBC or SQL/J to access the entity state in a relational database, classes that implement access to a non-relational data source, or classes that implement function calls to existing enterprise applications. The bean state is defined independently of how and where it will be stored and hence is more flexible across applications. The disadvantage is that sophisticated tools must be used at deployment time to map the enterprise bean's fields to a data source. These tools and containers are typically specific to each data source.

When a container supports container-managed persistence, it simplifies the task of writing entity beans because the container takes the responsibility of generating the code to access the data source. Bean developers should take advantage of this feature and delegate the task of saving the state of an entity bean to the container whenever possible. Some containers may not be capable of handling complex state objects (for example, objects representing multiple joins). In such cases, the Bean Provider may have to use bean-managed persistence.

5.4   Session Beans

Session beans are used to implement business objects that hold client-specific business logic. The state of such a business object reflects its interaction with a particular client and is not intended for general access. Therefore, a session bean typically executes on behalf of a single client and cannot be shared among multiple clients. A session bean is a logical extension of the client program that runs on the server and contains information specific to the client. In contrast to entity beans, session beans do not directly represent shared data in the database, although they can access and update such data. The state of a session object is non-persistent and need not be written to the database.

A session bean is intended to be stateful. However, the Enterprise JavaBeans specification allows stateless session beans as a way to provide server-side behavior that doesn't maintain any specific state. The next section discusses the properties and uses of both stateful and stateless session beans.

5.4.1   Stateful Session Beans

A stateful session bean contains conversational state on behalf of the client. A conversational state is defined as the session bean's field values plus all objects reachable from the session bean's fields. Stateful session beans do not directly represent data in a persistent data store, but they can access and update data on behalf of the client. As its name suggests, the lifetime of a stateful session bean is typically that of its client.

5.4.1.1   Uses of Stateful Session Beans

A Bean Provider can use the following session bean characteristics as guidelines when deciding whether to model a business object as a stateful session bean:

- Maintaining client-specific state

    Stateful session beans are designed to maintain a conversational state on behalf of a client, therefore business objects representing client-centric business logic should be modeled as stateful session beans. Since stateful session bean instances are tied to a client, system resources held by stateful session beans cannot be shared among multiple clients.

- Representing non-persistent objects

    Stateful session bean state is not stored in the persistent storage and cannot be recreated after the client's session with the server is over. Therefore, business objects that are relatively short-lived and non-persistent should be modeled as stateful session beans. In other words, a business object that does not need to live after a client's session with the server is over, or be present when the server comes back after a crash, should be modeled as a session bean.

- Representing work flow between business objects

    The business objects that manage the interaction of various business objects in a system are excellent candidates to be modeled as stateful session beans. Such objects usually exhibit both of the above characteristics, since they are client specific and represent data-neutral non-persistent behavior.

5.4.1.2 Example: A Shopping Cart Bean

A shopping cart object represents the collection of products selected by a particular user for purchase during a session. The state of the shopping cart object is specific to a particular user session and need not be saved unless the user is ready to place an order. The shopping cart object is short-lived. The data should not be shared, since it represents a particular interaction with a particular user and is alive only for the user's session with the server. The sample application models the concept of shopping cart as a stateful session bean.

As mentioned earlier, stateful session beans can also be used to model an object that manages the interaction of various objects in the work flow on behalf of a client. The sample application follows the MVC architecture. If the view (client) needs to read the data (model) it does it by directly interacting with the data. However, if the view needs to update the data, it uses the controller as a mediator. The controller interacts with multiple objects representing data on behalf of the view or user.

In the sample application, the controller is implemented as a stateful session bean named ShoppingClientController. As shown in Code Example 5.2, ShoppingClientController is responsible for managing the life cycle of model objects such as the shopping cart and account enterprise beans and processes business events. For example, when a user places an order, ShoppingClientController handles the order event.

```
public interface ShoppingClientController extends EJBObject {
    public Catalog getCatalog() throws RemoteException;
    public ShoppingCart getShoppingCart() throws RemoteException;
    public Account getAccount() throws RemoteException;
    public Collection getOrders() throws
        RemoteException, FinderException;
    public Order getOrder(int requestId) throws
        RemoteException, FinderException;
    // Returns a list of updated models
    public Collection handleEvent(EStoreEvent se) throws
```

```
                RemoteException, DuplicateAccountException;
    }
```

Code Example 5.2   `ShoppingClientController` Remote Interface

5.4.2   Stateless Session Beans

Stateless session beans are designed strictly to provide server-side behavior. They are anonymous in that they contain no user-specific data. In fact, the EJB architecture provides ways for a single stateless session bean to serve the needs of many clients. This means that all stateless session bean instances are equivalent when they are not involved in serving a client-invoked method. The term stateless means that it does not have any state information for a specific client. However, stateless session beans can have non-client specific state, for example, an open database connection.

5.4.2.1   Uses of Stateless Session Beans

A Bean Provider can use the following session bean characteristics as guidelines when deciding whether to model a business object as a stateless session bean:

- Modeling reusable service objects

    A business object that provides some generic service to all its clients can be modeled as stateless session beans. Such an object does not need to maintain any client specific state information, so the same bean instance can be reused to service other clients. For example, it would be appropriate to model a business object that validates an employee ID against a database as a stateless service.

- Providing high performance

    A stateless session bean can be very efficient as it requires fewer system resources by the virtue of being not tied to one client. Since stateless session beans minimize the resources needed to support a large number of clients, depending on the implementation of the EJB server, applications that use this approach may scale better than those using stateful session beans. However, this benefit may be offset by the increased complexity of the client application that uses the stateless session beans because the client has to perform the state management functions.

- Operating on multiple rows at a time

    A business object that manipulates multiple rows in a database and represents a shared view of the data is an ideal stateless session bean. An example of a such business object would be a catalog object that presents a list of various products and categories. Since all users would be interested in such information, the stateless session bean that represents it could easily be shared.

- Providing procedural view of data

    In a procedural view of data, methods of the business object do not operate on instance variables. Instead they behave like calls in a procedural language. The method caller provides all the input and the method returns all output to the caller. If a business object exhibits such functionality then it should be modeled as a stateless session bean.

5.4.2.2 Example: A Catalog Bean

The sample application uses a stateless session beans to model a catalog object. A catalog object represents different categories and products and provides browsing and searching services to its clients. Both of the primary functions of the catalog, browsing and searching, are generic services that are not tied to any particular client. Also, the catalog object operates on multiple rows in the database at the same time and provides a shared view of the data. Code Example 5.3 lists the services provided by a catalog object:

```
public interface Catalog extends EJBObject {
    public Collection getCategories()throws RemoteException;
    public Collection getProducts(String categoryId,
        int startIndex, int count)throws RemoteException;
    public Product getProduct(String productId)
        throws RemoteException;
    public Collection getItems(String productId,int startIndex,
        int count)throws RemoteException;
    public Item getItem(String itemId)
        throws RemoteException;
    public Collection searchProducts(Collection keyWords,
```

```
                    int startIndex,int count)throws RemoteException;
    }
```

Code Example 5.3   Catalog Remote Interface

Another example of a stateless session bean is the mailer object used to send confirmation mail to clients after their order has been placed successfully. Mailer provides a generic service that can be completed within a single method call with its state is not tied to any particular client. Also, since the instances can be shared among multiple clients, they are modeled as stateless session beans.

5.5   Design Guidelines

In addition to the guidelines discussed previously for choosing specific bean types, there are other design choices that Application Component Providers must make when developing objects for the EJB tier. These choices include what types of objects should be enterprise beans, and what role an enterprise bean may play in a group of collaborating components.

Since enterprise beans are remote objects that consume a significant amount of system resources and network bandwidth, it is not appropriate to model all business objects as enterprise beans. Only the business objects that need to be accessed directly by a client need to be enterprise beans; other objects can be modeled as data access objects, which encapsulate database access, and value objects, which model fine-grained objects that are dependent on enterprise beans.

It may not be appropriate to give clients direct access to all enterprise beans within an application. As a consequence, some enterprise beans may act as mediators of communication between clients and the EJB tier. A bean of this type can encapsulate work flow specific to an application or can serve as an entry point to a hierarchy of information keyed to an attribute of the entry-point bean.

5.5.1   Data Access Objects

To encapsulate access to data, the sample application uses *data access objects*. The use of separate objects to access databases was driven by following requirements:

- Keep session bean code clear and simple

- Ensure easier migration to container-managed persistence for entity beans

- Allow for cross-database and cross-schema portability

- Provide a mechanism that supports tools from different vendors

5.5.1.1 Clarifying Session Bean Implementations

Any session bean method that needs to access a database has a corresponding method in the data access object that implements the actual logic of fetching or updating data in the database. This makes the enterprise bean implementation much cleaner and readable by conveying the business logic at a glance without being cluttered up with JDBC calls.

For example, consider the `Catalog` session bean. The business method `getProducts` need to return all the products for a category. Whenever `getProducts` needs to operate on data residing in the database, it hands over control to a data access object. The data access object formulates the query, fetches the result set, and returns the data in the desired format to the calling method of the enterprise bean.

In the sample application, the implementation of the `Catalog` session bean is provided by `CatalogEJB`, which inherits from `CatalogImpl`. The code for `CatalogImpl.getProducts` appears in Code Example 5.4; the code for the corresponding data access object appears in Code Example 5.5.

```
public Collection getProducts(String categoryId,
    int startIndex, int count) {
    Connection con = getDBConnection();

    try {
        CatalogDAO dao = new CatalogDAO(con);
            return dao.getProducts(categoryId, startIndex, count);
    } catch (SQLException se) {
        throw new GeneralFailureException(se);
    } finally {
        try {
            con.close();
        } catch (Exception ex) {

            ...

        }
```

```
        }
    }
```

Code Example 5.4   `CatalogImpl.getProducts`

```
public Collection getProducts(String categoryId, int startIndex,
    int count) throws SQLException {

    String qstr =
        "select itemid, listprice, unitcost, " +
        "attr1, a.productid, name, descn " +
        "from item a, product b where " +
        "a.productid = b.productid and category =  "
         + "'" + categoryId + "' " + " order by name";

    ArrayList al = new ArrayList();
    Statement stmt = con.createStatement();
    ResultSet rs = stmt.executeQuery(qstr);
    HashMap table = new HashMap();
    // skip initial rows as specified by the startIndex parameter
    while (startIndex-- > 0 && rs.next());
    // Now get data as requested
    while (count-- > 0 && rs.next()) {
        int i = 1;
        String itemid = rs.getString(i++).trim();
        double listprice = rs.getDouble(i++);
        double unitcost = rs.getDouble(i++);
        ...
        Product product = null;
        if (table.get(productid) == null) {
            product = new Product(productid, name, descn);
            table.put(productid, product);
            al.add(product);
        }
    }
    rs.close();
    stmt.close();
```

```
        return al;
    }
```

Code Example 5.5   `CatalogDAO.getProducts`

5.5.1.2 Migrating to Container-Managed Persistence

Apart from neater, more maintainable code, the use of data access objects provides an easier migration path to container-managed persistence. To convert an entity bean from bean-managed persistence to container-managed persistence you simply need to discard corresponding the data access object along with references to it in the entity bean's code.

5.5.1.3 Database and Schema Portability

By encapsulating data access calls, data access objects allow adapting data access to different schemas or even to a different database types. Data access objects for different schemas and databases can share a common interface enabling the Application Assembler to choose the appropriate object from among several at assembly time.

In the sample application we have used the flexibility provided by data access objects to access different types of databases, namely Oracle, Sybase, and Cloudscape. In the order management module, a separate data access object is provided for each vendor. This allows the same enterprise bean code to run on all databases. The decision of which data access object to invoke is taken dynamically when a connection to the database is made. A similar approach can be used to access databases with different schemas.

5.5.1.4 Tool Compatibility

Data access objects fill a gap in the J2EE application architecture between responsibilities of application developers and those of Server Providers. They represent an excellent opportunity for the tool vendors to add value. Data access objects are a type of class that can be easily generated by sophisticated tools. In the future, custom data access objects, such as those in the sample application, will most likely be replaced by sophisticated object-relational tools.

5.5.2   Value Objects

As mentioned earlier, because enterprise beans are remote objects, they consume significant amount of system resources and network bandwidth to execute. Therefore, before modeling a business object as an enterprise bean, you should determine that there is a good case for doing so. For example, if a business object merely represents a structure to hold data fields, and the only behavior it provides are get and set methods for the fields, then it would be wasteful of system resources to implement it as an enterprise bean.

A better alternative would be to model it as a value object. A *value object* is a serializable Java object that can be passed by value to the client. A business concept should be implemented as a value object when it is:

- Fine-grained, which means it only contains methods to get the values of fields.

- Dependent, which means its life cycle is completely controlled by another object.

- Immutable, which means that its fields are not independently modifiable.

A client's request for a value object can be fulfilled by the server more simply than for an enterprise bean; the object is serialized and sent over the network to the client where the object is deserialized. The object can then be used as a local object. This conserves system resources by reducing the load on a remote object. It also reduces network traffic as the method calls to get fields of the object are all local.

In the sample application the details of an account are modeled as a value object representing the state of a particular account in the database and providing getter methods to query the state of this account. The client makes just one remote call to execute `getAccountDetails` on the remote object account and gets back the serialized `AccountDetails` object. The client can then query the state of this account locally via the methods provided with the `AccountDetails` object. Similarly, the state of an account object can be modified in just one remote call by passing a `ContactInformation` object to the remote method for updating contact information.

5.5.2.1 Example: An Address Value Object

In the sample application, an address and credit card information are modeled as value objects. The definition of the `Address` class is shown in Code Example 5.6.

```
public class Address implements java.io.Serializable {
    public Address (String streetName1, String streetName2,
        String city, String state, String zipCode, String country){
        this.streetName1 = streetName1;
        this.streetName2 = streetName2;
    ...
    }
    public String getStreetName1() {
        return streetName1;
    }
    ...
    private String streetName1;
    private String streetName2;
    ...
}
```

Code Example 5.6   `Address`

An `Address` does not exhibit complex behavior, but is merely a data structure that contains only data fields. An address is fine-grained, having only get and set methods. Also, it is a dependent object; it only has meaning if it is associated with an account.

When making the object pass-by-value it is important to make it immutable to reinforce the idea that the dependent object is not a remote object and changes to its state will not be reflected on the server; in other words, it is just a copy and not the remote reference. To make an `Address` object immutable, all its instance data is declared private and it only has methods to get fields. To change a pass-by-value object the client must first remove it and then create a new object with the desired field values.

5.5.3   Session Beans as a Facade to Entity Beans

A facade provides a unified interface to a set of interfaces. This section describes when and how to use an session bean as a facade to entity beans.

Entity beans represent an object-oriented view of data and provide business logic to manipulate this data. In an enterprise environment, entity beans often need to be shared among different applications representing different work flows. In such cases, use of application-specific stateful session beans to manage the interaction of various entity beans provides a simpler interface to the client, by giving the client a central point of entry. The client always interacts with this session bean and is unaware of the existence of other entity beans in the system.

Stateful session beans are logical extensions of the client programs. Whether to use one or many session bean facades depends on the types of clients the application supports. Since the sample application has only one kind of client for the application, namely the shopping client, the sample application uses a single stateful session bean called `ShoppingSessionController`. It's easy to imagine another client that would provide administration functionality such as inventory and order status monitoring. The work flow of such a client would be entirely different from a shopping client. Therefore, defining another stateful session bean that encapsulates this work flow would be advisable. However, creating a session bean for every entity bean in the system would waste server resources and is not recommended.

Where the client interacts with only a few entity beans in a relatively simple way, the entity beans can be exposed directly. For example, in the sample application the client that converts pending orders to XML (for use by business-to-business transactions) interacts with the order entity bean directly.

5.5.4   Master-Detail Modeling Using Enterprise Beans

In a master-detail relationship, one object serves as a pointer to another. Typically such a relationship is represented to the user as a list of items from which to select. This list is called a master record and its contents are provided by the master object. Selecting an item from this list leads to an expanded view of that item. The expanded view is provided by a detail object.

A master-detail relationship is a one-to-many type relationship among data sets. For example, if we have a set of customers and a set of orders placed by each customer, a master-detail relationship is created by having customer number as a common field between the two. An application can use this master-detail relationship to enable users to navigate through the customer data set and see the detail data for orders placed by the selected customer.

When modeling a master-detail relationship as enterprise beans, the guidelines for using entity or session beans still hold. The choice is not affected by the master-detail relationship. However, the relationship is relevant when designing the behavior of the master. For example, suppose the master object should be modeled as a session bean and the details object should be an entity bean. In this case, the issue to be decided is how to implement the behavior of the master:

- Expose the underlying entity beans to its clients when the client wants the detail object.

- Implement the logic of collecting the details in the master.

In analyzing various possible combinations of session beans, entity beans, or value objects, to represent master and detail objects, these questions are relevant only when the details are entity beans. For this case there are two possible scenarios:

- If the client modifies the detail entity object, then the master object needs to expose the underlying entity object to the clients.

- If the client does not modify the detail entity object, then the master object can have the necessary business logic to know which detail bean to access to construct the logical master/detail object. The client should not be exposed to the logic associated with accessing and aggregating the entity beans representing the details.

5.6 Summary

There are a number of common services that distributed enterprise applications require. These include maintaining state, operating on shared data, participating in transactions, servicing a large number of clients, providing remote access to data, and controlling access to data. The middle tier of enterprise computing has evolved as the ideal place to provide these services. The J2EE platform promotes the Enterprise JavaBeans architecture as a way to provide the system services that most enterprise applications need. The EJB architecture frees enterprise application developers from concerns about these services enabling them to concentrate on providing business logic.

The Enterprise JavaBeans architecture provides various types of enterprise beans to model business objects: entity beans, stateful session beans, and stateless session beans. When choosing a particular enterprise bean type to model a business concept, the choice depends on a number of factors such as the need to provide robust data handling, the need to provide efficient behavior, and the need to maintain client state during a user session.

An entity bean provides an object-oriented view of relational data stored in a database; a stateless session bean gives a procedural view of the data. An Application Component Provider should use entity beans to model logical entities such as individual records in a database. When implementing behavior to visit multiple rows in a database and present a read-only view of data, stateless session beans are the best choice. They are designed to provide generic services to multiple clients.

Some business concepts actually require more than one view of data. An example would be a catalog that provides browsing and searching services as well as mechanisms to update the product information. In such cases, you can use a stateless session bean to operate on a product information as a whole and an entity bean to provide access to a particular product.

Because enterprise beans are remote objects that consume significant amount of system resources and network bandwidth, they are not appropriate for modeling all business objects. An Application Component Provider can use data access objects to encapsulate database access and value objects to model objects that are dependent on enterprise beans.

Also, it may not be appropriate to give clients direct access to all enterprise beans used by an application. Some enterprise beans may act as mediators for communication between clients and the EJB tier. Such beans can encapsulate work flow specific to an application or can serve as an entry point to a hierarchy of information.

About the Author

RAHUL SHARMA is a Staff Engineer with Sun Microsystems, where he is the lead architect for the J2EE Connector architecture 1.0. Before this, Rahul has worked in the areas of Java computing, Web technologies, distributed computing, CORBA, databases, and object-oriented programming. Rahul received a degree in Computer Science from Delhi University in India. He is presently pursuing his M.B.A. from Haas School of Business, University of California at Berkeley.

CHAPTER 6

The Enterprise Information System Tier

by Rahul Sharma

ENTERPRISE applications require access to applications running on enterprise information systems. These systems provide the information infrastructure for an enterprise. Examples of enterprise information systems include enterprise resource planning systems, mainframe transaction processing systems, relational database management systems, and other legacy information systems. Enterprises run their businesses using the information stored in these systems; the success of an enterprise critically depends on this information. An enterprise cannot afford to have an application cause inconsistent data or compromise the integrity of data stored in these systems. This leads to a requirement for ensuring transactional access to enterprise information systems from various applications.

The emergence of the e-business model has added another dimension to information system access: enterprises want their information to be accessible over the Web to their partners, suppliers, customers, and employees. Typically enterprises develop Web-enabled applications that access and manage information stored in their information systems. These enterprises can use J2EE applications to extend the reach of their existing information systems and make them accessible over the Web. Enterprises also develop new e-business applications. The sample application described in this book is one example of this class of application.

This added dimension requires an enterprise to ensure secure access to its enterprise information systems because any break in security can compromise critical information. An increase in the number of relationships that an enterprise has to establish with its suppliers, buyers, and partners leads to a requirement that

J2EE applications accessing enterprise information systems be scalable and support a large number of clients.

This chapter describes the application programming model for accessing enterprise information system resources from enterprise applications in a secure, transactional, and scalable manner.

6.1   Enterprise Information System Capabilities and Limitations

Some enterprise information systems provide advanced support for transaction and security. For example, some systems support controlled access to their resources through transactions. These systems can participate in transactions with others by supporting two-phase commit protocol, managed by a transaction manager supported by a J2EE server. Other systems offer limited or almost no support for transactional access. For example, a system may only support transactions that are coordinated internally.

Legacy systems or applications that have been in existence for a long time may impose specific technology and administrative restrictions. For example, it may be difficult to create new user accounts in a legacy system or to extend this system to support development of new applications. In this case, an Application Component Provider has to live with what exists and enable access to such systems under restrictions. This may be a very typical situation.

When developing an application to integrate enterprise information systems, an Application Component Provider has to be aware of its functional and system capabilities, and design application components taking into account possibilities and limitations of the system. For example, application components should not be developed and deployed so that they require transactions spanning multiple resource managers if the J2EE server cannot really provide support for such transactions due to the fact that the participating enterprise information system resource managers do not support the two-phase commit protocol. In other cases, application components may need to limit their security requirements due to constraints of the underlying system.

6.2   Enterprise Information System Integration Scenarios

There are any number of configurations in which a J2EE application might be structured to access an enterprise information system. The following sections illustrate a few typical enterprise information system integration scenarios.

6.2.1   An Internet E-Store Application

Company A has an e-store application based on the J2EE platform. This application is composed of a set of enterprise beans, JSP pages, and servlets that collaborate to provide the overall functionality of the application. The database stores data related to product catalogs, shopping carts, customer registration and profiles, transaction status and records, and order status.

The architecture of this application is illustrated in Figure 6.1.

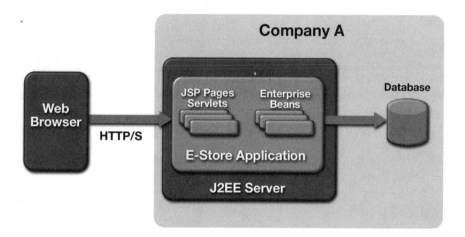

Figure 6.1   An Internet E-Store Application

A customer uses a Web browser to initiate an e-commerce transaction with the e-store application. A customer browses the catalog, makes a selection of products, puts the product selection into a shopping cart, enters a user name and password to initiate a secure transaction, fills in order related information, and finally places an order. In this scenario, the e-store application uses an existing database that already contains product and inventory information to store all persistent information about customers and their transactions.

6.2.2   An Intranet Human Resources Application

Company B has developed and deployed an employee self-service application based on the J2EE platform. This application supports a Web interface to existing human resources applications supported by the enterprise resource planning system from vendor X and provides additional business processes that are customized to the needs of company B.

Figure 6.2 illustrates an architecture for this application. The middle tier is composed of enterprise beans and JSP pages that provide customization of business processes and support a company standardized Web interface. This application enables an employee (under the different roles of Manager, HR manager, and Employee) to perform various personnel management functions: personal information management, payroll management, compensation management, benefits administration, travel management, and cost planning.

The IT department of company B deploys this application and enterprise resource planning system in a secure environment at a single physical location. Access to the application is permitted only to employees of the organization based on their roles and access privileges, and within the confines of the organization-wide intranet.

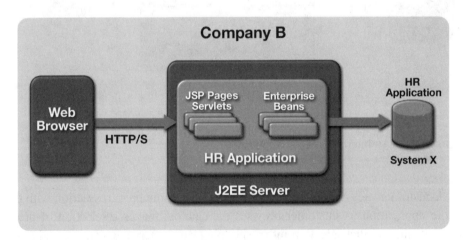

Figure 6.2   An Intranet Human Resources Application

6.2.3 A Distributed Purchasing Application

Company C has a distributed purchasing application. This application enables an employee to use a Web-based interface to perform multiple purchasing transactions. An employee can manage the whole procurement process, from creating a purchase requisition to getting invoice approval. This application also integrates with the existing financial applications in the enterprise for tracking financial aspects of the procurement business processes.

Figure 6.3 illustrates an architecture for this application. The application as developed and deployed on the J2EE platform, is composed of JSP pages, enterprise beans, and existing information systems. The enterprise beans integrate a logistics application that provides integrated purchasing and inventory management functions from vendor X and another that provides financial accounting functions from vendor Y.

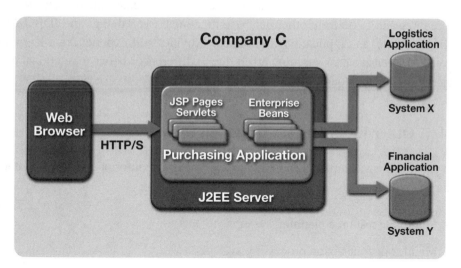

Figure 6.3　A Distributed Purchasing Application

Company C is a large decentralized enterprise with geographically distributed business units and departments. In this scenario, system X and system Y are managed by different IT departments and have been deployed at secured data centers in different geographic locations. The integrated purchasing application is deployed at a location different from either system X or system Y.

System X and System Y are in different security domains; they use different security technologies and have their own specific security policies and mechanisms. The distributed purchasing application is deployed in a security domain that is different from either that of system X or system Y.

6.3   Relational Database Management System Access

Application Component Providers use the JDBC 2.0 API for accessing relational databases to manage persistent data for their applications. The JDBC API has two parts: a client API for direct use by developers to access relational databases and a standard contract between J2EE servers and JDBC drivers for supporting connection pooling and transactions. The latter contract is not directly used by the developers, it is used by J2EE server vendors to automatically provide pooling and transaction services to J2EE components.

An Application Component Provider uses the JDBC client-level API to get a database connection, to retrieve database records, to execute queries and stored procedures and to perform other database functions. Even though the JDBC API is quite simple, an Application Component Provider still experiences a learning curve and intensive programming effort due to differences between relational and object-oriented methodologies.

6.4   Other Enterprise Information System Access

An enterprise environment invariably includes enterprise information systems other than relational database systems:

- Enterprise resource planning systems
- Mainframe transaction processing systems
- Legacy applications
- Non-relational database systems

Currently, there is no standard architecture for integration of a J2EE server with enterprise information systems; most enterprise information system vendors and J2EE Server Providers use vendor-specific architectures to support enterprise information system integration. For example, a J2EE Server Provider can specialize its container to support integration with an enterprise resource planning system.

A major disadvantage of developing enterprise information system integration applications for deployment on specialized containers is that application components become tied to mechanisms and programming models defined by the specialized container. As a result, such components are not portable across different types of containers.

The J2EE Connector architecture (described in Section 6.10 on page 161) is a standard architecture for the integration of J2EE products and applications with heterogeneous enterprise information systems. This architecture is currently under development and will be part of the next version of the J2EE platform. In this document, we make no specific recommendations based on the Connector architecture.

In the interim, an Application Component Provider can use vendor-specific architectures to integrate with enterprise information systems. However, while developing various types of application components we suggest following the guidelines that are discussed in the subsequent sections in this chapter in order to ensure that the migration path to the Connector architecture will be smooth.

6.5   Application Component Provider Tasks

The task of an Application Component Provider assumes different levels of complexity and effort depending on whether the programming model used is based on the J2EE application programming model or not. In either case, an Application Component Provider has to write the business and application logic for the application.

In the absence of J2EE platform support, the Component Provider faces significant complexity when programming access to enterprise information system resources (data and functions managed by an enterprise information system). This complexity comes from dealing with security, transaction, and application programming models that are specific to an enterprise information system. A Component Provider has to manage transactions using a transaction demarcation API specific to an enterprise information system, such as the transaction demarcation API defined in the `java.sql.Connection` interface in the JDBC 2.0 API. In the application, the Application Component Provider has to explicitly code security checks to restrict enterprise information system access to valid users.

Using the J2EE application programming model, an Application Component Provider faces reduced complexity by relying on the Web and EJB containers to handle transactions, security, and scalability related to enterprise information system access. The Application Component Provider can focus on the task of writing business and application logic and use a simple client-oriented API for accessing the enterprise information system. The task of accessing enterprise information system resources from the application code is made even easier through the use of enterprise application development tools.

By letting J2EE containers manage transactions, security, and scalability, Application Component Providers focus on what they do the best: writing business and application logic. The J2EE platform vendors focus on their core strengths: multiuser, secure, transactional, scalable implementations of J2EE platform that enable different enterprise information systems to plug into the J2EE platform. Together Application Component Providers and J2EE Platform Providers succeed in ensuring that enterprises can rely on J2EE applications to extend their enterprise information systems without compromising the information stored in these systems.

6.6   Application Programming Model

The J2EE application programming model for enterprise information system access lays down a set of design choices, guidelines, and recommendations for Application Component Providers. These guidelines enable an Application Component Provider to develop an application based on its overall functional and system requirements. The application programming model focuses on the following aspects:

- Accessing enterprise information system resources from components

- Using tools to simplify and reduce application development effort involved in accessing enterprise information systems

- Getting connections to an enterprise information system and managing connections

- Supporting the security requirements of an application

- Supporting the transactional requirements of an application

The following sections describe each of these aspects from the perspective of relational database access using JDBC 2.0 API, with the exception of transactions, which are discussed in Chapter 8. An important point to note is that the following sections are not meant to be a programmer's guide to using the JDBC API.

6.7   Programming Access to Data and Functions

In an application that requires access to an enterprise information system, an Application Component Provider is responsible for programming access to resources managed by the enterprise information system, including tables, stored procedures, business objects, and transaction programs. The Application Component Provider also has to write the business and application logic when developing functionality of applications that target enterprise information system.

The API for accessing an enterprise information system belongs to two categories: a client-level API to access data and execute functions (for example, `java.sql.PreparedStatement` and `java.sql.ResultSet` in JDBC 2.0) and a system-level API for getting connections and demarcating transactions (for example, `javax.sql.DataSource` in JDBC 2.0).

In the J2EE programming model, a container assumes primary responsibility for managing connection pooling, transactions, and security. The level of service provided is based on the declarative specification of application requirements by an Application Component Provider or Deployer. This leaves an Application Component Provider to concentrate on programming access to data and functions being managed by an enterprise information system.

6.7.1   Client API for Enterprise Information System Access

A client API for accessing data and functions can be difficult to understand and use for one or more of the following reasons:

- The client API may be tied to a specific enterprise information system programing model.

- The client API may not present object-oriented abstractions. For example, it may require remote function calls to access business functions on an ERP system.

- An Application Component Provider who is proficient with the JavaBeans component model and visual application composition and development tools may see any API that does not support such functionality as being difficult to use.

- The lack of application development tool support for a specific client API may force Application Component Providers to hand-code all data and/or function access.

These factors increase the need for tools to support end-to-end application development. Application Component Providers also have to use additional programming techniques to simplify enterprise information system integration.

6.7.2   Tools for Application Development

The J2EE programming model recognizes that Application Component Providers will rely on enterprise development tools for simplifying development during enterprise information system integration. These tools will come from different vendors, provide varied functionalities, and serve various steps in the application development process. A number of these tools will be integrated together to form an end-to-end development environment. The tools include:

- Data and function mining tools, which enable Application Component Providers to look at the scope and structure of data and functions in an existing information system.

- Object-oriented analysis and design tools, which enable Application Component Providers to design an application in terms of enterprise information system functionality.

- Application code generation tools, which generate higher level abstractions for accessing data and functions. A mapping tool that bridges different programming models, such as an object to relational mapping, will fall into this category.

- Application composition tools, which enable Application Component Providers to compose application components from generated abstractions (such as those described in previous bullets). These tools will use the JavaBeans component model to enhance ease of programming and composition.

- Deployment tools, which are used by Application Component Providers and Deployers to set transaction, security, and other deployment time requirements.

Since programming access to enterprise information system data and functions is a complex application development task in itself, we recommend that application development tools should be used to reduce the effort and complexity involved in enterprise information system integration.

6.7.3   Access Objects

A component can access data and functions in an enterprise information system in a couple of ways, either directly by using the corresponding client API or indirectly by abstracting the complexity and low-level details of enterprise information system access API into higher level *access objects*. An Application Component Provider comes across these access objects in different forms, scopes, and structure.

The use of access objects provides several advantages:

- An access object can adapt the low-level programming API used for accessing enterprise information system data and/or functions to an easy-to-use API that can be designed to be consistent across various types of enterprise information systems. For example, an access object may follow a design pattern that maps function parameters to setter methods and return values to getter methods. The Application Component Provider uses a function by first calling the appropriate setter methods, then calling the method corresponding to the enterprise information system function, and finally calling the getter methods to retrieve the results.

- A clear separation of concern between access objects and components will enable a component to be adapted to different enterprise information system resources. For example, a component can use an access object to adapt its persistent state management to a different database schema or to a different type of database.

- Since access objects can be made composable through support for the Java-Beans model, components can be composed out of access objects or can be linked with generated access objects using application development tools. This simplifies the application development effort.

Since access objects primarily provide a programming technique to simplify application development through one or more of the above advantages, we recommend that Application Component Providers consider using them anywhere they need to access data or functions in an enterprise information system. In some cases tools may be available to generate such access objects. In other cases they will need to be hand-coded by Application Component Providers.

6.7.3.1 Guidelines for Access Objects

Here are some guidelines to follow in developing access objects:

- An access object shouldn't make assumptions about the environment in which it will be deployed and used.

- An access object should be designed to be usable by different types of components. For example, if an access object follows the set-execute-get design pattern described previously, then its programming model should be consistent across both enterprise beans and JSP pages.

- An access object shouldn't define declarative transaction or security requirements of its own. It should follow the transaction and security management model of the component that uses it.

- All programming restrictions that apply to a component apply to the set of access objects associated with it. For example, an enterprise bean isn't allowed to start new threads, to terminate a running thread, or to use any thread synchronization primitives. Therefore, access objects should conform to the same restrictions.

6.7.3.2 Examples of Access Objects

Access objects can be used in a number of ways, as represented in the following examples:

- Encapsulating functions

    An access object can encapsulate one or more enterprise information system functions, such as business functions or stored procedures. The following code implements an access object that drives a purchase requisition business process on an enterprise resource planning system by mapping purchasing functions to method calls on a purchase function object.

```
PurchaseFunction pf = // instantiate access object for PurchaseFunction
// set fields for this purchase order
pf.setCustomer("Wombat Inc");
pf.setMaterial(...);
pf.setSalesOrganization(...);
```

```
po.execute();
// now get the result of purchase requisition using getter methods
```

- Encapsulating persistent data

    A data access object can encapsulate access to persistent data such as that stored in a database management system. Data access objects can provide a consistent API across different types of such systems. Data access objects used by the sample application (see Section 5.5.1 on page 130) are used to access order objects stored in different types of databases.

- Aggregating behaviors

    An access object can aggregate access to other access objects, providing a higher level abstraction of application functionality. For example, a `Purchase-Order` aggregated access object can drive its purchase requisition business process through the `PurchaseFunction` access object and use a data access object `PurchaseData` to maintain persistent attributes of the purchase order.

6.7.3.3 Usage Scenarios for Access Objects

A component can use access objects in different ways depending on the functionality they offer. A couple of common ways to use access objects would be:

- Define a one-to-one association between components and access objects. That is, each access object encapsulates the enterprise information system functionality required by a particular component. This usage scenario will typically be used to enable Web access to enterprise information system resources being encapsulated by an access object.

- Define components to aggregate the behavior of multiple access objects. This will happen often where a component accesses multiple enterprise information system resources or adds additional business logic to the functionality defined by multiple enterprise information system resources.

6.8   Connections

Virtually all enterprise information systems are accessed via objects called connections. The following discussions provide pointers on efficient techniques for getting and managing connections.

6.8.1   Establishing a Connection

A component is responsible for getting a connection to an enterprise information system. Once a connection to the enterprise information system is established, the component uses the connection to access enterprise information system resources. After the component is finished, it closes the connection.

The specific steps in establishing a connection to an enterprise information system are:

1. The Deployer configures a connection factory instance in the JNDI name space. This connection factory instance is tied to the connection factory requirements specified in the deployment descriptor by the Application Component Provider.

2. A component looks up a connection factory from the JNDI name space. After a successful lookup, the component calls a connection factory method to create a connection to the enterprise information system.

3. The connection factory returns a connection instance. The component uses the connection instance to access enterprise information system resources.

4. Having established a connection to the enterprise information system, the component manages this connection and its life cycle.

5. Once the component is finished using the connection, it closes the connection instance.

Code Example 6.1 illustrates how a component gets a connection to a relational database using the JDBC 2.0 API.

```java
public void getConnection(...) {
        // obtain the initial JNDI context
        Context initctx = new InitialContext();

        // Perform JNDI lookup to obtain factory
        javax.sql.DataSource ds =
            (javax.sql.DataSource)initctx.lookup(
                "java:comp/env/jdbc/MyDatabase");

        // Invoke factory to get a connection
        java.sql.Connection cx = ds.getConnection();
```

```
        // Use the Connection to access the resource manager
        ...
    }
```

Code Example 6.1   Establishing a Database Connection

6.8.2   Guidelines for Connection Management

If each component were to acquire an enterprise information system connection and hold it until it gets removed, it would be difficult to scale up an application to support thousands of users. Since holding on to an enterprise information system connection across long-lived instances or transactions is expensive, components should manage connections more efficiently. To avoid scaling problems, almost every J2EE server should support connection pooling. However, an Application Component Provider still needs to follow sound connection management practices.

When an application is migrated from a two-tier structure to a multitier component-based structure, the issue of connection management becomes especially important. For example, a two-tier JDBC application may share a single connection across an entire application. After migration to a component-based partitioning, the application will need to deal with shared connections across multiple component instances.

This section provides guidelines for addressing application programming model issues related to connections using a JDBC connection to a relational database as an example.

6.8.2.1 Connection Life Cycle and Connection Pooling

A component can get a connection to a database in any client- or container-invoked method. We recommend that components open and close their connections within a single method, rather than holding connection state across methods. Only when the design of an application requires components to share connections across component instances or method invocations should connections be retained.

A component can retain a connection across methods at the cost of additional system resources and added programming model complexity required to manage the connection. One example might be a stateful session bean instance that retains the results of queries and database access operations across methods. The session bean gets a connection and starts a transaction through it. The transaction itself is handled internally by database with no external transaction management. Since the session bean wants to have this transaction span multiple methods, it must keep the connection open across method invocations.

Ideally, containers should take care of connection sharing. But currently the J2EE platform defines no standardized way of implementing connection sharing across different containers. Until a connection sharing mechanism is standardized for containers, a component can choose to do connection sharing through vendor-specific mechanisms offered by different containers and JDBC drivers. This comes at the cost of portability across containers.

6.8.2.2 Connection Management by Component Type

A J2EE application is typically composed of components of different types: JSP pages, servlets, and enterprise beans. These component types vary in terms of support for container-managed activation and passivation, execution of an instance for multiple clients, sharing of an instance across multiple clients, long-lived nature, and other factors. The Application Component Provider has to account for such differences across component types when deciding on a connection management model for an application. Here are a few examples that illustrate these differences.

A JSP page or servlet acquires and holds on to a JDBC connection in relation to the life cycle of its HTTP session. It can handle multiple HTTP requests across a single HTTP session from Web clients using the same JDBC connection.

A stateful session bean can share an open connection and its client-specific query results across multiple methods. However stateless session beans are designed to have no state specific to a client. So if stateless session beans share a connection across methods, they are required to maintain no client-specific state associated with the connection.

For entity beans, the EJB specification identifies methods that are allowed to perform enterprise information system access through a connection. These include `ejbCreate`, `ejbPostCreate`, `ejbRemove`, `ejbFind`, `ejbActivate`, `ejbLoad`, `ejbStore`, and business methods from the remote interface. An entity bean cannot access enterprise information systems from within the `setEntityContext` and `unsetEntityContext` methods because a container does not have a meaningful transaction or security context when they are called.

6.8.2.3 Multiple Connections

Some JDBC drivers don't support multiple concurrent connections under a single transaction. To be portable, components should avoid opening multiple concurrent connections to a single database. However, multiple component instances can access the same database using different connections.

6.9   Security

An enterprise has a critical dependency on its information systems for its business activities. Loss or inaccuracy of information or unauthorized access to an enterprise information system can be extremely costly. So, enterprises require that the security of their enterprise information systems should never be compromised. Applications need to provide access to enterprise information systems without creating security threats to these valuable resources.

Enterprise applications should clearly establish the requirements and architecture for secure enterprise information system integration environment. For example, an application should require only the level of protection needed by the enterprise: reducing the level of protection for less sensitive information or where the system is less vulnerable to threats. The cost of implementing, administering, and running a secure system should also be weighed against the security needs of an application. This trade-off, based on the security benefits and cost, is difficult to make for an enterprise application. However, this trade-off is important to make for the security architecture for enterprise information system integration.

6.9.1   Security Architecture

A security architecture for enterprise information system integration should fulfill a variety of requirements to ensure seamless support for distributed applications:

- Support a consistent end-to-end security architecture across Web, EJB, and enterprise information system tiers for applications based on the J2EE platform.

- Fit with the existing security environment and infrastructure supported by an enterprise information system.

- Support authentication and authorization of users who are accessing enterprise information systems.

- Be transparent to application components. This includes support for enabling end-users to log on only once to the enterprise environment and access multiple enterprise information systems.

- Enable applications to be portable across security environments that enforce different security policies and support different mechanisms.

The relative importance of achieving these goals depends on the cost/benefit trade-off for the security requirements. The more an architecture takes care of these security requirements for the application, the easier the application development effort.

6.9.2   Application Programming Model

While developing and deploying application components, an Application Component Provider follows the security model defined for the corresponding J2EE component—EJB, JSP, or servlet. We recommend the following application programming model for all types of components:

- An Application Component Provider should specify security requirements for an application declaratively in the deployment descriptor. The security requirements include security roles, method permissions, and authentication approach for enterprise information system signon.

- A security-aware Application Component Provider can use a simple programmatic interface to manage security at an application level. This programmatic interface allows the Application Component Provider to make access control decisions based on the security context (principal, role) associated with the caller of a method and to do programmatic signon to an enterprise information system (described in Section 6.9.3.2 on page 160).

- Other development roles—J2EE Server Provider, Deployer, System Administrator—should satisfy an application's security requirements (as specified in the deployment descriptor) in the operational environment.

6.9.3   Resource Signon

From a security perspective, the mechanism for getting a connection to a resource is referred to as *resource signon*. A user requests a connection to be established under its security context. This security context includes various attributes, such as role, access privileges, and authorization level for the user. All application-level invocations to the database using this connection are then provided through the security context associated with the connection.

If the resource signon mechanism involves authentication of the user, then an Application Component Provider has the following two choices:

- Allow the Deployer to set up the resource signon information. For example, the Deployer sets the user name and password for establishing the database connection. The container then takes the responsibility of managing the database signon.

- Implement sign on to the database from the component code by providing explicit security information for the user requesting the connection.

We recommend that a component let the container manage resource signon. This takes the burden of managing security information for the signon off of the Application Component Provider. It also enables J2EE servers to provide additional useful security services, such as single signon across multiple enterprise information systems and principal mapping across security domains.

Container-managed resource signon enables the Application Component Provider to avoid hard-coding security details in the component code. A component with hard-coded security logic is less portable because it is difficult to deploy on containers with different security policies and mechanisms. The following sections illustrate how to sign on using both approaches.

6.9.3.1 Container-Managed Signon

In this example, the Application Component Provider delegates the responsibility of setting up and managing resource signon to the container. The Deployer sets up the resource signon so that the user account for connecting to the database is always eStoreUser. The Deployer also configures the user identification and authentication information—user name and password—that is needed to authenticate eStoreUser to the database.

As shown in Code Example 6.2, the component code invokes the connection request method on the javax.sql.DataSource with no security parameters. The component instance relies on the container to do the signon to the database using the security information configured by the Deployer. Code Example 6.3 contains the corresponding connection factory reference deployment descriptor entry, where the res-auth element specifies that signon is performed by the container.

```
// Obtain the initial JNDI context
Context initctx = new InitialContext();
```

```
// Perform JNDI lookup to obtain connection factory
javax.sql.DataSource ds = (javax.sql.DataSource)initctx.lookup(
                           "java:comp/env/jdbc/MyDatabase");

// Invoke factory to obtain a connection. The security
// information is not given, and therefore it will be
// configured by the Deployer.
java.sql.Connection cx = ds.getConnection();
```

Code Example 6.2   Container-Managed Signon

```
<resource-ref>
    <description>description</description>
    <res-ref-name>jdbc/MyDatabase</res-ref-name>
    <res-type>javax.sql.DataSource</res-type>
    <res-auth>Container</res-auth>
</resource-ref>
```

Code Example 6.3   Connection Factory Reference Element

6.9.3.2 Application-Managed Signon

In this example, the Application Component Provider performs a programmatic signon to the database. The component passes explicit security information (user name, password) to the connection request method of the javax.sql.DataSource.

```
// Obtain the initial JNDI context
Context initctx = new InitialContext();

// Perform JNDI lookup to obtain factory
javax.sql.DataSource ds = (javax.sql.DataSource)initctx.lookup(
                           "java:comp/env/jdbc/MyDatabase");

// Get connection passing in the security information
java.sql.Connection cx = ds.getConnection("eStoreUser",
                                           "password");
```

Code Example 6.4   Application-Managed Signon

6.9.3.3 Authorization Model

An Application Component Provider relies on the container and enterprise information system for authorizing access to enterprise information system data and functions. The Application Component Provider specifies security requirements for application components declaratively in a deployment descriptor. A set of security roles and method permissions can be used to authorize access to methods on a component. For example, an Application Component Provider declaratively specifies the `PurchaseManager` role as the only security role that is granted permission to call the `purchase` method on a `PurchaseOrder` enterprise bean. The `purchase` method in turn drives its execution through an ERP Logistics application by issuing a purchase requisition. So in effect, this application has authorized only end-users with the `PurchaseManager` role to do a purchase requisition. This is the recommended authorization model.

An Application Component Provider can also programmatically control access to enterprise information system data and functions based on the principal or role associated with the client who initiated the operation. For example, the EJB specification allows component code to invoke `getCallerPrincipal` and `isCallerInRole` to get the caller's security context. An Application Component Provider can use these two methods to perform security checks that cannot be expressed declaratively in the deployment descriptor.

An application can also rely on an enterprise information system to do access control based on the security context under which a connection to the enterprise information system has been established. For example, if all users of an application connect to the database as `dbUser`, then a database administrator can set explicit permissions for `dbUser` in the database security domain. The database administrator can deny `dbUser` permission to execute certain stored procedures or to access certain tables.

6.10   J2EE Connector Architecture

The J2EE Connector architecture is an API under development to define a standard for connecting the J2EE platform to heterogeneous enterprise information systems such as enterprise resource planning, mainframe transaction processing, and database systems. This API defines a set of scalable, secure, and transactional mechanisms to support the integration of enterprise information systems with J2EE servers and enterprise applications.

The Connector architecture enables an enterprise information system vendor to provide a standard connector for its enterprise information system. This connector is plugged into a J2EE server to provide the underlying infrastructure for integration with an enterprise information system. The J2EE server that is extended to support the Connector architecture is then assured of connectivity to multiple enterprise information systems. Likewise, an enterprise information system vendor provides one standard connector that will plug into any J2EE server supporting the Connector architecture.

The J2EE server and enterprise information system collaborate through the connector to keep all system-level mechanisms—transactions, security, connection management—transparent to the application components. This enables an application component developer to focus on the business and presentation logic for the application components without getting involved in the system-level issues related to enterprise information system integration. This leads to an easier and faster cycle for the development of scalable, secure, and transactional enterprise applications that require integration with multiple enterprise information systems. The Connector architecture will be supported in the J2EE platform, version 1.3.

6.11   Summary

This chapter has described a set of design choices, guidelines, and recommendations for integrating enterprise information systems into enterprise applications. These guidelines enable an Application Component Provider to develop an enterprise application based on its overall functional and system requirements for enterprise information system integration. The focus has been on accessing enterprise information system resources from the component, using tools to simplify and reduce application development effort involved in accessing enterprise information systems, getting and managing connections to enterprise information systems, and supporting the security requirements of an application.

The current version of the J2EE platform provides full support for database systems through the JDBC API. In the next version of J2EE platform, the Connector architecture will support integration with enterprise information systems other than database systems.

About the Author

INDERJEET SINGH is a Staff Engineer with Sun Microsystems where he leads the technical aspects of the J2EE Blueprints program. He also designed and implemented the Web-caching and proxy-service module of the Java Web Server. In another incarnation, he designed fault-tolerance software for large-scale distributed telecommunications switching systems. Inderjeet holds an M.S. in Computer Science from Washington University at Saint Louis, and a B.Tech. in Computer Science and Engineering from Indian Institute of Technology at Delhi.

CHAPTER 7

Packaging and Deployment

by Inderjeet Singh

T HE J2EE platform enables developers to create different parts of their applications as reusable components. The process of assembling components into modules and modules into enterprise applications is called packaging. In good software design, reusable components can be customized to the operational environment. The process of installing and customizing an application in an operational environment is called deployment. To enable customization, the components of an application need to be configurable. However, application developers should not have to reinvent a configuration mechanism over and over again. They need a standard mechanism that provides flexibility for configuration and supports tools to help the process.

The J2EE platform provides facilities to make the packaging and deployment process simple. It uses JAR files as the standard package for modules and applications, and XML-based deployment descriptors for customizing components and applications. This chapter begins by providing an overview of the J2EE packing and deployment process. It describes how to perform each stage in the process and provides guidelines for each stage. It concludes by discussing requirements for tools that support the deployment process.

7.1   Roles and Tasks

The J2EE packaging and deployment process involves three different development roles: Application Component Providers, Application Assemblers, and Deployers. The packaging and deployment tasks that each role performs are summarized in Figure 7.1.

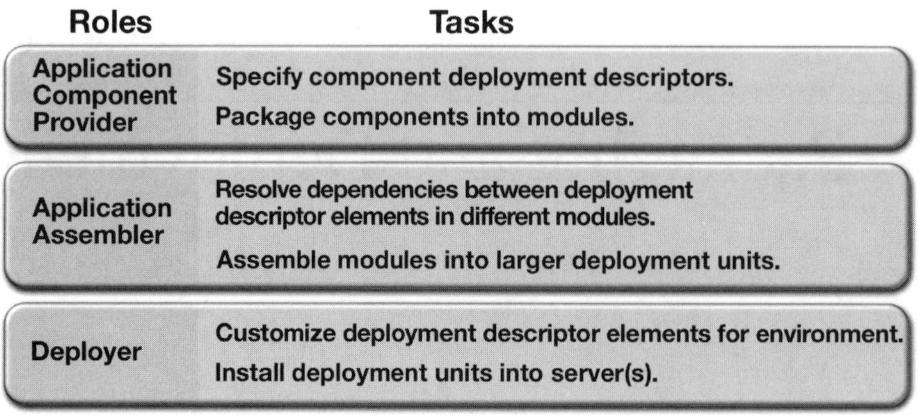

Roles	Tasks
Application Component Provider	**Specify component deployment descriptors.** **Package components into modules.**
Application Assembler	**Resolve dependencies between deployment descriptor elements in different modules.** **Assemble modules into larger deployment units.**
Deployer	**Customize deployment descriptor elements for environment.** **Install deployment units into server(s).**

Figure 7.1   J2EE Packaging and Deployment Tasks

Application Component Providers develop enterprise beans, HTML and JSP pages, and their associated helper classes. They supply the structural information of the deployment descriptor for each component. This information includes the home and remote interfaces and implementation classes of enterprise beans, the persistence mechanisms used, and the type of resources the components use, information typically hard coded in the application and not configurable at deployment time. Code Example 7.1 contains an excerpt from the sample application's enterprise bean deployment descriptor:

```
<entity>
    <display-name>TheAccount</display-name>
    <ejb-name>TheAccount</ejb-name>
    <home>com.sun.estore.account.ejb.AccountHome</home>
    <remote>com.sun.estore.account.ejb.Account</remote>
    <ejb-class>
        com.sun.estore.account.ejb.AccountEJB
    </ejb-class>
    <persistence-type>Bean</persistence-type>
    <prim-key-class>java.lang.String</prim-key-class>
    <reentrant>False</reentrant>
    <resource-ref>
        <description>description</description>
        <res-ref-name>jdbc/EstoreDataSource</res-ref-name>
```

```
            <res-type>javax.sql.DataSource</res-type>
            <res-auth>Container</res-auth>
        </resource-ref>
    </entity>
```

Code Example 7.1   Descriptor Elements for an Entity Bean

Application Assemblers provide information related to the application as a whole. In the sample application, the Application Assembler configures the file Main.jsp to handle requests coming to the URL namespace, (/control/*), the error pages the application uses, its security constraints and roles, and so on. Code Example 7.2 contains excerpts from the sample application's Web deployment descriptor:

```
<web-app>
    <display-name>JavaPetStoreDemoWebTier</display-name>
    <servlet>
        <servlet-name>webTierEntryPoint</servlet-name>
        <display-name>centralJsp</display-name>
        <description>central point of entry for the Web app
        </description>
        <jsp-file>Main.jsp</jsp-file>
    </servlet>
    <servlet-mapping>
        <servlet-name>webTierEntryPoint</servlet-name>
        <url-pattern>/control/*</url-pattern>
    </servlet-mapping>
    ...
    <error-page>
        <exception-type>java.lang.Exception</exception-type>
        <location>/errorpage.jsp</location>
    </error-page>
    ...
</web-app>
```

Code Example 7.2   Descriptor Elements for Web Application

A Deployer is responsible for deploying J2EE components and applications into an operational environment. Deployment typically involves two tasks:

1. Installation: The Deployer moves the media to the server, generates the additional container-specific classes and interfaces that enable the container to manage the components at runtime, and installs the components and additional classes and interfaces into the J2EE server.

2. Configuration: The Deployer resolves all the external dependencies declared by the Application Component Provider and follows the application assembly instructions defined by the Application Assembler. For example, the Deployer is responsible for mapping the security roles defined by the Application Assembler to the user groups and accounts that exist in the operational environment into which the components and applications are deployed. In some cases a qualified Deployer may customize the business logic of the application's components at deployment time by using tools provided with a J2EE product. For example, a Deployer may write application code that wraps an enterprise bean's business methods or customizes the appearance of a JSP page, for example, by adding a company's logo or other graphics to a login page.

7.2   Packaging J2EE Applications

A J2EE application is packaged as an Enterprise ARchive (EAR) file, a standard Java JAR file with an .ear extension. The goal of this file format is to provide an application deployment unit that is assured of being portable.

A J2EE application file contains one or more J2EE modules and a J2EE application deployment descriptor. Therefore, creation of a J2EE application is a two-step process. First, the Application Component Providers create the J2EE modules: EJB, Web, and application client modules. Second, the Application Assembler packages these modules together to create the J2EE application. In this section, we will discuss the issues involved in both of these steps.

It is important to note that all J2EE modules are independently deployable units. This enables component providers to create units of functionality without having to implement full scale applications.

To assemble an application, an Application Assembler edits deployment descriptors for the J2EE modules to link dependencies between components within each archive and between components in different archives. All such dependencies must be linked before deployment. For example, in the sample application, the Web components in the WAR file need to refer to `ShoppingClientController`, `Catalog`, `Account`, `Order`, and `ShoppingCart` enterprise beans present in the EJB JAR file. The role of the Application Assembler is to make sure that the description of the enterprise beans in the WAR file matches with their description in the EJB JAR file.

Once the application assembly is complete, we recommend that the Application Assemblers run J2EE verifier tools (one is provided with the J2EE SDK) on the EAR file to ensure that its contents are well-formed. The verifiers perform a number of static checks to ensure that the deployment descriptor and the archive file contents are consistent with the EJB, Servlet, and J2EE specifications. While verification is not a guarantee of correct behavior at runtime, it is useful for catching some errors early on.

The following sections discuss the different types of J2EE modules and give some heuristic rules and practical tips on how best to package the different component types into modules.

7.2.1   EJB Modules

An EJB module is the smallest deployable and usable unit of enterprise beans. An EJB module is packaged and deployed as an EJB JAR file, a JAR file with a .jar extension. It contains:

- Java class files for the enterprise beans and their remote and home interfaces. If the bean is an entity bean, its primary key class must also be present in the EJB module.

- Java class files for any classes and interfaces that the enterprise bean code depends on that are not included with the J2EE platform. This may include superclasses and superinterfaces and the classes and interfaces used as method parameters, results, and exceptions.

- A EJB deployment descriptor that provides both the structural and application assembly information for the enterprise beans in the EJB module. The application assembly information is optional and is typically included only with assembled applications.

An EJB JAR file differs from a standard JAR file in one key aspect: it is augmented with a deployment descriptor that contains meta-information about one or more enterprise beans.

The EJB JAR file producer can create a client JAR file to be used by the clients of the enterprise beans contained in the EJB JAR file. The client JAR file consists of all the class files that a client program needs to use to access the enterprise beans that are contained in the EJB JAR file.

7.2.2   Packaging Components Into EJB Modules

A typical enterprise application will contain many enterprise beans. Some of these enterprise beans could be off-the-shelf components while others may use third-party libraries. The Application Assembler, therefore, has to choose from the following packaging options:

1. Package each enterprise bean for an application in its own EJB module. In this approach, each enterprise bean has its own deployment descriptor and is packaged in one EJB module along with its dependent classes. One advantage of this approach is the maximum reusability of each enterprise bean, by leaving the Application Assembler free to pick and choose among these EJB modules to compose additional J2EE applications. This option is recommended if your enterprise beans are each highly reusable. In such a case, the Application Assemblers will be able to reuse precisely those enterprise beans that they wish to, and no more.

2. Package all enterprise beans for an application in one EJB module. In this approach all enterprise beans and their dependent classes are packaged together in one EJB module. This approach is the simplest to implement. The Application Assembler does not have to specify references to the enterprise beans present in this EJB module as unresolved. This makes the job of Application Assemblers easier in the case when they wish to use all the enterprise beans. Application Assemblers who only wish to use a subset of the enterprise beans in the EJB module will still be able to do so, but may end up with a bloated application. The Deployer in this case may have to deploy superfluous enterprise beans.

3. Package all related (closely-coupled) enterprise beans for an application in one EJB module. In this approach, all off-the-shelf components are used as is (that is, in their own EJB modules). All in-house enterprise beans are grouped based on their functional nature and put in one EJB module. For example, all enterprise beans related to account management can be put in one EJB module.

Because its more modular, the third option is recommended for reasonably-sized J2EE applications. It strikes the right balance between maximum reusability (option 1) and maximum simplicity (option 2). It promotes the black-box use of third-party components, which is especially important when such third-party components that are digitally signed. Another value of the third option arises when a J2EE server deploys each EJB module on a separate Java virtual machine for load balancing. In such cases, the third option is most efficient since it groups closely-coupled enterprise beans together, allowing many remote calls to be optimized to local calls. Another advantage of option 3 is that it promotes reusability at the functional level rather than at the enterprise bean level. For example, making a single Account enterprise bean reusable is more difficult than providing a reusable set of classes that provide account management functionality collectively. Logical grouping also makes sense from a tool point of view. A deployment or assembly tool may show the EJB module as a group under a single icon. The following discussions provide guidelines on grouping enterprise beans.

7.2.2.1 Grouping by Related Functionality

Once a group of enterprise beans is packaged into the same EJB module, they may not be easily separated without knowing significant implementation details of each enterprise bean. To reuse one bean from an EJB module, you would generally have to deploy all of them. So, it makes good sense to package together a group of enterprise beans only if they will be commonly deployed and used together.

The utility classes used by a bean must be packaged into the EJB module of that bean in order for the bean to function correctly at runtime. If you package related beans together, you reduce the number of copies of utility classes which would otherwise increase the virtual machine size of most J2EE servers and could cause potential conflicts during upgrades.

EJB modules will commonly be displayed in a palette of reusable components in a J2EE application assembly tool. Tools will commonly group together enterprise beans from the same EJB module in a user interface. For example, it makes sense to group server-side components related to accounting functionality or specialized database functionality in a single code library or EJB module.

7.2.2.2 Grouping Interrelated Beans

Enterprise beans can call one another at runtime, and one enterprise bean can delegate some of its functionality to another. Though some J2EE servers will support highly efficient cross-application dependencies, enterprise beans that depend on one another should be grouped together in the same JAR file for both organizational and performance reasons. Where beans call one another, the EJB module may be delivered preassembled, with all the enterprise bean cross-references resolved within the same unit. This makes the tasks of both the Assembler and the Deployer much easier. Locating an appropriate accounting bean for use by a teller bean across a number of servers may prove tedious despite the best efforts and user interface wizardry of the authors of a J2EE deployment tool. Where one bean delegates to another, many servers will partition deployed EJB modules across different process and even machine boundaries. If a bean makes frequent calls on another bean, there may be performance issues when they are run within separate address spaces.

7.2.2.3 Grouping for Circular References

When two enterprise beans refer to each other, the result is a circular dependency. Neither bean can function without the other and so neither is reusable without the other. In some cases redesign may eliminate these dependencies. When circular references are necessary, you should also package the components together in the same EJB module to ensure reusability.

7.2.2.4 Groupings with Common Security Profiles

While each EJB module allows a number of abstract security roles to be specified, enterprise beans are often written with a discrete set of users in mind. Enterprise beans that have the same security profile should be grouped together to reduce negotiation of security role names across EJB modules.

7.2.3   Web Modules

A Web module is the smallest deployable and usable unit of Web resources. A Web module is packaged and deployed as a Web ARchive (WAR) file, a JAR file with a .war extension. It contains:

- Java class files for the servlets and the classes that they depend on, optionally packaged as a library JAR file

- JSP pages and their helper Java classes

- Static documents (for example, HTML, images, sound files, and so on)

- Applets and their class files

- A Web deployment descriptor

The WAR file format does not conform to all the requirements of the JAR format because the classes in a WAR file are not usually loadable by a classloader if the JAR is added to a classpath.

7.2.4   Packaging Components Into Web Modules

The Web module is the smallest indivisible unit of Web resources functionality that Application Component Providers will supply to the Application Assembler. Therefore, an Application Component Provider needs to choose how to package Web tier components into Web modules. This section contains guidelines for doing so.

7.2.4.1 Cross-Dependent Servlets

Servlets may directly call each other via HTTP. The URL by which a servlet is known on the J2EE platform depends on the J2EE application in which it was deployed. For reasons of robustness, servlets that call one another should be deployed together. It is therefore recommended that you put them in the same Web module.

7.2.4.2 Cross-Linked Static Content

Since a WAR file is typically deployed under its own context root, cross-linked Web pages must be packaged in a single Web module to avoid broken links. Moreover, cross-linked HTML Web pages are typically reusable as a bundle, so it makes sense to package them together.

7.2.4.3 Logical Grouping of Functionality

A Web module that has a clearly defined purpose is easier to reuse in different scenarios than one with less well-defined overall behavior. For example, a well-designed Web module concerned purely with inventory management can be reused in many e-commerce applications that need inventory management capability. Such a module would be ideal for adding a Web-based interface for inventory management to the sample application.

7.2.5   Application Client Modules

Application client modules are packaged in JAR files with a .jar extension. Application client modules contain:

- Java classes that implement the client

- An application client deployment descriptor

An application client will use a client JAR file created by the EJB JAR file producer. The client JAR file consists of all the class files that a client program needs to use to access the enterprise beans that are contained in an EJB module.

Figure 7.2 illustrates the various types of J2EE packages and how they can be deployed. Although the figure only shows an independently deployed EJB module, all three types of J2EE modules can be deployed independently.

7.3   Deployment Descriptors

A *deployment descriptor* is an XML-based text file whose elements describe how to assemble and deploy the unit into a specific environment. Each element consists of a tag and a value expressed in the following syntax: `<tag>value</tag>`. Usually deployment descriptors are automatically generated by deployment tools, so you will not have to manage them directly. Deployment descriptor elements contain behavioral information about components not included directly in code. Their purpose is to tell the Deployer how to deploy an application, not tell the server how to manage components at runtime.

There are different types of deployment descriptors: EJB deployment descriptor described in the Enterprise JavaBeans specification, Web deployment descriptor described in the Servlet specification, and application and application client deployment descriptors described in the J2EE specification.

Deployment descriptors specify two kinds of information:

- Structural information describes the different components of the JAR file, their relationship with each other, and their external dependencies. An Application Assembler or Deployer risks breaking the functionality of the component if this information is changed. Environment entries and resource requirements are part of structural information.

- Assembly information describes how contents of a JAR file can be composed into a deployable unit. Assembly information is optional. Assembly information can be changed without breaking the functionality of the contents, although doing so may alter the behavior of the assembled application.

The remainder of this section describes how to specify the most commonly used deployment descriptor elements.

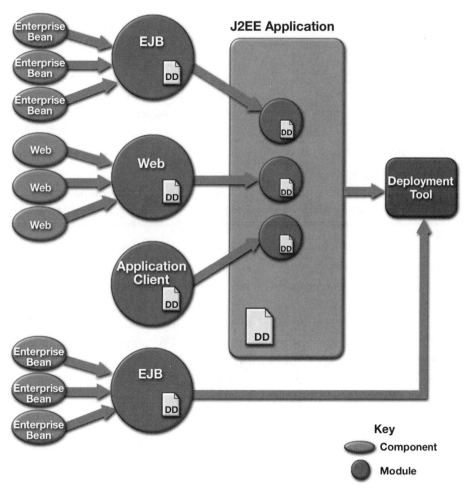

Figure 7.2   J2EE Packages

7.3.1   Specifying Deployment Descriptor Elements

This section describes how to specify commonly used elements in the various deployment descriptors. First we describe elements common to various J2EE component types. Then we describe elements specific to enterprise beans, in particular, the elements related to transactions and persistence. Finally we cover Web component elements. For the definitions of each type of deployment descriptor, see the J2EE, EJB, and servlet specifications.

7.3.1.1   Common Elements

This section describes the deployment descriptor elements common across the different J2EE component types. These include environment entries, references to enterprise beans, references to connection factories, and security-related elements.

Naming Environment Entries

Naming environment entries allow customization of a component during deployment or assembly without the need to access or change the component's source code. The container implements the naming environment, and provides it to the component instance through a JNDI naming context.

The Deployer must ensure that the values of all the environment entries declared by a component are set to meaningful values. The Deployer can modify values of environment entries that have been previously set by the Application Component Provider and/or Application Assembler. The Deployer must set the values of those environment entries for which no value has been specified. The description elements provided by the Application Component Provider or Application Assembler help the Deployer with this task.

Naming environment entries are specified with the env-entry element. Code Example 7.3 uses an environment entry to determine whether confirmation email is sent when an order is processed. Code Example 7.4 shows how to set the value of the environment entry.

```
public static boolean sendConfirmationMail() {
    boolean boolVal = false;
    try {
        InitialContext ic = new InitialContext();
        Boolean bool = (Boolean)
            ic.lookup("java:comp/env/sendConfirmationMail");
        if (bool != null) {
```

```
            boolVal = bool.booleanValue();
        }
    } catch (NamingException ne) {
        ...
    }
    return boolVal;
}
```

Code Example 7.3   Looking up a Naming Environment Entry

```
<env-entry>
    <env-entry-name>sendConfirmationMail</env-entry-name>
    <env-entry-type>java.lang.Boolean</env-entry-type>
    <env-entry-value>false</env-entry-value>
</env-entry>
```

Code Example 7.4   Environment Entry Element

References to Enterprise Beans

There are two parts to the mechanism for establishing connections to enterprise beans in a J2EE application: the Java language interface for accessing a bean and the deployment descriptor declarations for identifying those references. The Application Component Provider looks up the references in the source code of the referring component using the Java interfaces, then identifies these references in the deployment descriptor when packaging the component. A Deployer binds enterprise bean references to the enterprise beans' homes in the target environment. The deployment descriptor also allows an Application Assembler to link an enterprise bean reference declared in one enterprise bean to other enterprise beans contained in the same EJB module, or in other EJB modules in the same J2EE application unit. The link is an instruction to the tools used by the Deployer that the enterprise bean reference must be bound to the home of the specified enterprise bean.

Code Example 7.5 illustrates how a component obtains a reference to the home interface of another enterprise bean. In the example, the Application Component Provider of the ShoppingClientControllerEJB assigned the environment entry cart as the name to refer to the home of another enterprise bean, Shopping-CartHome. ShoppingClientControllerEJB calls a utility method getShopping-CartHome, which performs a JNDI lookup of cart in the ejb subcontext of the environment naming context java:comp/env. ShoppingClientControllerEJB caches the reference to the home interface in the cart variable so that the lookup need only be performed once.

```java
public class ShoppingClientControllerEJB implements SessionBean {
    public ShoppingCart getShoppingCart() {
        if (cart == null) {
            try {
                ShoppingCartHome cartHome =
                    EJBUtil.getShoppingCartHome();
                cart = cartHome.create();
            } catch (CreateException ce) {
                ...
            }
        }
        return cart;
    }
}

public static ShoppingCartHome getShoppingCartHome() {
    try {
        InitialContext initial = new InitialContext();
        Object objref = initial.lookup("java:comp/env/ejb/cart");
        return (ShoppingCartHome) PortableRemoteObject.
            narrow(objref, ShoppingCartHome.class);
    } catch (NamingException ne) {
        throw new GeneralFailureException(ne);
    }
}
```

Code Example 7.5   Locating a Home Interface

An Application Component Provider must use the ejb-ref element of the deployment descriptor to declare all enterprise bean references. Similarly, the deployment descriptor for a Web component must contain ejb-ref elements for the enterprise beans that it uses. Such declarations allow the EJB module consumer (that is, Application Assembler or Deployer) to discover all the enterprise beans used by the components.

Code Example 7.6 illustrates the declaration of an enterprise bean reference to ShoppingCart in the deployment descriptor for ShoppingClientController. Note the ejb-ref-name element, which contains string ejb/cart used in the JNDI lookup performed in Code Example 7.5.

```
<session>
    <display-name>TheShoppingClientController</display-name>
    <ejb-name>TheShoppingClientController</ejb-name>
    <home>com.sun.estore.control.ejb.
        ShoppingClientControllerHome</home>
    <remote>com.sun.estore.control.ejb.
        ShoppingClientController</remote>
    <ejb-class>com.sun.estore.control.ejb.
        ShoppingClientControllerEJB</ejb-class>
    ...
    <ejb-ref>
        <ejb-ref-name>ejb/cart</ejb-ref-name>
        <ejb-ref-type>Session</ejb-ref-type>
        <home>com.sun.estore.cart.ejb.ShoppingCartHome</home>
        <remote>com.sun.estore.cart.ejb.ShoppingCart</remote>
        <ejb-link>TheCart</ejb-link>
    </ejb-ref>
    ...
</session>
```

Code Example 7.6 Enterprise Bean Reference Element

An Application Assembler uses the ejb-link element in the deployment descriptor to link an enterprise bean reference to a target enterprise bean. The ejb-link element is a subelement of the ejb-ref element. The value of the ejb-link element is the name of the target enterprise bean, that is, the name defined in the ejb-name element of the target enterprise bean. The target enterprise bean can be in the same EJB module or in another EJB module in the same J2EE application as the referencing enterprise bean. The Application Assembler needs to ensure that the target enterprise bean is type compatible with the declared enterprise bean reference. This means that the target enterprise bean must be of the type indicated in the ejb-ref-type element, and that the home and remote elements of the target enterprise bean must be type compatible with the home and remote elements declared in the enterprise bean reference.

The ejb-link element in Code Example 7.6 indicates that the enterprise bean reference cart declared in ShoppingClientController is linked to the enterprise bean TheCart shown in Code Example 7.7.

```
<session>
    <display-name>TheCart</display-name>
    <ejb-name>TheCart</ejb-name>
    <home>com.sun.estore.cart.ejb.ShoppingCartHome</home>
    <remote>com.sun.estore.cart.ejb.ShoppingCart</remote>
    <ejb-class>com.sun.estore.cart.ejb.ShoppingCartEJB</ejb-class>
    <session-type>Stateful</session-type>
    transaction-type>Container</transaction-type>
</session>
```

Code Example 7.7   Enterprise Bean Element

References to Connection Factories

A connection factory is an object used to create connections to a resource manager. For example, an object that implements the javax.sql.DataSource interface is a connection factory for java.sql.Connection objects which provide connections to database management systems.

An Application Component Provider must obtain connections to resources as follows:

* Declare a connection factory reference in the component's naming environment.

   For each connection factory that is used by a component, an Application Component Provider declares a connection factory reference in the deployment descriptor using the resource-ref element. This allows the EJB module consumer (that is, Application Assembler or Deployer) to discover all the connection factory references used by an enterprise bean. All connection factory references should be organized in the subcontexts of a component's environment, using a different subcontext for each resource manager type. For example, all JDBC DataSource references might be declared in the java:comp/env/jdbc subcontext (see Section 6.9.3.1 on page 159), and all email sessions in the java:comp/env/mail subcontext. Connection factory references are also used to refer to URL resources and JMS connections.

- Look up the connection factory object in the component's naming environment using the JNDI interface.

- Invoke the appropriate method on the connection factory method to obtain a connection to the resource. The factory method is specific to the resource type. It is possible to obtain multiple connections by calling the factory object multiple times.

A Deployer binds connection factory references to actual connection factories that are configured in the Container.

Code Example 7.8 illustrates the mail connection factory reference in the entry for the `Mailer` enterprise bean.

```
<session>
    <display-name>TheMailer</display-name>
    <ejb-name>TheMailer</ejb-name>
    <home>com.sun.estore.mail.ejb.MailerHome</home>
    <remote>com.sun.estore.mail.ejb.Mailer</remote>
    ...
    <resource-ref>
        <res-ref-name>mail/MailSession</res-ref-name>
        <res-type>javax.mail.Session</res-type>
        <res-auth>Container</res-auth>
    </resource-ref>
</session>
```

Code Example 7.8   Connection Factory Reference Element

Note that the connection factory type must be compatible with the type declared in the `res-type` element. The `res-auth` subelement of the `resource-ref` element specifies whether resource signon is managed by an application component or its container. See Section 6.9.3 on page 158 for more information on resource signon.

The `Mailer` enterprise bean calls `MailHelper` to open a mail session. Code Example 7.9 contains the code from the `MailHelper` class that requests a mail session object declared as java:comp/env/mail/MailSession in the JNDI context.

```
public void createAndSendMail(String to, String subject,
                                String htmlContents) {
    try {
            InitialContext ic = new InitialContext();
            Session session = (Session) ic.
                lookup("java:comp/env/mail/MailSession");
            ...
    }
}
```

Code Example 7.9   Looking Up a Connection Factory

The Deployer must bind the connection factory references to the actual resource factories configured in the target environment. A Deployer can use the JNDI LinkRef mechanism to create a symbolic link to the actual JNDI name of the connection factory. The Deployer also needs to provide any additional configuration information that the resource manager needs for opening and managing the resource.

Security Elements

An Application Component Provider uses the security-role element to define logical security roles that can be assumed by an authenticated principal. Code Example 7.10 illustrates how the sample application defines the gold_customer security role.

```
<security-role>
    <role-name>gold_customer</role-name>
</security-role>
```

Code Example 7.10   Security Role Element

The security-role-ref element is used to link a role name used by the isCallerInRole method with a security role. In the sample application, this method is used by the `Order` entity bean to enforce business rules based on whether the user is a preferred customer.

Code Example 7.11 and Code Example 7.12 illustrate how the `security-role-ref` element establishes a link between the string `GOLD_CUSTOMER` used by the `isCallerInRole` method and the security role named `gold_customer`.

```
private int getBonusMiles() {
    int miles = (totalPrice >= 100) ? 1000 : 500;
    if (context.isCallerInRole("GOLD_CUSTOMER"))
        miles += 1000;
    return miles;
}
```

Code Example 7.11   Referencing a Security Role Name

```
<security-role-ref>
    <role-name>GOLD_CUSTOMER</role-name>
    <role-link>gold_customer</role-link>
</security-role-ref>
```

Code Example 7.12   Linking a Security Role Name and Security Role

An Application Component Provider declaratively controls access to an enterprise bean's methods by specifying the `method-permission` element in the enterprise bean's deployment descriptor. The component provider defines this element to list the set of methods that can be accessed by each security role. The authorization scenario described in Section 9.3.8 on page 232 illustrates how `method-permission` elements affect the execution of enterprise bean methods.

7.3.1.2 Enterprise Bean Elements

The component-specific elements that must be specified for an enterprise bean are those related to transactions and those related to persistence.

Transaction Elements

Two transaction elements must be specified: whether the bean uses container- or bean-managed transaction demarcation, and for container-managed demarcation, the transaction attributes of the bean's methods.

An Application Assembler must ensure that the methods of the deployed enterprise beans with container-managed transaction demarcation have been assigned a transaction attribute. If the transaction attributes have not been assigned by the Application Component Provider, they must be assigned by the Application Assembler. Code Example 7.13 illustrates how transaction attributes are declared for an `Account` entity bean. Recall that entity beans can only use container-managed transactions. The `container-transaction` element for `Account` specifies that when the `changeContactInformation` method is invoked, it must be within the scope of a transaction. See Section 8.7.2.1 on page 205 for detailed information about the values that a transaction attribute can take.

```
<container-transaction>
    <method>
        <ejb-name>TheAccount</ejb-name>
        <method-intf>Remote</method-intf>
        <method-name>changeContactInformation</method-name>
        <method-params>
            <method-param>com.sun.estore.util.
                ContactInformation</method-param>
        </method-params>
    </method>
    <trans-attribute>Required</trans-attribute>
</container-transaction>
```

Code Example 7.13   Transaction Elements

Persistence Elements

The Application Component Provider must specify whether a bean manages its own persistence or uses container-managed persistence. When a bean uses container-managed persistence, the Application Component Provider must specify the fields of the bean. Code Example 7.14 illustrates how the `Account` entity bean uses the `persistence-type` element to declare that it will manage its own persistence.

```
<entity>
    <description>Account of a shopper</description>
    <display-name>TheAccount</display-name>
    ...
    <persistence-type>Bean</persistence-type>
</entity>
```

Code Example 7.14 Persistence Element

7.3.1.3 Web Component Elements

Some of the more commonly used Web component deployment descriptor elements are discussed in this section.

Servlet

The one deployment descriptor element that *must* be specified for a Web component is the servlet element, shown in Code Example 7.15. This element associates a logical identifier (servlet-name) with the name of the servlet class or the JSP file associated with the component.

```
<servlet>
    <servlet-name>webTierEntryPoint</servlet-name>
    <display-name>centralJsp</display-name>
    <jsp-file>Main.jsp</jsp-file>
</servlet>
```

Code Example 7.15 Servlet Element

Servlet Mapping

The servlet-mapping element specifies the URLs that the Web component is aliased to handle. While the element is called servlet-mapping, it is used to map URLs to both servlets and JSP pages. Code Example 7.16 aliases Main.jsp to handle all requests coming to the set of URLs /control/*.

```
<servlet-mapping>
    <servlet-name>webTierEntryPoint</servlet-name>
```

```
    <url-pattern>/control/*</url-pattern>
</servlet-mapping>
```

Code Example 7.16   Servlet Mapping Element

Error Pages

The `error-page` element can be used to invoke an error page automatically when the Web application throws a Java language exception. Code Example 7.17 shows how to enable the J2EE server to send `errorpage.jsp` to the browser client if the Web application ever throws any exception of the type `java.lang.Exception` or its subclass.

```
<error-page>
    <exception-type>java.lang.Exception</exception-type>
    <location>/errorpage.jsp</location>
</error-page>
```

Code Example 7.17   Error Page Element

Form-Based Authentication Configuration

Form-based authentication is the preferred mechanism for authenticating application users in the J2EE platform. Code Example 7.18 illustrates how to configure a Web application to activate form-based authentication when the Web server receives a request for the URL /control/placeorder. The `security-constraint` element specifies that the URL /control/placeorder is a protected resource. The `login-config` element specifies that the URL `formbasedloginscreen` will be displayed when an unauthenticated user tries to access /control/placeorder. This page contains an HTML form that prompts for a user name and password.

```
<security-constraint>
    <web-resource-collection>
        <web-resource-name>MySecureBit0</web-resource-name>
        <description>no description</description>
        <url-pattern>/control/placeorder</url-pattern>
        <http-method>POST</http-method>
        <http-method>GET</http-method>
    </web-resource-collection>
```

```
<auth-constraint>
    <description>no description</description>
    <role-name>gold_customer</role-name>
    <role-name>customer</role-name>
</auth-constraint>
<user-data-constraint>
    <description>no description</description>
    <transport-guarantee>NONE</transport-guarantee>
</user-data-constraint>
</security-constraint>
<login-config>
    <auth-method>FORM</auth-method>
    <realm-name>default</realm-name>
    <form-login-config>
        <form-login-page>formbasedloginscreen</form-login-page>
        <form-error-page>formbasedloginerrorscreen
            </form-error-page>
    </form-login-config>
</login-config>
```

Code Example 7.18 Form-Based Authentication Configuration

7.4   Deployment Tools

Although deployment can be performed directly by editing XML text files, the process best handled by specialized tools. This section describes the actions that a deployment tool performs and outlines requirements on packaging and development tools. The requirements serve as recommendations to vendors of packaging and deployment tools and determine what developers can expect from such tools.

7.4.1   Deployment Tool Actions

This section discusses what happens behind the scenes when a J2EE application is deployed on a J2EE server. Since there can be many J2EE applications deployed on the same J2EE server, the J2EE servers typically register each application under a different identifier. The deployment of a J2EE application involves three different types of components: enterprise beans, Web components, and application clients.

For each enterprise bean, the J2EE server must perform the following tasks:

1. Generate and compile the stubs and skeletons for the enterprise bean.

2. Set up the security environment to host the enterprise bean according to its deployment descriptor. This is needed so that the access to the methods of the enterprise bean can be regulated according to the security policy of the application.

3. Set up the transaction environment for the enterprise bean according to its deployment descriptor. This is needed so that the calls to the methods of the enterprise bean happen in the correct transaction context.

4. Register the enterprise bean, its environment properties, resources references, and so on, in the JNDI name space.

5. Create database tables for enterprise beans that use container-managed persistence.

For each Web component, the J2EE server must perform the following tasks:

1. Transfer the contents of the Web component underneath the document root of the server. Since there can be more than one J2EE application installed, the server may install each under a specific directory. For example, the J2EE SDK installs each application under a context root specified at the deployment time. The sample application is installed under the `estore` directory.

2. Initialize the security environment of the application. This involves configuring the form-based login mechanism, role-to-principal mappings, and so on.

3. Register environment properties, resource references, and EJB references in the JNDI name space.

4. Set up the environment for the Web application. For example, it performs the alias mappings and configures the servlet context parameters.

5. Precompile JSP pages as specified in the deployment descriptor.

The tool used to deploy an application client, and the mechanism used to install the application client, is not specified by the J2EE specification. Very sophisticated J2EE products may allow the application client to be deployed on a J2EE server and automatically made available to some set of (usually intranet) clients. Other J2EE products may require the J2EE application bundle containing the application client to be manually deployed and installed on each client machine. And yet another approach would be for the deployment tool on the J2EE server to produce an installation package that could be taken to each client to install the application client.

7.4.2   Deployment Tool Requirements

When considering the requirements on deployment tools, it is important to consider the deployment process at two different times: during application development and during production deployment. A developer's deployment needs are different than the needs of a Deployer installing a production application on a mission-critical system. When an application is being developed, it must be deployed before it can be tested. Developers want fast response times, and the ability to undeploy, redeploy, and partially deploy applications easily and quickly. They will often make minor changes to Java classes, and hence will not want to go through a lengthy deployment process over and over again. They also need extensive debugging facilities. Many Java development environments will contain a J2EE server optimized for these purposes.

When deploying a production application on a mission-critical server, the priorities are robustness, performance, and stability. Often, to avoid downtime and unforeseen problems, the application is first brought up on parallel systems. The foremost consideration of the Deployer is to be able to connect all legacy systems to the newly developed application. A Deployer may also want detailed logging of the deployment process.

The following sections explore packaging and deployment issues from a tools perspective and point out differences, if any, in the light of the two different deployment times.

7.4.2.1 Vendor-Specific Information

The J2EE platform specification specifies file formats for each of the three J2EE component types and for a J2EE application itself. This specification defines how such files must be structured to be correctly handled by a J2EE deployment tool. A certain amount of information must be available to each container along with the application code and deployment descriptor for proper runtime support of an application. This information is usually related to bindings of the application in a vendor-specific or environment specific setting. Here is a partial list of information the deployment tool of the J2EE SDK solicits from the Deployer after consuming an application EAR file:

- A JNDI name for each enterprise bean's home interface

- A mapping of abstract security roles of the application to user and group names

- JNDI lookup names and account information for all databases

- JavaMail session configuration information

Note that these issues only come up at deployment time—they in no way affect the ability to deploy an application on servers from different J2EE Product Providers.

There are many ways to represent this information. The J2EE SDK represents this information in an XML document held as a separate entry within the application archive. Code Example 7.19 is an example of the XML document that represents runtime information for the sample application after the runtime bindings have been made with the J2EE SDK:

```
<j2ee-ri-specific-information>
    <server-name>localhost</server-name>
    <rolemapping>
        <role name="gold_customer">
            <groups>
                <group name="gold" />
            </groups>
        </role>
        <role name="customer">
            <principals>
                <principal>
                    <name>j2ee</name>
                </principal>
            </principals>
            <groups>
                <group name="cust" />
            </groups>
        </role>
    </rolemapping>
    <enterprise-beans>
        <ejb>
            <ejb-name>TheAccount</ejb-name>
            <jndi-name>estore/account</jndi-name>
            <resource-ref>
                <res-ref-name>jdbc/EstoreDataSource</res-ref-name>
                <jndi-name>jdbc/EstoreDB</jndi-name>
                <default-resource-principal>
                    <name>estoreuser</name>
```

```
            <password>estore</password>
        </default-resource-principal>
      </resource-ref>
    </ejb>
  </enterprise-beans>
</j2ee-ri-specific-information>
```

Code Example 7.19 Runtime Deployment Descriptor

Different J2EE product vendors will also need to add similar information in the deployment process of a J2EE application. Vendors may find it useful to take advantage of the attribute ID mechanism afforded by document type definitions to link vendor-specific information to components and entities within a J2EE application.

The output of a deployment tool should remain compliant with the J2EE specifications in order that it may be easily opened in other deployment tools even when such extra information has been added. We recommend that the deployment descriptors within an application remain as unchanged as possible to support this. We also recommend that the tools preserve vendor-specific information added to an application across sessions. This can be done by storing such information with or inside the J2EE application file or using an IDE-like project structure.

EJB and Web modules are independently deployable units and hence any deployment tools should be able to accept and deploy them. Although the archive files may be augmented with vendor-specific information, we recommend that other deployment tools be able to accept and deploy these augmented EJB and Web modules and J2EE applications even though they may not understand a particular vendor's runtime binding information. We recommend that the vendor-specific information that the deployment tool expects have reasonable fall-back default options for this purpose.

7.4.2.2 Single Point of Entry for Deployment

A high-end mission-critical server often consists of multiple physical servers. Often the number of Web containers is greater than the number of EJB containers. In such cases, the Deployer to shouldn't have to install applications individually on each machine. We recommend that the deployment process has a single point of entry— either a stand-alone deployment tool or the deployment component of a J2EE server. For example, the J2EE SDK has a deployment tool that provides a single point of entry to the J2EE server. This central component then takes care of distributing appropriate components on both the Web and the EJB containers.

This approach has following benefits:

- It simplifies the deployment process since the Deployer has to interact with only one deployment tool. The Deployer also has a clear understanding of when deployment is complete. The tool also handles determining which components are required to be deployed on each machine.

- It provides a way to perform centralized logging and auditing.

- It provides better fault tolerance. Since the deployment tool has complete control over all application components on all servers, it can detect server failures and handle them by dynamic load balancing. It can also detect when a server comes back up and redeploy the application to bring it in sync. An added advantage is that the Deployer does not have to worry about load-balancing.

- It simplifies undeployment and upgrading.

7.4.2.3 Remotely Accessible Deployment

Deployers often need to deploy multiple applications on multiple J2EE servers. To handle such scenarios more easily, the deployment tool should be remotely accessible as either a Web-based or client-server application. The deployment tool bundled with the J2EE SDK takes a client-server approach, using RMI-IIOP to communicate with the administration back-end of the J2EE server. The tool has the capability to access multiple J2EE servers and deploy applications on them.

7.4.2.4 Undeployment Capability

In development-time deployment, it is critical to have undeployment capability for quicker updating of new application components. In a high-end implementation, it isn't acceptable to have to bring down the server to add or remove new software applications, so that high-end servers will likely support dynamic deployment and dynamic undeployment. Low-end J2EE servers may not need to support this capability.

For many J2EE servers, deploying a J2EE application may be an atomic process, with no support for incremental deployment of J2EE application components. However, at stages of the application development process, it may be desirable to test portions of an application. This requires the ability to divide a component application into smaller units so that each can be deployed and re-deployed without the wait associated with deploying a full scale application.

7.4.2.5 JNDI Name Space Management

Deployers will need to bind external references in a J2EE application to entities in their environment. Examples of such references include databases and enterprise beans in the system. Since binding happens through the JNDI name space, Container Providers need to provide tools to create and manage the JNDI name space. These tools also need to control the access to the JNDI name space according to the security policy of their environment.

7.4.2.6 Name Collision Management

Application Assemblers may use third-party enterprise beans, without control over the names used for such enterprise beans. As a result, name collisions are bound to occur. Packaging tools should automatically detect and handle such name collisions by adjusting names through the `ejb-link` element of the bean's deployment descriptors.

7.4.2.7 Deployment Descriptor Versioning

The lifetime of many enterprise applications may be measured in years and even decades. An important goal of the J2EE platform is to provide compatibility even when systems and application components are upgraded. Packaging and deployment tools need to ensure that they do not add anything that is against the general direction of evolution of deployment descriptors. They also need to follow the versioning conventions described in the J2EE, EJB, and servlet specifications.

7.5   Summary

The J2EE platform provides facilities to make the deployment process simple. It uses JAR files as the standard package for components and applications, and XML-based deployment descriptors for customizing parameters. For the most part, the facilities provided by the platform support simplified application development through the use of tools that can read and write deployment descriptor files. These tools present users with a more intuitive view of the structure of an application and the capabilities of its components.

The J2EE packaging and deployment process involves three different J2EE roles: Application Component Provider, Application Assembler, and Deployer.

Application Component Providers specify component deployment descriptors and package components into modules. Application Component Providers should ensure that the Application Assembler and the Deployer can customize an enterprise bean's business logic via deployment descriptors rather than modifying source code. When packaging components into modules, Application Component Providers need to balance between the competing goals of reusability and simplicity.

Application Assemblers resolve dependencies between deployment descriptor elements in different modules and assemble modules into larger deployment units. Deployers customize deployment descriptor elements for environment in which the application is deployed and install deployment units. The Deployer must ensure that the values of all the environment entries declared by an enterprise bean are set to meaningful values.

The packaging and deployment process is best handled by specialized tools. Both Component Providers and Deployers need to deploy applications; however, their deployment needs are different. Component Providers want fast response times, and the ability to undeploy, redeploy, and partially deploy applications easily and quickly. In production, the priorities are robustness, performance, and stability. Deployment tools need to address both sets of requirements, as well as J2EE goals such as portability and backwards compatibility.

About the Author

TONY NG is a Staff Engineer at Sun Microsystems. He is part of the J2EE Reference Implementation team, where he leads the development of the J2EE Connector architecture, distributed transaction, and database connection management in the reference implementation. Tony also participated in the development of the J2EE programming model and the Java Transaction Service. Formerly, he worked on Java Blend, an object-relational database mapping product. Tony has a B.S. in Computer Science from the University of Illinois at Urbana-Champaign and an M.S. in Electrical Engineering and Computer Science from the Massachusetts Institute of Technology.

CHAPTER 8

Transaction Management

by Tony Ng

Transactions are a mechanism for simplifying the development of distributed multiuser enterprise applications. By enforcing strict rules on an application's ability to access and update data, transactions ensure data integrity. A transactional system ensures that a unit of work either fully completes or the work is fully rolled back. Transactions free an application programmer from dealing with the complex issues of failure recovery and multiuser programming.

The chapter begins with a general overview of transaction properties and J2EE platform support for transactions. Then it describes the Java Transaction API, the interface used by the J2EE platform to manage and coordinate transactions. Finally, the chapter describes the J2EE transactional model available to the different types of J2EE components and to enterprise information systems.

8.1 Properties of Transactions

All transactions share the properties of atomicity, consistency, isolation, and durability. These properties are denoted by the acronym ACID.

Atomicity requires that all of the operations of a transaction are performed successfully for the transaction to be considered complete. If all of a transaction's operations cannot be performed, then none of them may be performed.

Consistency refers to data consistency. A transaction must transition the data from one consistent state to another. The transaction must preserve the data's semantic and physical integrity.

Isolation requires that each transaction appear to be the only transaction currently manipulating the data. Other transactions may run concurrently. However, a transaction should not see the intermediate data manipulations of other transactions until and unless they successfully complete and commit their work. Because of interdependencies among updates, a transaction might get an inconsistent view of the database were it to see just a subset of another transaction's updates. Isolation protects a transaction from this sort of data inconsistency.

Durability means that updates made by committed transactions persist in the database regardless of failures that occur after the commit operation and it also ensures that databases can be recovered after a system or media failure.

8.2   J2EE Platform Transactions

Support for transactions is an essential element of the J2EE architecture. The J2EE platform supports both programmatic and declarative transaction demarcation. The component provider can use the Java Transaction API to programmatically demarcate transaction boundaries in the component code. Declarative transaction demarcation is supported in enterprise beans, where transactions are started and completed automatically by the enterprise bean's container. In both cases, the burden of implementing transaction management is on the J2EE platform. The J2EE server implements the necessary low-level transaction protocols, such as interactions between transaction manager and JDBC database systems, transaction context propagation, and optionally distributed two-phase commit. Currently, the J2EE platform only supports flat transactions. A flat transaction cannot have any child (nested) transactions.

The J2EE platform supports a transactional application that is comprised of a combination of servlets and/or JSP pages accessing multiple enterprise beans within a single transaction. Each component may acquire one or more connections to access one or more shared resource managers. Currently, the J2EE platform is only required to support access to a single JDBC database within a transaction (multiple connections to the same database are allowed). It is not required to support access to multiple JDBC databases within a single transaction. It is also not required to support access to other types of enterprise information systems such as enterprise resource planning systems. However, some products might choose to provide these extra transactional capabilities. For example, the J2EE SDK supports access to multiple JDBC databases in one transaction using the two-phase commit protocol.

It is important for developers to understand and distinguish which transaction capabilities are required and which are optional in a J2EE product. To write a truly portable application, developers should only use features required by the J2EE specification. For example, if a J2EE application needs to access multiple databases under a single transaction, it will not run properly on a J2EE product that does not support two-phase commit.

8.3 Scenarios

The following scenarios illustrate the use of transactions in a J2EE environment.

8.3.1 Accessing Multiple Databases

In Figure 8.1, a client invokes enterprise bean X. Bean X accesses database A using a JDBC connection. Then enterprise bean X calls another enterprise bean Y. Y accesses database B. The J2EE server and resource adapters for both database systems ensure that updates to both databases are either all committed, or all rolled back.

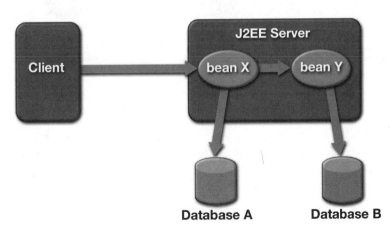

Figure 8.1   Accessing Multiple Databases in the Same Transaction

An Application Component Provider does not have to write extra code to ensure transactional semantics. Enterprise beans X and Y access the database systems using the JDBC client access API. Behind the scenes, the J2EE server enlists the connections to both systems as part of the transaction. When the transaction is committed, the J2EE server and the resource managers perform a two-phase commit protocol to ensure atomic update of the two systems.

8.3.2 Accessing Multiple Enterprise Information Systems From Multiple EJB Servers

In Figure 8.2, a client invokes the enterprise bean X, which updates data in enterprise information system A, and then calls another enterprise bean Y that is installed in another J2EE server. Enterprise bean Y performs read-write access to enterprise information system B.

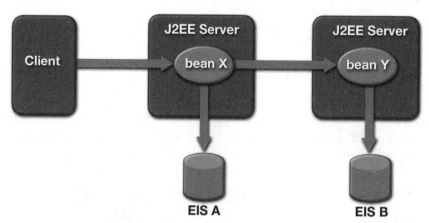

Figure 8.2   Accessing Multiple Enterprise Information Systems in the Same Transaction

When X invokes Y, the two J2EE servers cooperate to propagate the transaction context from X to Y. This transaction context propagation is transparent to the application code. At transaction commit time, the two J2EE servers use a distributed two-phase commit protocol to ensure that the two enterprise information systems are updated under a single transaction.

8.4   JTA Transactions

A *JTA transaction* is a transaction managed and coordinated by the J2EE platform. A J2EE product is required to support JTA transactions according to the transaction requirements defined in the J2EE specification. A JTA transaction can span multiple components and enterprise information systems. They are propagated automatically between components and to enterprise information systems accessed by components within that transaction. For example, a JTA transaction may be comprised of a servlet or JSP page accessing multiple enterprise beans, some of which access one or more relational databases.

There are two ways to begin a JTA transaction. A component can begin a JTA transaction using the JTA `javax.transaction.UserTransaction` interface. For an enterprise bean, a JTA transaction might also be started automatically by the EJB container if the bean uses container-managed transaction demarcation.

The main benefit of using JTA transactions is the ability to combine multiple components and enterprise information system accesses into one single transaction with little programming effort. For example, if a component A begins a JTA transaction and invokes a method of component B, the transaction will be propagated transparently from component A to B by the platform. Similarly, if component A updates a table in a relational database, the update will automatically be under the scope of the same transaction. No extra programming is required to propagate transactions between multiple components and enterprise information systems. In addition, enterprise beans using container-managed transaction demarcation will not need to begin or commit transactions programmatically as the demarcation is handled automatically by the EJB container.

It is recommend that an enterprise information system, such as a database, be accessed within the scope of a JTA transaction. Accessing an enterprise information system within a transaction provides some guarantee on the consistency and integrity of the data. In addition, using a JTA transaction allows work performed by multiple components through multiple enterprise information system connections to be grouped as an atomic unit. It also allows work performed on one or more independent enterprise information systems to be grouped as an atomic unit if the J2EE product supports two-phase commit.

8.4.1   JTA and JTS

JTA allows applications to access transaction management in a manner that is independent of a specific implementation. JTA specifies standard Java interfaces between a transaction manager and the parties involved in a distributed transaction system: the transactional application, the J2EE server, and the manager that controls access to the shared resources affected by the transactions.

JTS specifies the implementation of a transaction manager that supports JTA and implements the Java mapping of the OMG Object Transaction Service (OTS) 1.1 specification at the level below the API. JTS propagates transactions using IIOP. A JTS transaction manager provides the services and management functions required to support transaction demarcation, transactional resource management, synchronization, and transaction context propagation.

An Application Component Provider uses the JTA UserTransaction interface to demarcate JTA transaction boundaries in components. The JTS TransactionManager and XAResource interfaces are low-level APIs between a J2EE server and enterprise information system resource managers and are not intended to be used by applications.

A J2EE platform might choose to use a JTS implementation to support the transaction semantics defined in J2EE specification. An example is the J2EE SDK. The JTS implementation is transparent to J2EE components. Components should never interact directly with JTS. Instead, they should use the JTA UserTransaction interface for transaction demarcation.

8.5   Transactions in Applets and Application Clients

The J2EE platform does not require transaction support in applets and application clients, though like distributed transactions, a J2EE product might choose to provide this capability for added value. So, whether applets and application clients can directly access a UserTransaction object depends on the capabilities provided by the container. To ensure portability, applets and application clients should delegate transactional work to enterprise beans.

8.6   Transactions in Web Components

A servlet or JSP page can use JNDI to lookup a UserTransaction object, then use the UserTransaction interface to demarcation transactions. This is useful in a two-tier application where a Web component needs to access enterprise information systems under the scope of a JTA transaction.

Code Example 8.1 illustrates the use of the JTA interface to demarcate transactions within a Web component:

```
Context ic = new InitialContext();
UserTransaction ut =
    (UserTransaction) ic.lookup("java:comp/UserTransaction");
ut.begin();
```

```
// perform transactional work here
ut.commit();
```

Code Example 8.1   Web Component Using JTA Transactions

A Web component may only start a transaction in its `service` method. A transaction that is started by a servlet or JSP page must be completed before the `service` method returns. In other words, transactions may not span Web requests.

There are many subtle and complex interactions between the use of JTA transactions, threads, and JDBC connections. Web components should follow the guidelines stated in the transaction management chapter of the J2EE specification:

- JTA transactions should be started and completed only from the thread in which the `service` method is called. If the Web component creates additional threads for any purpose, these threads should not attempt to start JTA transactions.

- JDBC connections may be acquired and released by a thread other than the `service` method thread, but should not be shared between threads.

- JDBC `Connection` objects should not be stored in static fields.

- For Web components implementing `SingleThreadModel`, JDBC `Connection` objects may be stored in class instance fields.

- For Web components not implementing `SingleThreadModel`, JDBC `Connection` objects should not be stored in class instance fields, and should be acquired and released within the same invocation of the `service` method.

In a multitier environment, servlets and JSP pages are mainly responsible for the presentation of the application and dealing with browser interaction. In this case, the use of JTA transactions in the Web tier is not recommended. Instead, transactional work such as database access should be delegated to enterprise beans in the EJB tier.

8.7   Transactions in Enterprise Beans

There are two types of transaction demarcation in enterprise beans: bean-managed and container-managed. In container-managed transaction demarcation, six different transaction attributes—Required, RequiresNew, NotSupported, Supports, Mandatory, and Never—can be associated with an enterprise bean's method. An Application Component Provider or Assembler specifies the type of transaction demarcation and transaction attributes for the methods of the enterprise beans in the deployment descriptor. The use of deployment descriptors to specify transaction elements is discussed and illustrated in "Transaction Elements" on page 184.

This section discusses the types of transactions and the attributes of container-managed transactions and then presents guidelines for choosing among the available options.

8.7.1   Bean-Managed Transaction Demarcation

With bean-managed transaction demarcation, an enterprise bean uses the javax.transaction.UserTransaction interface to explicitly demarcate transaction boundaries. Only session beans can choose to use bean-managed demarcation. An entity bean must always use container-managed transaction demarcation.

The following code illustrates the use of JTA interface to demarcate transactions in an enterprise bean with bean-managed transaction demarcation.

```
UserTransaction ut = ejbContext.getUserTransaction();
ut.begin();
// perform transactional work here
ut.commit();
```

Code Example 8.2   Enterprise Bean Using a JTA Transaction

8.7.2   Container-Managed Transaction Demarcation

For an enterprise bean with container-managed transaction demarcation, the EJB container is responsible for managing transaction boundaries. The transaction attribute for a method determines what the EJB container needs to do in terms of transaction management. For example, if a method has a transaction attribute RequiresNew, the EJB container will begin a new JTA transaction every time this method is called and attempt to commit the transaction before the method returns. The same transaction attribute can be specified for all the methods of an enterprise bean or different attributes can be specified for each method of a bean. Refer to Section 8.7.2.1 on page 205 for more information on transaction attributes.

Even in container-managed demarcation, an enterprise bean has some control over the transaction. For example, an enterprise bean can choose to roll back a transaction started by the container using the method `setRollbackOnly` on the `SessionContext` or `EntityContext` object.

There are several benefits of using container-managed transaction demarcation:

- The transaction behavior of an enterprise bean is specified declaratively instead of programmatically. This frees the Application Component Provider from writing transaction demarcation code in the component.

- It is less error-prone because the container handles transaction demarcation automatically.

- It is easier to compose multiple enterprise beans to perform a certain task with specific transaction behavior. An Application Assembler that understands the application can customize the transaction attributes in the deployment descriptor without code modification.

8.7.2.1 Transaction Attributes

A *transaction attribute* is a value associated with a method of an enterprise bean that uses container-managed transaction demarcation. In most cases, all methods of an enterprise bean will have the same transaction attribute. For optimization purposes, it is possible to have different attributes for different methods. For example, an enterprise bean may have methods that don't need to be transactional.

A transaction attribute must be specified for the methods in the remote interface of a session bean and for the methods in the remote and home interfaces of an entity bean.

Required

If the transaction attribute is `Required`, the container ensures that the enterprise bean's method will always be invoked with a JTA transaction. If the calling client is associated with a JTA transaction, the enterprise bean method will be invoked in the same transaction context. However, if a client is not associated with a transaction, the container will automatically begin a new transaction and try to commit the transaction when the method completes.

RequiresNew

If the transaction attribute is RequiresNew, the container always creates a new transaction before invoking the enterprise bean method and commits the transactions when the method returns. If the calling client is associated with a transaction context, the container suspends the association of the transaction context with the current thread before starting the new transaction. When the method and the transaction complete, the container resumes the suspended transaction.

NotSupported

If the transaction attribute is NotSupported, the transactional context of the calling client is not propagated to the enterprise bean. If a client calls with a transaction context, the container suspends the client's transaction association before invoking the enterprise bean's method. After the method completes, the container resumes the suspended transaction association.

Supports

It the transaction attribute is Supports, and the client is associated with a transaction context, the context is propagated to the enterprise bean method, similar to the way the container treats the Required case. If the client call is not associated with any transaction context, the container behaves similarly to the NotSupported case. The transaction context is not propagated to the enterprise bean method.

Mandatory

The transaction attribute Mandatory requires the container to invoke a bean's method in a client's transaction context. If the client is not associated with a transaction context when calling this method, the container throws javax.transaction.TransactionRequiredException. If the calling client has a transaction context, the case is treated as Required by the container.

Never

The transaction attribute Never requires that the enterprise bean method not be called within a transaction context. If the client calls with a transaction context, the container throws the java.rmi.RemoteException. If the client is not associated with any transaction context, the container invokes the method without initiating a transaction.

8.7.3   Transaction Guidelines

As mentioned previously, the recommended way to manage transactions is through container-managed demarcation. Declarative transaction management provides one of the major benefits of the J2EE platform, by freeing the Application Component Provider from the burden of managing transactions. Furthermore, the transaction characteristics of an application can be changed without code modification by switching the transaction attributes. Transaction demarcation should be selected with great care, by someone who understands the application well. Bean-managed transaction demarcation is only for advanced users who want more control over the work flow.

8.7.3.1 Transaction Attributes Guidelines

Most enterprise beans perform transactional work (for example, accessing a JDBC database). The default choice for a transaction attribute should be `Required`. Using this attribute ensures that the methods of an enterprise bean are invoked under a JTA transaction. In addition, enterprise beans with the `Required` transaction attribute can be easily composed to perform work under the scope of a single JTA transaction.

The `RequiresNew` transaction attribute is useful when the bean method needs to commit its results unconditionally, whether or not a transaction is already in progress. An example of this requirement is a bean method that performs logging. This bean method should be invoked with `RequiresNew` transaction attribute so that the logging records are created even if the calling client's transaction is rolled back.

The `NotSupported` transaction attribute can be used when the resource manager responsible for the transaction is not supported by the J2EE product. For example, if a bean method is invoking an operation on an enterprise resource planning system that is not integrated with the J2EE server, the server has no control over that system's transactions. In this case, it is best to set the transaction attribute of the bean to be `NotSupported` to clearly indicate that the enterprise resource planning system is not accessed within a JTA transaction.

We do not recommend using the transaction attribute `Supports`. An enterprise bean with this attribute would have transactional behavior that differed depending on whether the caller is associated with a transaction context, leading to possibly a violation of the ACID rules for transactions.

The transaction attributes `Mandatory` and `Never` can be used when it is necessary to verify the transaction association of the calling client. They reduce the composability of a component by putting constraints on the calling client's transaction context.

8.8   Transactions in Enterprise Information Systems

Most enterprise information systems support some form of transactions. For example, a typical JDBC database allows multiple SQL updates to be grouped in an atomic transaction.

Components should always access an enterprise information system under the scope of a transaction since this provides some guarantee on the integrity and consistency of the underlying data. Such systems can be accessed under a JTA transaction or a resource manager (RM) local transaction.

8.8.1   JTA Transactions

When an enterprise information system is accessed under the scope of a JTA transaction, any updates performed on the system will commit or roll back depending on the outcome of the JTA transaction. Multiple connections to information systems can be opened and all updates through the connections will be atomic if they are performed under the scope of a JTA transaction. The J2EE server is responsible for coordinating and propagating transactions between the server and the enterprise information system.

If the J2EE product supports multiple enterprise information systems in one transaction, a J2EE application can access and perform updates on multiple enterprise information systems atomically, without extra programming effort, by grouping all updates within a JTA transaction. Code Example 8.3 illustrates this use:

```
InitialContext ic = new InitialContext("java:comp/env");
DataSource db1 = (DataSource) ic.lookup("OrdersDB");
DataSource db2 = (DataSource) ic.lookup("InventoryDB");
Connection con1 = db1.getConnection();
Connection con2 = db2.getConnection();

UserTransaction ut = ejbContext.getUserTransaction();
ut.begin();
// perform updates to OrdersDB using connection con1
```

```
// perform updates to InventoryDB using connection con2
ut.commit();
```

Code Example 8.3   Accessing Multiple Databases

8.8.2   Resource Manager Local Transactions

A *resource manager local transaction* (or *local transaction*) is a transaction specific to a particular enterprise information system connection. A local transaction is managed by the underlying enterprise information system resource manager. The J2EE platform usually does not have control or knowledge about any local transactions begun by components. Typically access to a transactional enterprise information system will be under a local transaction if no JTA transaction has been initiated. For example, if a servlet accesses a JDBC database without starting a JTA transaction, the database access will be under the scope of a local transaction, specific to the database.

Another scenario where enterprise information system access is under the scope of a local transaction is when the enterprise information system is not supported by the J2EE platform. For example, a standard J2EE platform is not required to support object-oriented databases. As a result, the platform would not be able to propagate any JTA transactions to the object-oriented databases and any access will be under local transactions.

8.8.3   Choosing Between JTA and Local Transactions

It is recommended that enterprise information systems, such as databases, be accessed under the scope of a transaction. Accessing an enterprise information system under a transaction provides some guarantee on the consistency and integrity of the data.

We recommend that a component use JTA transactions whenever possible to access enterprise information systems. Using a JTA transaction allows multiple components accessing enterprise information systems to be grouped in a single transaction without adding extra logic. If a component marks the transaction as rollback only, all enterprise information system work will be rolled back automatically. With local transactions, each enterprise information system accessed will have to be committed or rolled back explicitly. In addition, components need extra logic to deal with individual enterprise information system rollbacks or failures.

8.8.4   Compensating Transactions

A *compensating transaction* is a transaction or a group of operations that is used to undo the effect of a previously committed transaction. In the case where multiple access to enterprise information systems need to be grouped under a single transaction, but not all of the systems support JTA transactions, it will be necessary to define a compensating transaction for each enterprise information system access that is under the scope of a local transaction.

Compensating transactions are useful if a component needs to access an enterprise information system that does not support JTA transactions or access an enterprise information system that is not supported by a particular J2EE platform. In both cases, the enterprise information system will be accessed under the scope of a RM local transaction. If multiple enterprise information systems are involved, this creates the challenge of having to group all the work to multiple enterprise information systems into an atomic unit.

For example, suppose an application needs to perform an atomic operation that involves updating three enterprise information systems: two JDBC databases that supports JTA transactions and an enterprise resource planning system that does not. The application would need to define a compensating transaction for the update to the enterprise resource planning system. The approach is illustrated in Code Example 8.4.

```
updateERPSystem();
try {
    UserTransaction.begin();
    updateJDBCDatabaseOne();
    updateJDBCDatabaseTwo();
    UserTransaction.commit();
}
catch (RollbackException ex) {
    undoUpdateERPSystem();
}
```

Code Example 8.4   Compensating Transaction

The methods `updateERPSystem`, `updateJDBCDatabaseOne`, and `updateJDBCDatabaseTwo` contain code to access and perform work on enterprise information systems. The `undoUpdateERPSystem` method contains code to undo the effect of `updateERPSystem` if the JTA transaction does not commit successfully.

This compensation logic should be encapsulated in a session enterprise bean with a bean-managed transaction. If the enterprise information system access logic is relatively simple, they can all reside in this bean. Otherwise, the enterprise bean can invoke other enterprise beans to access the enterprise information system. If an enterprise bean's only responsibility is to access an enterprise information system that does not support JTA transactions, its transaction attribute should be set to `NotSupported`. This denotes that a JTA transaction will not be used in the enterprise bean.

There are a few pitfalls regarding the use of compensating transactions:

- It is not always possible to undo the effect of a committed transaction. Consider Code Example 8.4. If the JTA transaction does not commit and for some reason the method `undoUpdateERPSystem` does not succeed, the data will be left in an inconsistent state.

- Atomicity could also be broken if the server crashes when a compensating transaction is used. For example, if the system crashes after the method `updateERPSystem`, the updates to the two databases will not happen.

- Inconsistent data might be seen by concurrent enterprise information system access. In this approach, non-JTA transactions are actually committed but may be undone subsequently. In the previous example, a concurrent enterprise information system access might see the update to the enterprise resource planning system which might be rolled back later. In other words, it sees uncommitted data.

An application that depends on compensating transactions must have extra logic to deal with potential failures and inconsistencies. The extra work and pitfalls of compensating transactions mean applications should avoid using them if possible. Instead, JTA transactions should be used as they provide a simple and safe way to achieve the ACID properties across multiple components and enterprise information systems.

8.8.5   Isolation Level

An *isolation level* defines how concurrent transactions to an enterprise information system are isolated from one another. Enterprise information systems usually support the following the isolation levels:

- ReadCommitted: This level prevents a transaction from reading uncommitted changes from other transactions.

- RepeatableRead: This level prevents a transaction from reading uncommitted changes from other transactions. In addition, it ensures that reading the same data multiple times will receive the same value even if another transaction modifies the data.

- Serializable: This level prevents a transaction from reading uncommitted changes from other transactions and ensures that reading the same data multiple times will receive the same value even if another transaction modifies the data. In addition, it ensures that if a query retrieves a result set based on a predicate condition and another transaction inserts data that satisfy the predicate condition, re-execution of the query will return the same result set.

Isolation level and concurrency are closely related. A lower isolation level typically allows greater concurrency, at the expense of more complicated logic to deal with potential data inconsistencies. A useful guideline is to use the highest isolation level provided by enterprise information systems that gives acceptable performance.

For consistency, all enterprise information systems accessed by a J2EE application should use the same isolation level. Currently, the J2EE specification does not define a standard way to set isolation levels when an enterprise information system is accessed under JTA transactions. If a J2EE product does not provide a way to configure the isolation level, the enterprise information system default isolation level will be used. For most relational databases, the default isolation level is ReadCommitted.

We recommend that you not change the isolation level within a transaction, especially if some work has already been done. Some enterprise information systems will force a commit if you attempt to change the isolation level.

8.9   Summary

This chapter provides the guidelines for using transactions on the J2EE platform. It describes the J2EE transactional model available to each J2EE component type—application clients, JSP pages and servlets, and enterprise beans—and enterprise information systems.

The J2EE platform provides powerful support for writing transactional applications. It contains the Java Transaction API, which allows applications to access transactions in a manner that is independent of specific implementations and a means for declaratively specifying the transactional needs of an application. These capabilities shift the burden of transaction management from J2EE Application Component Providers to J2EE product vendors. Application Component Providers can thus focus on specifying the desired transaction behavior, and rely on a J2EE product to implement the behavior.

About the Author

Ron MONZILLO is a Senior Staff Engineer at Sun Microsystems where he is the J2EE security specification lead. Prior to joining Sun, Ron worked for the Open Group where he contributed to the evolution of the Distributed Computing Environment. Ron has also worked for BBN, where he developed Network Management systems, and as a Principal Investigator for the MITRE Corporation where he researched fault-tolerant distributed database systems and multi-processor architectures. Ron received an M.S. in Computer Science from the University of Connecticut and a B.S. in Biology from Bates College.

CHAPTER 9

Security

by Ron Monzillo

IN an enterprise computing environment, failure, compromise, or lack of availability of computing resources can jeopardize the viability of the enterprise. An organization must take steps to identify threats to security. Once they are identified, steps should be taken to reduce these threats.

It is unreasonable to assume that J2EE products, and hence J2EE applications, can displace existing enterprise security infrastructures. The J2EE application programming model attempts to leverage existing security services rather than require new services or mechanisms.

This discussion begins with a review of some security concepts and mechanisms. We describe the security concerns and characteristics of enterprise applications and explore the application of J2EE security mechanisms to the design, implementation, and deployment of secure enterprise applications.

9.1 Security Threats and Mechanisms

Threats to enterprise-critical assets fall into a few general categories:

- Disclosure of confidential information

- Modification or destruction of information

- Misappropriation of protected resources

- Compromise of accountability

- Misappropriation that compromises availability

Depending on the environment in which an enterprise application operates, these threats may manifest themselves in different forms. For example, in a traditional single system environment, a threat of disclosure might manifest itself in the vulnerability of information kept in files. In a distributed environment with multiple servers and clients, a threat of disclosure might also result from exposures occurring as the result of networking.

Although not all threats can or need be eliminated, there are many circumstances where exposure can be reduced to an acceptable level through the use of the following security mechanisms: authentication, authorization, signing, encryption, and auditing. The following sections describe J2EE platform security mechanisms and indicate how the mechanisms are used to support security policies in an operational environment.

9.2   Authentication

In distributed component computing, *authentication* is the mechanism by which callers and service providers prove to one another that they are acting on behalf of specific users or systems. When the proof is bidirectional, we refer to it as *mutual authentication.* Authentication establishes the call identities and proves that the participants are authentic instances of these identities. An entity that participates in a call without establishing and/or proving an identity (that is, *anonymously*), is called *unauthenticated.*

When calls are made from a client *program* being run by a user, the caller identity is likely to be that of the *user.* When the caller is an *application component* acting as an intermediary in a call chain originating with some user, the identity may be associated with that of the user, in which case the component would be *impersonating* the user. Alternatively, one application component may call another with an identity of its own and unrelated to that of its caller.

Authentication is often achieved in two phases. First, service-independent authentication requiring knowledge of some secret is performed to establish an *authentication context* that encapsulates the identity and is able to fabricate *authenticators* (proofs of identity*).* Then, the authentication context is used to authenticate with other (called or calling) entities. Controlling access to the authentication context, and thus the ability to authenticate as the associated identity, becomes the basis of authentication. Among the possible policies and mechanisms for controlling access to an authentication context are:

- Once the user performs an initial authentication, the processes the user starts inherit access to the authentication context.

- When a component is authenticated, access to the authentication context may be available to other related or trusted components, such as those that are part of the same application.

- When a component is expected to *impersonate* its caller, the caller may *delegate* its authentication context to the called component.

9.2.1   Protection Domains

Some entities may communicate without requiring authentication. A *protection domain* is a set of entities that are assumed or known to trust each other. Entities in such a domain need not be authenticated to one another.

Figure 9.1 illustrates that authentication is only required for interactions that cross the boundary of a protection domain. When a component interacts with components in the same protection domain, no constraint is placed on the identity that it can associate with its call. The caller may *propagate* the caller's identity, or *choose* an identity based on knowledge of authorization constraints imposed by the called component, since the caller's ability to *claim* an identity is based on trust, not authentication. If the concept of protection domains is employed to avoid the need for authentication, there must be a means to establish the boundaries of protection domains, so that trust in unproven identities does not cross these boundaries. Entities that are universally trusting of all other entities should not be trusted as a member of any protection domain.

In the J2EE architecture, a container provides an authentication boundary between external callers and the components it hosts. The boundaries of protection domains don't always align with those of containers. Containers enforce the boundaries, and implementations are likely to support protection domains that span containers. However, a container is not required to host components from different protection domains, although an implementation may choose to do so.

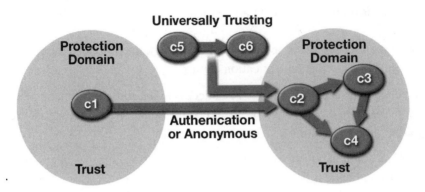

Figure 9.1   Protection Domain

For *inbound* calls, it is the container's responsibility to make an authentic representation of the caller identity available to the component in the form of a *credential*. An X.509 certificate and a Kerberos service ticket are examples of credentials. A passport or a driver's licence are analogous artifacts used in person-to-person interactions.

For *outbound* calls, the container is responsible for establishing the identity of the calling component. In general, it is the job of the container to provide bidirectional authentication functionality to enforce the protection domain boundaries of the deployed applications.

Without proof of component identity, the interacting containers must determine if there is sufficient inter-container trust to accept the container-provided representations of component identity. In some environments, trust may simply be presumed, in others it may be more explicitly evaluated based on inter-container authentication and possibly the comparison of container identities to lists of trusted identities. If a required proof of identity is not provided, and in the absence of a sufficient inter-container trust relationship, a container should reject or abandon a call.

Figure 9.2 illustrates these authentication concepts in two scenarios: an authenticated user scenario and an unauthenticated user scenario.

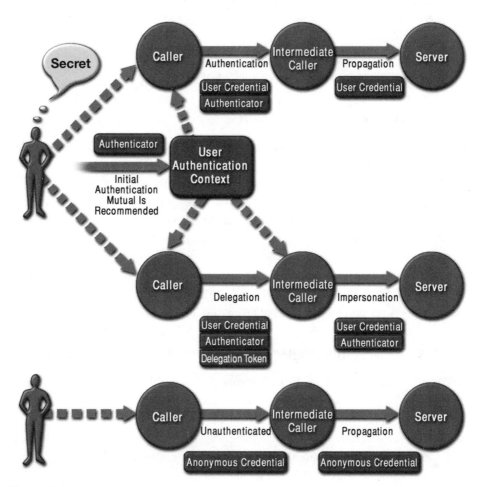

Figure 9.2   Authentication Scenarios

The authenticated user invokes a calling component that employs the user's authentication context to prove its identity to an intermediate component. When the called component makes a call it propagates the identity of its caller. The propagated identity is unproven, and so will be accepted only if the targets trust the caller, that is, if they reside in the same protection domain. The figure also differentiates identity propagation from delegation and subsequent impersonation. In propagation, the service providers bear the burden of determining whether they should accept propagated identities as authentic. In delegation, the user provides the called component with access to its authentication context, enabling the called component to impersonate the user in subsequent calls. Impersonation requires the user to trust the impersonator to act in its behalf. The lower portion of the figure depicts the propagation of an unauthenticated user identity in the form of an anonymous credential. An anonymous credential is the one form of unproven identity that may be propagated independent of trust.

9.2.2   Authentication Mechanisms

In a typical J2EE application, a user would go through a client container to interact with enterprise resources in the Web or EJB tiers. Resources available to the user may be protected or unprotected. Protected resources are distinguished by the presence of *authorization rules* (see Section 9.3 on page 225) that restrict access to some subset of non-anonymous identities. To access a protected resource, a user must present a non-anonymous credential such that its identity can be evaluated against the resource authorization policy. In the absence of a trust relationship between the client and resource containers, the credential must be accompanied by an authenticator that confirms its validity. This section describes the various authentication mechanisms supported by the J2EE platform and how to configure them.

9.2.2.1   Web Tier Authentication

An Application Component Provider can designate that a collection of Web resources (Web components, HTML documents, image files, compressed archives, and so on) is protected by specifying an authorization constraint (described in Section 9.3.7.1 on page 230) for the collection. When an anonymous user tries to access a protected Web resource, the Web container will prompt the user for a password to authenticate with the Web container. The request will not be accepted by the Web container until the user identity has been proven to the Web container and shown to be one of the identities granted permission to access the resource. Caller authentication performed on the first access to a protected resource is called *lazy authentication.*

When a user tries to access a protected Web-tier resource, the Web container activates the authentication mechanism defined in the application's deployment descriptor. J2EE Web containers must support three authentication mechanisms: HTTP basic authentication, form-based authentication, and HTTPS mutual authentication, and are encouraged to support HTTP digest authentication.

In *basic authentication,* the Web server authenticates a principal using the user name and password obtained from the Web client. In *digest authentication* a Web client authenticates to a Web server by sending the server a message digest along its HTTP request message. The digest is computed by employing a one-way hash algorithm to a concatenation of the HTTP request message and the client's password. The digest is typically much smaller than the HTTP request, and doesn't contain the password.

Form-based authentication lets developers customize the authentication user interface presented by an HTTP browser. Like HTTP basic authentication, form-based authentication is not secure, since the content of the user dialog is sent as plain text, and the target server is not authenticated.

In single-signon environments, discretion must be exercised in customizing an application's authentication interface. It may be preferable to provide a single enterprise-wide custom user authentication interface, rather than implementing a set of application-specific interfaces.

With *mutual authentication*, the client and server use X.509 certificates to establish their identity. Mutual authentication occurs over a channel protected by SSL. Hybrid mechanisms featuring either HTTP basic authentication, form-based authentication, or HTTP digest authentication over SSL are also supported.

Authentication Configuration

An authentication mechanism is configured using the `login-config` element of the Web component deployment descriptor. Code Example 9.1, Code Example 9.2, and Code Example 9.3 illustrate the declaration of each type of authentication mechanism.

```
<web-app>
    <login-config>
        <auth-method>BASIC|DIGEST</auth-method>
        <realm-name>jpets</realm-name>
    </login-config>
</web-app>
```

Code Example 9.1   HTTP Basic and Digest Authentication Configuration

```
<web-app>
    <login-config>
        <auth-method>FORM</auth-method>
        <form-login-config>
```

```
        <form-login-page>login.jsp</form-login-page>
        <form-error-page>error.jsp</form-error-page>
    </form-login-config>
  </login-config>
</web-app>
```

Code Example 9.2   Form-Based Authentication Configuration

```
<web-app>
  <login-config>
      <auth-method>CLIENT-CERT</auth-method>
  </login-config>
</web-app>
```

Code Example 9.3   Client Certificate Authentication Configuration

Hybrid Authentication

In both HTTP basic and form-based authentication, passwords are not protected for confidentiality. This vulnerability can be overcome by running these authentication protocols over an SSL-protected session, which ensures that all message content, including the client authenticators, are protected for confidentiality. Code Example 9.4 demonstrates how to configure HTTP basic authentication over SSL using the `transport-guarantee` element. Form-based authentication over SSL is configured in the same way.

```
<web-app>
  <security-constraint>
      ...
      <user-data-constraint>
          <transport-guarantee>CONFIDENTIAL</transport-guarantee>
      </user-data-constraint>
  </security-constraint>
</web-app>
```

Code Example 9.4   SSL Hybrid Authentication Mechanism

9.2.2.2 EJB Tier Authentication

The J2EE 1.2 platform specification doesn't require interoperable caller authentication at the EJB container. Also, network firewall technology may prevent direct Internet interaction (via RMI) between client containers and enterprise beans. One way that an EJB container can protect access to enterprise beans is to entrust the Web container to vouch for the identity of users accessing the beans via protected Web components. As illustrated in Figure 9.3, such configurations use the Web container to enforce protection domain boundaries for Web components and the enterprise beans that they call.

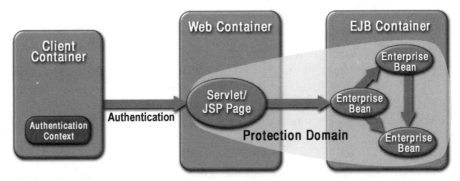

Figure 9.3   Typical J2EE Application Configuration

9.2.3 Authentication Call Patterns

In a multitier, multicomponent application, certain call patterns should be avoided for security reasons. For example, an application that calls protected EJB resources from unprotected Web resources can run into problems, because the Web tier's lazy authentication paradigm doesn't require user authentication except when the user attempts to access a protected resource. While the protection requirement can be moved to the EJB tier, care must be taken to ensure that users who are capable of authenticating can do so. With lazy authentication, a user who wants to visit a protected EJB resource must have visited a protected Web resource. One way to ensure this would be to front every protected EJB resource with a protected Web resource. Another approach would be to link to a protected Web resource (perhaps appearing as an authenticate button) on every Web resource that calls EJB resources. This approach gives the user the option of authenticating (by visiting the protected Web resource linked behind the button) prior to accessing an EJB resource, especially after having been denied access by the EJB resource through an unprotected page.

When an application is deployed with a hybrid authentication mechanism, the Deployer must ensure that the `transport-guarantee` element of each protected Web resource is set to `CONFIDENTIAL`. Otherwise, the client authenticator won't be fully protected.

9.2.3.1 Enterprise Information System Tier Authentication

In integrating with enterprise information systems, J2EE components may use different security mechanisms and operate in different protection domains than the resources they access. In these cases, the calling container can be configured to manage the authentication to the resource for the calling component. This form of authentication is called *container-managed resource manager signon*. The J2EE architecture also recognizes that some components require an ability to manage the specification of caller identity, and the production of a suitable authenticator directly. For these applications, the J2EE architecture provides a means for an application component to engage in what is called *application-managed resource manager signon*. Application-managed resource manager signon is used when manipulating the authentication details is a fundamental aspect of the component's functionality.

The `resource-ref` elements of a component's deployment descriptor (described in greater detail in Section 9.3 on page 225) declares the resources used by the component. The subelement `res-auth` specifies the type of signon authentication. Components can use the `EJBContext.getCallerPrincipal` and `HttpServletRequest.getUserPrincipal` methods to obtain the identity of their caller. The component may map the caller identity to a new identity and/or authentication secret as required by the target enterprise information system.

With container-managed resource manager signon, the container would perform the *principal mapping* on behalf of the calling component. Container-managed principal mapping isn't explicitly defined in any of the J2EE specifications. Whether it is performed by the container or embedded in the caller, the mapping of caller identity to an identity and authentication secret capable of accessing resources in the enterprise information system tier should be modeled as a protected resource, and secured by appropriate authorization rules (see Section 9.3.6 on page 229).

The Connector architecture discussed in Section 6.10 on page 161 offers a standard API for application-managed resource manager signon. The Connector provided API will ensure portability of components that authenticate with enterprise information systems.

9.2.4   Auto-Registration

Many e-commerce applications are designed to make it as easy as possible for a user to become a customer. In contrast to typical computer user authentication environments, where a user must wait for an administrator to set up the user's account, many e-commerce applications enable users to set up their own accounts without administrative intervention. Frequently the user is required to provide his or her identity and location, agree to some contractual obligations, provide credit card information for payment, and establish a password to protect the account.

Once the registration dialog is complete, the user can access the protected resources of the site. In the future, client certificates will replace the identity and password elements of the registration to improve the accountability of the authentication. This transition will also relieve users from the risks they assume when they reuse a single password with multiple vendors as their own form of single signon. Mechanisms to support auto-registration are not specified by the J2EE platform and are thus specific to the container implementation.

Web resources that provide the user interface for auto-registration must be protected. This is accomplished by setting the `transport-guarantee` of these resources to `CONFIDENTIAL`.

9.2.5   Exposing Authentication Boundaries with References

The Application Component Provider is responsible for declaring references made by each component to other J2EE components and to external resources. These declarations are made in the deployment descriptor. In addition to their role in locating services, such declarations serve to inform the Deployer of all the places in the application where authentication may be necessary. Enterprise bean references are declared using `ejb-ref` elements. Enterprise information system references are declared with `resource-ref` elements. In both cases, the declarations are made in the scope of the calling component, and the collection of declared references serves to expose the application's inter-component/resource call tree.

9.3   Authorization

Authorization mechanisms limit interactions with resources to collections of users or systems for the purpose of enforcing integrity, confidentiality, or availability constraints. Such mechanisms allow only authentic caller identities to access components. Mechanisms provided by the J2SE platform can be used to control access to code based on identity properties, such as the location and signer of the calling code. In the J2EE distributed component programming model, additional authorization mechanisms are required to limit access to called components based on who is *using* the calling code. As mentioned in the section on authentication, caller identity can be established by selecting from the set of authentication contexts available to the calling code. Alternatively, the caller may propagate the identity of its caller, select an arbitrary identity, or make the call anonymously.

In all cases, a credential is made available to the called component. The credential contains information describing the caller through its identity attributes. In the case of anonymous callers, a special credential is used. These attributes uniquely identify the caller in the context of the authority that issued the credential. Depending on the type of credential, it may also contain other attributes which define shared authorization properties (for example, group memberships) that distinguish collections of related credentials. The identity attributes and shared authorization attributes appearing in the credential are referred to together as the caller's *security attributes*. In the J2SE platform, the identity attributes of the code used by the caller may also be included in the caller's security attributes. Access to the called component is determined by comparing the caller's security attributes with those required to access the called component.

In the J2EE architecture, a container serves as an authorization boundary between callers and the components it hosts. The authorization boundary exists inside the container's authentication boundary, so that authorization is considered in the context of successful authentication. For inbound calls, the container compares security attributes from the caller's credential with the access control rules for the target component. If the rules are satisfied, the call is allowed. Otherwise, the call is rejected.

There are two fundamental approaches to defining access control rules: *capabilities* and *permissions*. The capabilities approach focuses on what a caller can do. The permissions approach focuses on who can do something. The J2EE application programming model focuses on permissions. In the J2EE architecture, the job of the Deployer is to map the permission model of the application to the capabilities of users in the operational environment.

9.3.1   Declarative Authorization

The container-enforced access control rules associated with a J2EE application are established by the Deployer. The Deployer uses a deployment tool to map an application permission model (typically) supplied by the Application Assembler to policy and mechanisms that are specific to the operational environment. The application permission model is contained in a deployment descriptor.

The deployment descriptor defines logical privileges called *security roles* and associates them with components to define the privileges required to be granted permission to access components. The Deployer assigns these logical privileges to specific callers to establish the capabilities of users in the runtime environment. Callers are assigned logical privileges based on the values of their security attributes. For example, a Deployer might map a security role to a security group in the operational environment such that any caller whose security attributes indicate that it is a member of the group would be assigned the privilege represented by the role. As another example, a Deployer might map a security role to a list containing one or more principal identities in the operational environment such that a caller authenticated as one of these identities would be assigned the privilege represented by the role.

The EJB container grants permission to access a method only to callers that have at least one of the privileges associated with the method. Security roles also protect Web resource collections, that is, a URL pattern and an associated HTTP method, such as GET. The Web container enforces authorization requirements similar to those for an EJB container. When a resource has no associated security role, permission to access the resource will be granted to all.

In both tiers, access control policy is defined at deployment time, rather than application development. The Deployer can modify the policy provided by the Application Assembler. The Deployer refines the privileges required to access the components, and defines the correspondence between the security attributes presented by callers and the container privileges. In any container, the mapping from security attributes to privileges is scoped to the application, so that the mapping applied to the components of one application may be different from that of another application.

9.3.2 Programmatic Authorization

A J2EE container makes access control decisions before dispatching method calls to a component. As a result, the logic or state of a component doesn't affect the access decisions. However, a component can use two methods, EJBContext.isCallerIn-Role (for use by enterprise bean code) and HttpServletRequest.isUserInRole (for use by Web components), to perform finer-grained access control. A component uses these methods to determine whether a caller has been granted a privilege selected by the component based on the parameters of the call, the internal state of the component, or other factors such as the time of the call.

The Application Component Provider of a component that calls one of these functions must declare the complete set of distinct `roleName` values used in all of its calls. These declarations appear in the deployment descriptor as `security-role-ref` elements. Each `security-role-ref` element links a privilege name embedded in the application as a `roleName` to a security role. It is ultimately the Deployer who establishes the link between the privilege names embedded in the application and the security roles defined in the deployment descriptor. The link between privilege names and security roles may differ for components in the same application.

9.3.3   Declarative Versus Programmatic Authorization

There is a trade-off between the external access control policy configured by the Deployer and the internal policy embedded in the application by the Component Provider. The former is more flexible after the application has been written. The latter provides more flexibility, in the form of functionality, while the application is being written. The former is transparent and completely comprehensible. The latter is buried in the application such that it may only be completely understood by the those who developed the application. These trade-offs should be considered in choosing the authorization model for particular components and methods.

9.3.4   Isolation

When designing the access control rules for protected resources, take care to ensure that the authorization policy is consistently enforced across all the paths by which the resource may be accessed. When method-level access control rules are applied to a component, care must be taken that a less protected method does not serve to undermine the policy enforced by a more rigorously protected method. Such considerations are most significant when component state is shared by disparately protected methods. The simplifying rule of thumb is to apply the same access control rules to all the methods of a component, and to partition an application as necessary to enforce this guideline unless there's some specific need to architect an application otherwise.

9.3.5   Identity Selection

When setting an application's access control policy, the Application Component Provider bases policy decisions on assumptions about the call identities selected by the application callers. When a call passes through intermediary components, the caller identity at the destination component may depend on the identity selection decisions made by the intermediaries. The destination component may assume that caller identities have been propagated along the call chain such that the identity of its caller will be that of the caller who initiated the chain. In other cases, the called component must assume that one or more of the callers in its call path will employ an identity selection policy other than identity propagation. The Application Assembler is responsible for communicating these assumptions to the Deployer, while the Deployer configures the caller identity selection for inter-component calls. Unless the Deployer has other instructions from the Application Assembler, they should assume that each caller will propagate the identity of the caller's identity.

9.3.6   Encapsulation for Access Control

The component model of an application may be used to impose authorization boundaries around what might otherwise be unprotected resources. This can be done by using accessor components to implement the authorization barrier. If accessor components are used to create an authorization boundary, access control can either be done externally by the container, or internally by the component, or both.

An accessor component may encapsulate the mapping to an authentication context suitable for interacting with an external resource. Considered in the context of principal mapping for the purpose of authenticating and gaining access to enterprise information system resources, encapsulation for access control can be used to control who is authorized to access a mapping. Depending on the form of the mapping, the authorization rules may be more or less complex. For example, if all access to a resource is performed via a single conceptually omnipotent enterprise information system tier identity, then the J2EE application can implement secure access to the resource by limiting who can access the accessor. If the mapping of authentication context is many-to-many, then the authorization configuration of the accessor may need to define which of a collection of mappings are accessible to the caller, and which should be assumed by default (if the caller does not assert which mapping it requires).

9.3.7   Controlling Access to J2EE Resources

In a typical J2EE application, a client would go through its container to interact with enterprise resources in the Web or EJB tiers. Resources available to the user may be protected or unprotected. Protected resources are distinguished by the presence of authorization rules defined in deployment descriptors that restrict access to some subset of non-anonymous identities. To access a protected resource, a user must present a non-anonymous credential such that its identity can be evaluated against the resource authorization policy. In other words, caller authentication is required any time a caller tries to access a protected component.

9.3.7.1 Controlling Access to Web Resources

To control access to a Web resource, an Application Component Provider or Application Assembler specifies a `security-constraint` element with an `auth-constraint` subelement in the Web deployment descriptor. Code Example 9.5 illustrates the definition of a protected resource in a Web component deployment descriptor. The descriptor specifies that the URL `/control/placeorder` can only be accessed by users acting in the role of `customer`.

```
<security-constraint>
    <web-resource-collection>
        <web-resource-name>placeorder</web-resource-name>
        <url-pattern>/control/placeorder</url-pattern>
        <http-method>POST</http-method>
        <http-method>GET</http-method>
    </web-resource-collection>
    <auth-constraint>
        <role-name>customer</role-name>
    </auth-constraint>
</security-constraint>
```

Code Example 9.5   Web Resource Authorization Configuration

9.3.7.2 Controlling Access to Enterprise Beans

An Application Component Provider or Application Assembler that has defined security roles for an enterprise bean can also specify the methods of the remote and home interface that each security role is allowed to invoke. This is done in the form of `method-permission` elements. Ultimately, it is the assignment of users to roles that determines if a resource is protected. When the roles required to access the enterprise bean are assigned only to authenticated users, the bean is protected.

Code Example 9.6 contains two styles of method specifications. The first refers to all of the remote and home interface methods of an enterprise bean. The second is used for referring to a specific method of the remote or home interface of an enterprise bean. If there are multiple methods with the same overloaded name, this style refers to all of the overloaded methods. Method specifications can be further qualified with parameter names for methods with an overloaded name.

```
<method-permission>
    <role-name>admin</role-name>
        <method>
            <ejb-name>TheOrder</ejb-name>
            <method-name>*</method-name>
        </method>
</method-permission>

<method-permission>
    <role-name>customer</role-name>
    <method>
        <ejb-name>TheOrder</ejb-name>
        <method-name>getDetails</method-name>
    </method>
    <method>
    ...
</method-permission>
```

Code Example 9.6   Enterprise Bean Authorization Configuration

9.3.7.3 Unprotected Resources

Many applications feature unprotected Web-tier content, available to any caller without authentication. Some applications also feature unprotected enterprise beans. For example, the sample application (see Section 10.11 on page 301) allows anonymous, unauthenticated users to access certain EJB resources. In either tier, unprotected resources are characterized by the absence of a requirement that their caller be authenticated. In the Web tier, unrestricted access is provided simply by leaving out an authentication rule. In the EJB tier, unrestricted access is accomplished by mapping at least one role which is permitted access to the resource to the universal set of users independent of authentication.

9.3.8   Example

To understand how each application, and each component within an application can apply its own authorization requirements, consider the following examples.

One application is assembled from two enterprise beans, EJB 1 and EJB 2, each with one method. Each method calls `isCallerInRole` with the role name `MANAGER`. The deployment descriptor includes a `security-role-ref` element for the call to `isCallerInRole` in each enterprise bean. The `security-role-ref` for EJB 1 links `MANAGER` to the role `good-managers` and the `security-role-ref` element for EJB 2 links `MANAGER` to the role `bad-managers`. The deployment descriptor defines two method-permission elements, one establishes that the role `employees` can access all methods of EJB 1 and the other does the same for EJB 2. The deployment descriptor has 3 `security-role` elements: `employees`, `good-managers`, and `bad-managers`. The Deployer assigns User 1 to roles `employees` and `good-managers` and assigns User 2 to roles `employees` and `bad-managers`.

A second application, with one enterprise bean EJB 3, is also deployed in the container. EJB 3 also makes a call to `isCallerInRole` with the role name `MANAGER`. The deployment descriptor for this second application contains a `security-role-ref` element that links `MANAGER` to the role `good-managers`. Similarly, the deployment descriptor defines one `method-permission` element that establishes that the role `employees` can access all the methods of EJB 3. The deployment descriptor has 2 role elements, `employees` and `good-managers`. The Deployer assigns User 2 to roles `employees` and `good-managers`.

Figure 9.4 illustrates the configuration of method permissions as a relationship between roles and methods. It also illustrates the mapping of caller security attributes to roles, and the link between privilege names embedded in the application and roles.

Table 9.1 lists the authorization decisions that occur when different users initiate method calls on these enterprise beans. For example, when User 1 initiates a method call on EJB 2's method, the container dispatches the call because the `method-permission` element specifies the security roles `employees` and `good-managers`, and the Deployer has assigned User 1 to the former security role.However, the `isCallerInRole(MANAGER)` method returns false, because the `security-role-ref` element for EJB 2 links `MANAGER` to the security role `bad-managers`, which is not satisfied for User 1. When User 1 invokes a method on EJB 3, the call isn't even dispatched, because User 1 isn't assigned to any security roles.

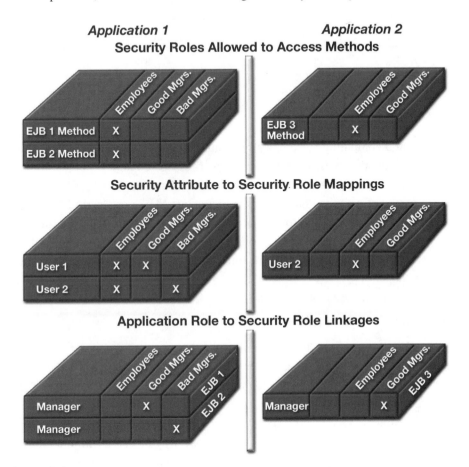

Figure 9.4 Authorization Scenario

Table 9.1 Authorization Decisions

Call	Call Dispatched?	isCallerInRole?
User 1 - EJB 1	yes	true
User 1 - EJB 2	yes	false
User 1 - EJB 3	no	never called
User 2 - EJB 1	yes	false

Table 9.1   Authorization Decisions (continued)

Call	Call Dispatched?	isCallerInRole?
User 2 - EJB 2	yes	true
User 2 - EJB 3	yes	true

9.4   Protecting Messages

In a distributed computing system, a significant amount of information is transmitted through networks in the form of messages. Message content is subject to three main types of attacks. Messages might be intercepted and modified for the purpose of changing the affects they have on their recipients. Messages might be captured and reused one or more times for the benefit of another party. Messages might be monitored by an eavesdropper in an effort to capture information that would not otherwise be available. Such attacks can be minimized by using integrity and confidentiality mechanisms.

9.4.1   Integrity Mechanisms

Integrity mechanisms ensure that communication between entities is not being tampered with by another party, especially one that can intercept and modify their communications. Integrity mechanisms can also be used to ensure that messages can only be used once.

Message integrity is ensured by attaching a *message signature* to a message. The message signature is calculated by using a one-way hash algorithm to convert the message contents into a typically smaller, fixed length *message digest* that is then *signed* (that is, cryptographically enciphered, typically using a public key mechanism). A message signature ensures that modification of the message by anyone other than the caller will be detectable by the receiver. Although there are always things a sender can do (including publishing its private authentication keys), to compromise a receiver's ability to hold it accountable for a received message, both parties to the communication would be wise to select an integrity mechanism that appends a message confounder (typically a sequence number and a timestamp) to the message before the digest. The purpose of the confounder is to make the message authenticator useful only once. This prevents a malicious recipient from claiming that it received a message more times than it did or from reusing an intercepted message for its own purpose. In exchange for these receiver-side limitations, a measure of accountability is transferred to the sender.

In the J2EE architecture, a container serves as an authentication boundary between callers and the components it hosts. Information may flow in both directions on a call (that is, a call may have input, output, or input and output parameters). The Deployer is responsible for configuring containers to safeguard interactions between components. A Deployer must configure the containers involved in a call to implement integrity mechanisms either because the call will traverse open or unprotected networks, or because the call will be made between components that do not trust each other. The latter is necessary to ensure that messages can only be used once, and to reduce the plausibility of arguments made by either of the communicants that they did not send the messages claimed to have been received. When integrity mechanisms are configured by the Deployer, the calling container must compute and attach a message signature to the call request, and verify the correspondence between the call response and the message signature attached to the call response. The called container must verify the correspondence between the call request and the attached message signature, and compute and attach a message signature to the call response. If either of the verifications fails, the call should be abandoned, and the caller notified (for example, by exception) of the failure.

The performance cost associated with applying integrity protection to all message communication is as much a property of the operational environment as it is a consequence of the cost of the protection. One way to safeguard the integrity of application messages without unnecessarily limiting the space of operational environments, is to capture application-specific knowledge identifying which messages must be integrity protected. The place to capture this information is in the application's deployment descriptor.

9.4.2   Confidentiality Mechanisms

Confidentiality mechanisms ensure that communication between entities is kept private. Privacy is achieved by encrypting the message contents. Because symmetric (that is, shared secret) encryption mechanisms are generally much less expensive (in terms of compute resources) than are asymmetric (that is, public key) mechanisms, it is quite common for an asymmetric mechanism to be used to secure the exchange of a symmetric encryption key, which is then used to encrypt the message contents.

The Deployer is responsible for configuring containers to apply confidentiality mechanisms to ensure that sensitive information is not disclosed to third parties. Despite the improved performance of the shared secret mechanisms, the costs of message encryption are significant, and should be expected to have an adverse effect on performance when confidentiality mechanisms are applied where they are not needed. The Application Assembler should supply the Deployer with information on which method calls of which components feature parameters or return values that should be protected for confidentiality. The Deployer then must configure the containers involved in a call to employ a confidentiality mechanism whenever one of the method calls identified by the Application Assembler will traverse open or unprotected networks. In addition to applying confidentiality mechanisms where appropriate, the Deployer should configure containers to reject call requests or responses with message content that should be protected but isn't protected. Message integrity is typically verified as a side effect of confidentiality.

9.4.3   Identifying Sensitive Components

We recommend that the Application Assembler identify the components whose method calls feature parameters or return values that should be protected for integrity and/or confidentiality. The deployment descriptor is used to convey this information. For enterprise beans, this would be done in a `description` subelement (most likely of a `method-permission` element). For servlets and JSP pages, this would be done in the `transport-guarantee` subelement of the `user-data-constraint` subelement of a `security-constraint`. In cases where a component's interactions with an external resource are known to carry sensitive information, these sensitivities should be described in the `description` subelement of the corresponding `resource-ref`.

9.4.4   Ensuring Confidentiality of Web Resources

In addition to understanding how to configure Web transport guarantees, it is important to understand the properties of HTTP methods, and the effects these properties have when a link is followed from one Web resource to another. When a resource contains links to other resources, the nature of the links determines how the protection context of the current resource affects the protection of requests made to the linked resources.

When a link is *absolute* (that is, the URL begins with `https://` or `http://`), the HTTP client container will ignore the context of the current resource and access the linked resource based on the nature of the absolute URL. If the URL of the link begins with `https://`, a protected transport will be established with the server before the request is sent. If the URL of the link begins with `http://`, the request will be attempted over an insecure transport. When the link is *relative*, the HTTP client container will protect an access to a linked resource based on whether the resource in which the link occurs was protected.

The application developer should consider these link properties most carefully when a linked request must carry confidential data back to the server. There are a few choices available to ensure security in such cases. For example, an application developer might choose to use secure absolute links to ensure the transport protection of requests that carry confidential data. This would solve the security problem, at the expense of constraining the application to a very specific naming environment.

Another option, assuming that an application opts for portability and uses relative links, is for the Deployer to configure the application so that wherever there is a confidential interaction from one resource to another, both are deployed with a confidential transport guarantee. This approach will ensure that an HTTP client container will not send a request to a protected resource without protecting it.

As a related point, the `POST` method is favored over the `GET` method for delivering confidential request data, since data sent via `GET` appears in both client- and server-side logs.

9.5   Auditing

Auditing is the practice of capturing a record of security-related events for the purpose of being able to hold users or systems accountable for their actions. A common misunderstanding of the value of auditing is evident when auditing is used solely to determine whether security mechanisms are serving to limit access to a system. When security is breached, it is usually much more important to know who has been allowed access than who has not. Only by knowing who has interacted with the system do we have a chance of determining who should be held accountable for a breach of security. Moreover, auditing can only be used to evaluate the effective security of a system when there is a clear understanding of what is audited and what is not.

The Deployer is responsible for configuring the security mechanisms that will be applied by the enterprise containers. Each of the configured mechanisms may be thought of as a constraint that the containers will attempt to enforce on interactions between components. It should be possible for the Deployer or System Administrator to review the security constraints established for the platform, and to associate an audit behavior with each constraint so that the container will audit one of the following:

- All evaluations where the constraint was satisfied

- All evaluations where it was not satisfied

- All evaluations independent of outcome

- No evaluations

It would also be prudent to audit all changes (resulting from deployment or subsequent administration) to the audit configuration or the constraints being enforced by the platform. Audit records must be protected so that attackers cannot escape accountability for their actions by expunging incriminating records or changing their content.

The J2EE programming model aims to shift the burden of auditing away from developers and integrators to those who are responsible for application deployment and management. Therefore, although not currently mandated by the J2EE specification, we recommend that J2EE containers provide auditing functionality that facilitates the evaluation of container-enforced security policy.

9.6   Summary

A primary goal of the J2EE platform is to relieve the application developer from the details of security mechanisms and facilitate the secure deployment of an application in diverse environments. The J2EE platform addresses this goal by defining a clear separation of responsibility between those who develop application components, those who assemble components into applications, and those who configure applications for use in a specific environment. By allowing the Component Provider and Application Assembler to specify which parts of an application require security, then letting the Deployer select the specific security mechanisms used for that protection at deployment time, deployment descriptors provide a means outside of code for the developer to communicate these needs to the Deployer. They also enable container-specific tools to give the Deployer easier ways to engage the security constraints recommended by the developer.

An Application Component Provider identifies all of the security dependencies embedded in a component including:

- The names of all the role names used by the component in calls to `IsCaller-InRole` or `isUserInRole`

- References to all of the external resources accessed by the component

- References to all the inter-component calls made by the component

An Application Component Provider may also provide a method permission model, along with information that identifies the sensitivity with respect to privacy of the information exchanged in particular calls.

An Application Assembler combines one or more components into an application package and then rationalizes the external view of security provided by the individual components to produce a consistent security view for the application as a whole. The objective of the Application Assembler is to provide this information so that it can inform the actions of a Deployer.

A Deployer is responsible for taking the security view of the application provided by the Application Assembler and using it to secure the application in a specific operational environment. The Deployer uses a platform-specific deployment tool to map the view provided by the assembler to the policies and mechanisms that are specific to the operational environment. The security mechanisms configured by the Deployer are implemented by containers on behalf of the components hosted in the containers.

J2EE security mechanisms combine the concepts of container hosting, plus the declarative specification of application security requirements, with the availability of application-embedded mechanisms. This provides a powerful model for secure, interoperable, distributed component computing.

About the Author

STEPHANIE BODOFF is a staff writer at Sun Microsystems. She has been involved with object-oriented enterprise software since graduating from Columbia University with an M.S. in electrical engineering. For several years she worked as a software engineer on distributed computing and telecommunications systems and object-oriented software development methods. During that period she co-authored *Object-Oriented Software Development: The Fusion Method*, Prentice Hall. For the past 4 years Stephanie has concentrated on technical writing, documenting object-oriented databases, application servers, and enterprise application development methods.

ABHISHEK CHAUHAN has been working on the design of scalable network services and distributed programs. At Sun Microsystems, Abhishek was involved in the evolution of the J2EE programming model from its inception. He pioneered work on Web access optimization techniques and implementation of the Java Web Server. He worked on the JavaServer Pages specification and Sun's JavaServer Pages implementations.

Abhishek was one of the founders and a lead architect at Vxtreme, where he worked on the design of its streaming server. Vxtreme was acquired by Microsoft in 1997. In a former life, Abhishek worked at Microsoft on the Office Visual Basic scripting engine. He has an M.S. from the University of Wisconsin at Madison and a Bachelor's degree from the Indian Institute of Technology at Delhi.

CHAPTER 10

The Sample Application

*by Stephanie Bodoff
and Abhishek Chauhan*

To conclude this discussion of the J2EE programming model, this chapter provides an in-depth description of a multitier Web application, an e-commerce Web site. We review the entire process of developing this application from specification to design to implementation, illustrating many of the principles discussed in the earlier chapters.

The first section describes some scenarios in which the sample application is used. Although the sample application supports administration and business-to-business interactions as well as shopping interactions, this chapter focuses mainly on shopping interactions.

The discussion then turns to the architecture of the sample application: the partitioning of functionality into modules, the assignment of functionality to tiers, and object decomposition within tiers. The architecture of the sample application conforms to the Model-View-Controller architecture. We describe the motivation for using this architecture and how each of these concepts is realized in the implementation of the sample application.

Finally, this chapter describes how the sample application uses the deployment, transaction, and security capabilities of the J2EE platform to simplify component development and provide richer functionality.

10.1   Application Functionality

The sample application models a typical e-commerce application, an online pet store. E-commerce sites like this are among the most common Web applications.

The application interface is presented to its customers through a Web site and a customer interacts with the application using a Web browser. Other potential users of the application include administrators responsible for maintaining inventory and performing other managerial tasks, and associated businesses such as suppliers. Each class of users would have access to specific categories of functionality, and each would interact with it through a specific user interface mechanism.

Like a typical e-commerce site, the pet store presents the customer with a catalog of products. The customer selects items of interest and places them in a shopping cart. When the customer has selected the desired items and indicates readiness to buy what is in the shopping cart, the sample application displays a bill of sale: a list of all selected items, a quantity for each item, the price of each item, and the total cost. The customer can revise or cancel the order. When the customer is ready to accept the order, the customer provides a credit card number to cover the costs and supplies a shipping address.

10.1.1   Scenarios

The following scenarios demonstrate a few key ways the pet store application could be used by describing a user's view of interactions with the system. By walking through these scenarios, you'll gain a better understanding of the requirements as well as the interactions that happen *within* the system.

The sample application could support three very different kind of scenarios. First, there is the shopping interface described earlier, that allows shoppers to buy items online. Second, there is an administration interface for carrying out store administration activities. Finally, there is a business-to-business interface through which the store can interact with suppliers. The scenarios in this section demonstrate all three types of interaction, while the remainder of this chapter focuses mainly on the shopping interactions.

10.1.1.1   Shopping Scenario

The primary function of the sample application is to provide an interface where customers can browse through and purchase items. This shopping interaction typically starts with the customer's visit to the application home page and ends when the customer orders from the site:

1. A customer connects to the application, by pointing the browser to the URL for the application's home page. This allows the customer to browse through the catalog or search for products through some search interface.

2. At any point during the whole interaction, the customer can sign into the application by providing an account identifier and a password. When the customer signs in, the application can recall information about the customer such as a preferred shipping address and billing information, buying preferences, and so on. Customers who don't have an account can create one at any time by providing an account identifier, customer name, password and some other personal details.

3. The customer browses through the catalog. The customer can select a category to see a list of all the products in that category. For example, the customer can select the category `Cats` to view all cats that the pet store sells. Alternatively, the customer can search for products using one or more keywords describing the product. For example searching with keywords `Persian` and `mammal` might bring a list of Persian dogs and cats.

4. The customer selects a particular product in the list. Now, the application displays detailed information about the selected product. The description and image of the product is shown along with pricing information. When there are several variants of the same product, each variant is shown as a separate item. For example, when showing details about an African parakeet, the items could be large male African parakeet, small female African parakeet, and so on.

5. The customer decides to purchase a particular item and clicks a button to add the item to the shopping cart. The customer may continue shopping, adding more items to the shopping cart. As the customer browses through the catalog, the application remembers all the items placed in the cart. The customer can recall the shopping cart at any time during the interaction to review or revise the contents of the cart.

6. The customer can choose to order the items in the shopping cart at any time. This is called checking out. A checkout button is presented along with the shopping cart. If the customer is not signed in, the application brings up a signin/signup screen. Here the customer can sign in, or set up a new account, if they don't have one. After the customer is signed in, order processing continues as before.

7. When the customer asks to check out, the application presents a summary of

all items that would be ordered along with their costs. At this point the customer must confirm the order.

8. When the customer confirms the order, the application begins to gather shipping and billing information for the order. First it presents a form, where the customer can enter shipping information. If the customer is signed into the application at this time, the form comes up filled in with the customer's preferred shipping address.

9. When the customer enters the shipping address, the customer is asked to enter billing information, including credit card details and a billing address. If the customer is signed in, the application recalls these details and the forms are returned filled in.

10. Finally the customer confirms the order and the application accepts the order for delivery. A receipt including a unique order number and other order details is presented to the customer. The application validates credit card and other information, updates its inventory database, and optionally sends a confirmation message via email.

This is a fairly typical shopping scenario. Some variations are possible, especially in the way the catalog is presented to the customer. For instance, the application could provide specialized lists of items such as best-sellers, or discounts on certain items. There may also be variations in order processing, such as reducing the steps for making an order when the customer is already signed in. The application developer needs to design the application to support these variations, as well as others that might arise as the application evolves.

Although this scenario presents the application from a single customer's point of view, the pet store application needs to simultaneously support a large number of shoppers.

10.1.1.2 Administration Scenario

The pet store application does most of the administrative work of managing orders, creating new accounts, and other details without manual intervention. However, there are some tasks where manual intervention is desirable or required. These are often administration tasks, such as managing the inventory, reestablishing forgotten customer passwords, rolling back orders, handling returned merchandise, and processing and shipping of orders.

The administration interface of the pet store application could use a Visual Basic client running in a Microsoft desktop application such as Microsoft Excel.

The application must be designed to support more than one administrator simultaneously using the administration interface.

The administration scenario models inventory management, where an administrator updates inventory when new shipments come in:

1. The administrator starts up the shopping client application. When the client starts, it asks the administrator to sign on to the system using a user name and password. The administrator enters information for one of the accounts that has administration privileges.

2. The client application then presents a list of products in the catalog, perhaps in order by category, with the product details such as description and name also shown.

3. The administrator clicks a product to see the items as well as their inventory status. For any item displayed, the administrator can modify the inventory status.

4. The administrator clicks an update button, causing the changes to inventory status to be committed to the inventory database.

10.1.1.3   Business-to-Business Scenario

Businesses often have a need to interact with other businesses through their custom applications. For example, a retailer needs to work with suppliers to procure inventory, with shipping agencies for managing shipments, and with billing agencies for handling its billing needs. In fact, significant pieces of the application such as inventory control could themselves be off-loaded to a separate business.

It would be desirable to have some of these interactions be automated. When businesses are tightly coordinated, perhaps under the same ownership or administration, these interactions could be *closely-coupled*. In such interactions, businesses expose their entities and data to each other. However, most of the time it is desirable to keep the businesses *loosely-coupled*. Here businesses interact by passing asynchronous messages to each other. This messaging approach also models the real world more closely, where businesses work together by sending faxes and packages, and so on, to each other.

An interaction between the pet store and one of its suppliers would illustrate a loosely-coupled business interaction. A typical scenario might be:

1. A customer places an order. This causes the inventory to fall below a pre-established low water mark, triggering the application to initiate an order to obtain more items from the supplier. This process happens asynchronously and does not interfere with the transaction being performed by the customer.

2. The application sends a purchase request message to the supplier. A typical purchase request message could say, "Send 100 male African parakeets."

3. At some later time, the supplier sends a message in response to the request. If the supplier does not have enough parakeets to fill the order, the message might say, "Can't fulfill request. Have 20 parakeets available."

4. The application, upon receipt of the message, might send another request for a smaller quantity. The message might say, "Send 20 male African parakeets."

5. The supplier initiates delivery of the shipment, and sends a message back to the application. This message might say, "Request completed. 20 parakeets shipped. Shipment number is 1234."

The interaction between the store and supplier is depicted in a timing diagram in Figure 10.1.

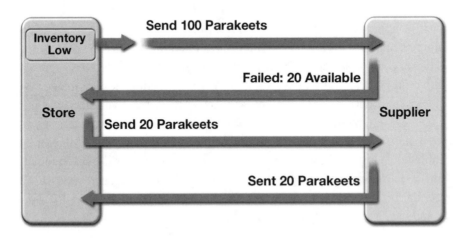

Figure 10.1   A Store-Supplier Business-to-Business Interaction

One thing to observe about this scenario that it is asynchronous. The action is initiated when a customer places an order. However, it proceeds without blocking the customer's interaction. Also note that neither the store nor the supplier is blocked waiting for the other to respond. While the procurement is in progress, the store's application and the supplier's system carry on with their activities as usual.

10.1.2   Functional Specification

With a clear understanding of the kind of scenarios in which the application would be used, let's create an initial specification of the user interface of the application. This section presents a sketch of the main user interface of an application that supports the shopping interactions. It is possible to create a similar sketch for a user interface for administration interactions. Business interactions typically do not require a user interface. As mentioned earlier, the remainder of this chapter focuses on the shopping functionality of the application.

Upon arriving at the main page of the online pet store, a customer would expect some of the following features:

- A set of links or navigation bars on each page that provide quick access to common navigational tasks.

- An organized view of the site's contents through a categorized catalog.

- A search mechanism to provide a way to locate items based on keyword descriptions. Other types of quick access could be in terms of popular items or new additions.

- A *master view* of the catalog that lists items of interest. This could be the result of the customer navigating through a catalog category or the outcome of a keyword search.

- A *detail view* that describes the details of a particular item. Shoppers click on an item in the master view to zoom in on details, including a description, a picture, the price, a link to the supplier's URL, and so on.

- A shopping cart view that lets customers review the contents of their shopping cart. The cart allows the customer to modify quantities of items in the cart, including removing items from the cart altogether.

- A checkout or bill-of-sales view that displays the total order cost and allows the customer to enter billing and shipping information. The customer will want assurance that order details including shipping and credit card information are transferred securely and accountably. The interaction must be authenticated to positively identify the customer for the purposes of accountability and encrypted through HTTPS to protect the privacy of the information the customer provides.

- A receipt view to provide confirmation of the purchase through a unique order identifier or other mechanism to track the newly placed order and review details of the order.

In addition to these user interface requirements, the application must also support some security requirements. We address these in Section 10.11 on page 301.

10.2   Application Architecture

This section describes the architecture of the pet store application; exploring the partitioning of functionality into modules, the assignment of functionality to tiers, and object decomposition within the tiers.

10.2.1   Application Modules

This discussion reviews the shopping interaction scenario once again, this time identifying actions within the application as it runs on the server. This replay is used to explore ways to divide the application into modules based on similar or related functionality. Dividing the problem in this manner reduces the dependency between modules, allowing them to be developed somewhat independently. Identifying the interface between modules enables some of the modules to be provided by third-party component providers, or subcontracted to specialists in a particular area of functionality.

Here's the scenario once again, with the various behaviors organized by modules:

1. A user connects to the application. If the user logs in, the *user account module* maintains user account information. It creates new user accounts and manages these accounts. Accounts include such information as user name, password, and account ID.

2. The *product catalog module* returns a list of products. The product catalog

module searches the product database for a list of possible matches to the search criteria and renders the products for the user.

3. The user views a specific product. The product catalog module also returns detailed information about the selected product, including pricing information. It optionally can check the *inventory module* for availability information, such as quantity in stock.

4. The user selects an item for purchase. The *shopping client module* creates a shopping cart for the user for the duration of the user's session.

5. The user chooses the checkout option and commits to buying the item. The *order processing module* manages this interaction.

6. The application determines whether the user is logged in and if not, calls the user account module to set up a new user account. Otherwise it instructs the user account module to extract account information such as credit card and shipping information.

7. The application then authenticates the user and validates the credit card and shipping information.

8. The application lets the user revise or cancel the order. If the user accepts the order, the order processing logic logs the order, notifies the *inventory module* to update the inventory database, and sends a confirmation message by email.

This time, the run-through of the scenario has identified the following modules and their responsibilities:

- User account module: The application tracks user account information. This includes a user identifier and password and various types (billing and email addresses, phone number, and so on) of contact information. The application saves user account information to a database so that it spans sessions.

- Product catalog module: The application allows the user to search for products or services and be able to display details of individual products. The product catalog includes descriptions of individual items.

- Order processing module: The application performs order processing. Order processing occurs when the user performs the check-out process and buys the items in the shopping cart.

- Messaging module: The application sends confirmation messages.

- Inventory module: The application maintains information on the number of each type of product in stock.

- Control module: The application allows users to browse the product catalog and add selected items to a shopping cart. At any time, the user can modify items in the shopping cart, add new items, or remove items already placed in the cart.

Figure 10.2 shows the interrelationship of the modules in the sample application.

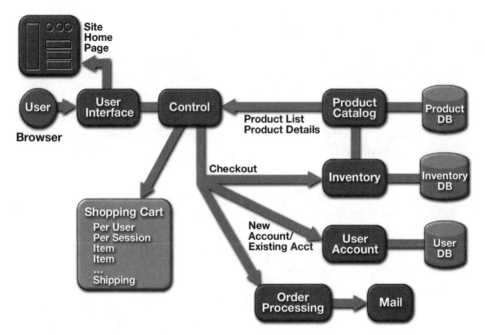

Figure 10.2   Functional Modules for the Sample Application

This modular decomposition of the pet store application is reflected in the subpackages of the sample application's top-level package `com.sun.estore`:

- `account`: user account
- `cart`: shopping cart
- `catalog`: product catalog
- `control`: controls

- `inventory`: product inventory

- `mail`: email messaging

- `order`: order processing

- `util`: utility classes

10.2.2   Application Design

Partitioning the application into logical modules is the first step in subdividing the overall problem. The next step is to begin the process of object-oriented design of the application, identifying units of business logic, data, and presentation logic and modeling each of them as a software object.

The process starts by identifying the options and approaches available at the highest level. Once these choices are clear and the decisions and design principles are established, the rest of the design will be simplified by leveraging these overall principles.

One of the first decisions to make concerns the tiers that the application uses. The J2EE platform is designed for multitier applications, and offers a lot of flexibility in choosing how to distribute application functionality across the tiers. In a Web-enabled application, such as the sample application, some tiers are always present: the client tier provided by the browser, the Web tier provided by the server and the enterprise information system or database tier which holds persistent application data. The first choice to make is whether the Web tier accesses the enterprise information system resources directly, or goes through an EJB tier. The decision depends on the functionality, complexity, and scalability requirements of the application. Since such requirements can change as the application evolves, one goal for the design is to make it amenable to migration to an EJB-centric approach.

After deciding what tiers constitute the application, the next decision is how to distribute application functionality across these tiers. This division is closely linked to how the application is divided into objects at the highest level and represents one of the most important decisions when designing enterprise applications. Some clear and simple guidelines to help with making this decision are addressed in the following discussions.

10.2.2.1 Application Tiers

In a Web-centric design, the Web tier communicates directly with the enterprise information system resources that hold application data. In this approach, the Web tier is responsible for almost all of the application functionality. It must take care of dynamic content generation and presentation and handling of user requests. It must implement core application functionality such as order processing and enforce business rules defined by the application. Finally, the components running in the Web tier must also manage transactions and connection pooling for data access. Because it must handle so many functions, Web-centric application software has a tendency to become monolithic. As a result, unless special efforts are taken, it does not scale well with increasing software complexity.

In an EJB-centric design, enterprise beans running on EJB servers encapsulate the enterprise information system resources and the core application logic. The Web tier communicates with the EJB tier instead of directly accessing the enterprise information system resources. This approach moves most of the core application functionality to the EJB tier, using the Web tier only as a front end for receiving client Web requests and for presenting HTML responses to the client.

The principal advantage of this approach is that enterprise beans have access to a broad set of enterprise-level services. Because of these services, managing transaction and security aspects of the application is easier. The EJB container provides a highly structured environment for the components that allows a developer to focus entirely on the application domain issues, while the EJB container takes care of system-level details. These standardized container-provided services also translate into better software reliability. The EJB architecture supports a programming discipline that promotes encapsulation and componentization, resulting in software that stays manageable as applications grow more complex.

The Web-centric approach is better for getting the application off to a quick start, while EJB-centric approach becomes more desirable when building a large scale application where code and performance scalability are prime factors. While the Web-centric approach may be more prevalent, with many applications implemented using it, it has limitations when building large scale, complex applications.

The ideal solution is an approach that benefits from the strengths of both approaches. The sample application demonstrates an approach that started out simple and small, but kept the option of growth open. Its extensible design started as Web-centric and migrated to an EJB-centric architecture. While most of its modules are implemented with an EJB-centric design, the catalog module uses the

Web-centric model. Strategies for migrating components from Web-centric to EJB-centric designs are described in detail in Section 4.7.1 on page 108.

Note that the discussion that follows describes a sample application design that evolves from Web-centric to EJB-centric. The actual code of the sample application reflects the final result of that migration. We have preserved the state of the catalog module before migration to provide an indication of how the migration was performed.

10.2.2.2 Application Objects

The next issue to address in developing the overall application architecture is how to subdivide the application into objects and how to the assign these objects to tiers. This process is referred to as object decomposition. While most of the objects are consigned to one tier or another, there are some that serve to connect the tiers and will need to span tiers, and their design needs to take this into account.

This discussion focuses primarily on large scale, complex applications. Smaller applications can probably get away with less rigorous treatment, but object design really becomes important as applications grow more complex. Large scale development of object-oriented software requires frameworks. It is important to have a framework, so that every time the design requires two objects to interact, a developer does not have to come up with a whole new notion of how the interaction works out.

This section looks at the issues to keep in mind when doing the object decomposition, and present techniques that we used in the sample application to determine an effective decomposition.

Design Goals

Consider the kind of goals that need to be addressed in object decomposition. Each of these considerations identifies criteria to use to divide the application. The framework must enable:

- Reuse of software designs and code

- Identification of the responsibility of each object. The division into objects must ensure that the responsibilities of each object—what the object represents and what it must accomplish—are easily and unambiguously identified.

While these requirements apply to object-oriented design in general, they become even more important for multitier enterprise applications. Our additional objectives were:

- Separate stable code from more volatile code. All parts of an enterprise application are not equally stable. The parts that deal with presentation and user interface change more often. The business rules and database schemas employed in the application have a much lower propensity to change. The overall architecture should separate stable portions of the application from parts that are more volatile.

- Divide development effort along skill lines. The people that comprise an enterprise development team typically represent a very diverse set of skills. There are HTML layout and graphics designers, programmers, application domain experts, and enterprise information system resource access specialists, among others. The decomposition should result in a set of objects that can be assigned to various subteams based on their particular skills. This division of labor allows work on each object to proceed in parallel.

- Ease migration from Web-centric to EJB-centric design. As mentioned earlier, the sample application starts out as a Web-centric application and migrates to being EJB-centric.

We have described these considerations from the point of view of a high-level division. However they are equally applicable even when we are working on identifying objects at a finer level. We will keep coming back to these considerations as we need to make choices about object decomposition.

MVC Architecture

When applying the considerations discussed above to the sample application, the first lines of division start becoming clear. At the highest level, the application divides into three logical categories of objects. These are objects that deal with *presentation* aspects of the application, objects that deal with the *business* rules and data, and objects that accept and interpret user requests and *control* the business objects to fulfill these request.

The look and feel of the application interface changes often, its behavior changes less frequently, and business data and rules are relatively stable. Thus objects responsible for control are often more stable than presentation objects while business rules and data are generally the most stable of all.

The implementation of presentation objects is typically handled by graphics designers, HTML and JSP technology experts, and application administrators after the application has been deployed. Control-related objects are implemented by application developers. Business rules and data objects are implemented by developers, domain experts, and database experts.

The presentation logic of a user interface can be handled by the Web tier or the client. In the Web tier, JSP pages are used to dynamically generate HTML for consumption by a browser. A stand-alone client, such as the one described in the administration scenario in Section 10.1.1.2 on page 244, provides its own presentation. Control-related objects are present in each tier to enable coordination of actions across tiers. Objects that model business data and rules live in the EJB tier in an EJB-centric approach, and in the Web tier when using a Web-centric approach.

As discussed in several chapters in this book, the MVC architecture can be easily applied to enterprise applications. The presentation, business, and control categories map respectively, to the view, model, and controller concepts defined in the MVC architecture. The following sections take a detailed look at the design, implementation, and interactions of the sample application objects that constitute the view, model, and controller.

10.3 The View

The view determines the presentation of the user interface of an application. In the sample application, the implementation of the view is contained completely in the Web tier. In the sample application, three kinds of components work together to implement the view: JSP pages, JSP custom tags, and JavaBeans components.

JSP pages are used for dynamic generation of HTML responses. Custom tags make it easier for JSP pages to use JavaBeans components when the underlying model is complex. Custom tags can also help encapsulate presentation logic and make it modular and more reusable.

JavaBeans components represent the contract between JSP pages and the model. JSP pages rely on these beans to read model data to be rendered to HTML, while elsewhere in the system, the model and controller coordinate to keep the JavaBeans components up to date.

This section describes the JSP pages and custom tags that implement the view. Because the classes that implement JavaBeans components are intimately tied to their corresponding model classes, the discussion of the implementation of Java-Beans components and model classes is deferred until after the discussion of the model.

10.3.1   Shopping Interaction Interface

The shopping scenario described in Section 10.1.1.1 on page 242 and the server-side scenario in Section 10.2.1 on page 248 provide a behavioral specification for the shopping interaction interface. This section translates this specification into the set of views that the customer sees when interacting with the pet store application.

10.3.1.1   Screens

The user interface for the shopping interaction consists of a set of screens. A *screen* is the total content delivered to the browser when the user requests an application URL. In other words, a screen is what customers see when they navigate to one of our application's URLs. A screen can be composed of several components each contributing a different part of its content.

The specification includes some notion of the kind of screens the application displays to the customer and the dialogs it carries on with them. Taking this process further, results in the specification of a complete set of screens, each with a unique name.The significance of the names will become clear later when the discussion turns to how the controller selects a view for each response. The following list identifies what model information it *presents* and what *user gestures* it can generate.

- Name: MAIN_SCREEN, DEFAULT_SCREEN

    This is the home page of the application. It displays a list of all product categories in the catalog, such as Dogs. The customer can click on any category to browse through a master view of products that belong in that category.

- Name: CATEGORY_SCREEN

    This screen displays a master view of all products that belong to a particular category. For each product it shows the product ID and its name. The customer can click on the name of any product on display to see further details of the product.

- Name: SEARCH_SCREEN

  This screen displays the results of a search. Searching the catalog is integral part of the application, and a search interface is displayed as part of every page. When the customer requests a search, the results are shown using the search screen. This screen is similar to the CATEGORY_SCREEN in that it displays a master view of the list of products that result from a search.

- Name: PRODUCT_SCREEN

  This screen displays information about a particular product. Each product can be offered for sale in several configurations. We call each of these an *item*. This screen lists inventory status for each item offered. The customer can click on any item in inventory to see further details about it.

- Name: PRODUCT_DETAILS_SCREEN

  This screen displays detailed information about a particular product item, including a description of the item and its image and the number of items in the inventory. It also provides an Add button. Clicking this button adds the product currently being shown to the shopping cart and displays the resulting shopping cart.

- Name: CART_SCREEN

  This screen displays the contents of the customer's shopping cart. For each item in the shopping cart, it includes a brief description of the item and its quantity. The customer can change the quantity of each item and delete items from the cart. This screen includes an update button to update the cart according to the changes made by the customer. It also has a checkout button. Clicking the checkout button initiates the process of placing an order.

- Name: CHECKOUT_SCREEN

  This screen displays the final unmodifiable contents of the customer's shopping cart once again and asks the customer to confirm everything before placing the order. A customer confirms the order by clicking the place order button.

- Name: PLACEORDER_SCREEN

  This screen displays a form where the customer can fill in details necessary to place the order. A customer places the order by clicking the submit button.

- Name: COMMIT_ORDER_SCREEN

  This screen displays the receipt after an order has been confirmed and committed. It shows a unique order identifier so that the customer can track the order later on. It also shows a complete list of items ordered, the total price and shipping charges if any, as well as shipping and billing information.

- Name: SIGNIN_SCREEN

  This screen displays a customer name and password, allowing the customer to sign into the application. The submit button initiates the signin process.

- Name: SIGNUP_SCREEN

  This screen displays a form allowing a new customer to sign up and register themselves with the application. Once registered the customer can conveniently recall personal information each time they place an order.

This completes the initial set of screens that are presented to the customer during the course of a shopping interaction with the application. As the application evolves, more screens may be added and existing screens modified.

10.3.1.2   Graphical Design

Since we already identified the major screens in the application and the data that needs to be shown as part of each screen, we can now involve graphic design and HTML specialists to create the layout, look, and feel of each of the screens.

There are two parts to this design: design of the custom content of each screen and design of a common template which remains consistent with each of the screens. The preceding scenarios have identified the data that needs to go into each of the screens as well as the dynamic portions of the template.

The artist needs an idea of the size and shape of each of the data element that needs to be shown in each of the screens. They can make good progress with the graphical design at this point using storyboarding techniques, even without an actual implementation of the rest of the application available to them. This is one major advantage of decoupling the design of the user interface from the rest of the application.

The *contract* with the graphic design artists is just how the application makes the model *data* required for each screen available to the screen. As we shall see later in this section, this is where the JavaServer Pages technology comes into play.

10.3.2   JSP Pages

The JSP pages provided by the pet store application use a generic template mechanism and application-specific JavaBeans components. This section describes the template mechanism and discusses several example JSP pages. The JavaBeans components are discussed in Section 10.5 on page 278. General guidelines on how to use JSP technology can be found in Chapter 4.

10.3.2.1   A Template Mechanism

While sketching out the shopping interaction interface of the application, it is clear that there are elements that we want to be part of each screen. Some of these are:

- The application logo and tag line.

- The search interface with a search text field and a search button.

- A help button to get information about the application.

- A show shopping cart button that provides immediate access to the shopping cart from any screen.

- A signin/signout status button that changes state based on whether the customer is signed in. If they are signed in, they are presented with a sign out button. If they are not signed in, they see a sign in button.

- Copyright notices and miscellaneous status information at the bottom of each page.

Among the elements that change on each page are the body and the title. Other elements, such as keywords and meta-headers, may also change with each screen as well.

To add headers and footers to every JSP page, the designer could create header and footer JSP files and have each JSP page include these at appropriate places. Such a technique is illustrated in Code Example 10.1.

```
<%@ include file="header.jsp" %>
    ...
    content of this screen
    ...
<%@ include file="footer.jsp" %>
```

Code Example 10.1   Templating Using JSP Include Statements

However, this approach runs into several limitations if we try to make the template more elaborate, using HTML tables, side bar, and so on. The header and footer files would have to be constructed and formatted properly to make sure the body appears where intended. For instance, correct HTML requires opening HTML tags in the header and a closing HTML tag in the footer so that the body can be enclosed between them. This requires either hand-coded HTML or specialized authoring tools to ensure correct design and correct HTML. The problem becomes compounded if we want more than just one contiguous chunk of HTML to change on each screen. For instance, each screen might want to provide its own HTML title as well as custom content. These features require a more flexible screen layout mechanism.

A template mechanism provides a way to separate the common elements that are part of each screen from the elements that change with each screen. Putting all the common elements together into one file makes it easier to maintain and enforce a consistent look and feel in all the screens. It also makes development of individual screens easier since the designer can focus on portions of a screen that are specific to that screen while the template takes care of the rest.

This section reviews the design and implementation of the sample application's screen template mechanism. The concept of a presentation template can be applied to almost any Web application in one form or another. The sample application's template mechanism is designed so that you can easily adapt it to other applications.

The template itself is a JSP page, with place holders for the parts that need to change with each screen. Each of these place holders is referred to as a *parameter* of the template. For example, a simple template could include a title text parameter for the top of the generated screen and a body parameter to refer to a JSP page for the custom content of the screen.

Once you have a template, you can generate different presentation screens from it simply by passing it different parameters. This process is called *instantiation* of the template. A specific screen is completely characterized by identifying the template page, and the parameters to pass to the template. The set of parameters that completely defines a screen is called a *screen definition.* While a large application could use multiple templates; the pet store application uses a single template for all its screens. However, the mechanism it uses is designed to support multiple templates.

From the templating mechanism's point of view a *screen* is the instantiation of a template according to its screen definition. Figure 10.3 illustrates the relationship between a template, a screen definition, and the resulting presentation screen.

Figure 10.3 Defining a Screen in Terms of a Template and Its Parameters

Code Example 10.2 shows the contents of template.jsp, the template file used in the sample application.

```
<%@ page errorPage="errorpage.jsp" %>
<%@ page import="com.sun.estore.control.Web.ScreenNames" %>
<%@ taglib uri="WEB-INF/tlds/taglib.tld" prefix="j2ee" %>
<%@ include file="ScreenDefinitions.jsp" %>
<HTML >
    <head>
        <title>
            <j2ee:insert template="template"
                parameter="HTML Title" />
        </title>
    </head>
    <body bgcolor="white">
        <j2ee:insert template="template" parameter="HTML Banner" />
        <j2ee:insert template="template"
```

```
            parameter="HTML TopIndex" />
        <j2ee:insert template="template" parameter="HTML Body" />
    </body>
</HTML >
```

Code Example 10.2 `template.jsp`

The template is instantiated by forwarding to or dynamically including the `template.jsp` page. Forwarding is performed using the `jsp:forward` standard action or by calling the `forward` method of a `RequestDispatcher`; inclusion is performed using an `include` directive or standard action or by calling the `include` method of a `RequestDispatcher`.

An appropriate screen definition must be set up in the request scope before invoking `template.jsp`. JSP pages can access objects in request, session, and application scopes. Since a screen is presented in the context of a specific URL request from the user, the appropriate screen definition needs to be set in the request scope before the template file is invoked. The other possible JSP scopes, session and application, are broader—they're more appropriate for setting general site and user-specific portions of the template.

The following examples show how `template.jsp` works. It uses the `j2ee:insert` custom tag to identify place holders in the template. This tag is responsible for extracting the screen definition from the request scope and inserting it into the page. Code Example 10.3 contains the implementation of the `insert` tag.

```
public class InsertTag extends TagSupport {
    private boolean directInclude = false;
    private String parameter = null;
    private String templateName = null;
    private Template template = null;
    private TemplateParameter templateParam = null;

    public void setTemplate(String templateName){
        this.templateName = templateName;
    }

    public void setParameter(String parameter){
        this.parameter = parameter;
```

```java
    }

    public int doStartTag() {
        try {
            if (templateName != null){
                template = (Template)pageContext.getRequest().
                            getAttribute("template");
            }
        } catch (NullPointerException e){
            ...
        }

        if (parameter != null && template != null)
            templateParam = (TemplateParameter)template.
                getParam(parameter);
        if (templateParam != null)
            directInclude = templateParam.isDirect();
        return SKIP_BODY;
    }

    public int doEndTag() throws JspTagException {
        try {
            pageContext.getOut().flush();
        } catch (Exception e){
            ...
        }
        try {
            if (directInclude && templateParam != null) {
                pageContext.getOut().
                    println(templateParam.getValue());
            } else if (templateParam != null)  {
                if (templateParam.getValue() != null)
                    pageContext.getRequest().
                        getRequestDispatcher(templateParam.
                            getValue()).include(pageContext.
                                getRequest(),
                                    pageContext.getResponse());
            }
        } catch (Throwable ex) {
```

```
                    ...
            }
            return EVAL_PAGE;
        }
    }
```

Code Example 10.3   Insert Tag Implementation

The insert tag gets values of the parameters passed to it. The parameters are automatically set by the JSP runtime environment and the tag focuses on inserting the appropriate parameters into the response. Parameters can be direct or indirect. Direct parameters are inserted as-is into the response stream. Indirect parameters are treated as the name of a JSP file, and that file is dynamically included into the response stream. This makes it possible to pass the title of a page as text using a direct parameter, and the body as the name of a JSP file to include using an indirect parameter.

10.3.2.2   View Selection

In a Web application, each screen presented to the user can be considered as a different view. However, unlike the classic MVC architecture, all these views share the same controller. There needs to be a mechanism that allows the controller to choose a particular view to render in response to a user request. In the sample application, the controller makes this selection by specifying the screen ID of the screen to present as the response. This screen ID is mapped to a screen definition, then the template is instantiated.

Recall that the file template.jsp defines the template for the sample application. This file includes another file, ScreenDefinitions.jsp, which defines all the screens of the sample application. When the controller invokes the template file at request time, it sets the appropriate screen definition in the request scope. The template file passes this information to the screen definitions file which then returns the appropriate screen definition for the request.

One goal in structuring template and screen definition files is to facilitate internationalization (discussed in Section 4.5 on page 88). This is achieved by separating text content from Java code. Since screen definitions that contain direct and indirect parameters are candidates for internationalization, we want to keep ScreenDefinitions.jsp devoid of Java technology code. We achieve this through the use of JSP custom tags. Code Example 10.4 contains an excerpt from Screen-

`Definitions.jsp`, which uses `Screen` and `Parameter` custom tags to pass text and the contents of files to the response.

```
<%@ page import="com.sun.estore.control.Web.ScreenNames" %>
<jsp:useBean
  id="screenManager"
  class="com.sun.estore.control.Web.ScreenFlowManager"
  scope="session"/>

<j2ee:CreateTemplate template="template"
    screen="<%=screenManager.getCurrentScreen(request)%>">
    <j2ee:Screen screen="<%=ScreenNames.MAIN_SCREEN%>">
        <j2ee:Parameter parameter="HTML Title"
            value="Welcome to Java Pet Store Demo" direct="true"/>
        <j2ee:Parameter parameter="HTML Banner"
            value="/banner.jsp" direct="false"/>
        <j2ee:Parameter parameter="HTML Body"
            value="/index.jsp" direct="false"/>
    </j2ee:Screen>
    <j2ee:Screen screen="<%=ScreenNames.SIGN_IN_SUCCESS_SCREEN%>">
        . . .
    </j2ee:Screen>
    . . .
</j2ee:CreateTemplate>
```

Code Example 10.4 `ScreenDefinitions.jsp`

When it is included at request time by the template file, `ScreenDefinitions.jsp` uses `ScreenFlowManager`, a component of the controller, to identify the view that the controller wishes to select. The nested custom tags arrange for that screen's definition to be set into the request scope when this file invoked.

In summary, the JSP pages `template.jsp` and `ScreenDefinitions.jsp` work together to create the page viewed by the user. Figure 10.4 depicts the process of view selection and instantiation in the sample application.

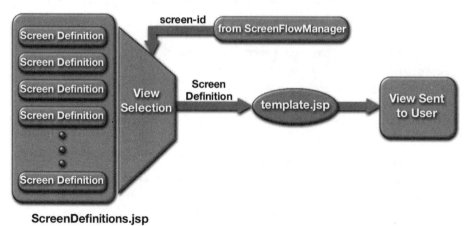

Figure 10.4   View Selection and Instantiation

10.3.3   Examples

For the most part, the sample application's presentation JSP pages use fairly straightforward JSP elements. This section examines three example presentation JSP pages: the home screen page (`index.jsp`), the products-by-category page (`productcategory.jsp`), and the shopping cart page (`cart.jsp`).

10.3.3.1   Home Screen

The home screen of the Java Pet Store Demo application is shown in Figure 10.5.

The JSP source used to generate the screen, contained in the file `index.jsp`, appears in Code Example 10.5. The screen is composed of the banner that appears in all the Java Pet Store Demo screens, a list of the product categories (`sideindex.jsp`) supported by the application, and an imagemap (`splash.jsp`) of the categories. The banner does not appear explicitly, because it is constructed by the template described in Section 10.3.2.1 on page 259.

Figure 10.5 Home Screen

```
<table border="0"  cellspacing="0" width="600" >
  <tr>
    <td>
      <%@ include file="sideindex.jsp"%>
    </td>
    <td bgcolor="white" height="300">
      <%@ include file="splash.jsp" %>
    </td>
  </tr>
</table>
</HTML >
```

Code Example 10.5 `index.jsp`

10.3.3.2 Product Category Screen

The screen that lists all the products in a category is shown in Figure 10.6.

The JSP source used to generate the screen, contained in the file `productcategory.jsp`, appears in Code Example 10.6. In this code sample, the first statement sets the `catalog` variable to point to an instance of the JavaBeans component `CatalogWebImpl`. This component is used to retrieve the catalog entries for a particular product category. The category is retrieved from the implicit `request` object with the `getParameter("category_id")` method. Once the category and its products are retrieved, JSP scriptlets are used to generate the table of products.

Figure 10.6 Product Category Screen

```
<jsp:useBean
  id="catalog"
  type="com.sun.estore.catalog.model.CatalogModel"
  class="com.sun.estore.catalog.web.CatalogWebImpl"
  scope="application"/>


<%
String key = request.getParameter("category_id");
Category category = null;
if (key != null)  category = catalog.getCategory(key);
if (category != null) {
    Collection products = null;
    products = catalog.getProducts(key, 0, 20);
%>
<p>
<font size="5" color="green"><%= category.getDescription()%></font>
<p>

<table border="0" bgcolor="#336666">
<tr background="../images/bkg-topbar.gif">
    <th><font color="white" size="3">Category ID</font></th>
```

```
        <th><font color="white" size="3">Category Name</font></th>
    </tr>

    <%
        Iterator it = null;
        if (products != null) it =products.iterator();
        while (it.hasNext()) {
            Product product = (Product)it.next();
    %>
        <tr bgcolor="#eeebcc">
        <td><%= product.getId() %></td>
        <td>
            <a href="product?product_id=<%= product.getId() %>">
            <%= product.getName()%></a>
        </td>
        </tr>

    <% } %>
    </table>
    <%
        } else {
        // Category was not found:
    %>
    <p>
    <font size="5" color="red">Unable to Locate Category ID <%= key
    %></font>

    <% } %>
```

Code Example 10.6 `productcategory.jsp`

10.3.3.3 Shopping Cart Screen

The screen that displays the contents of a user's shopping cart is shown in Figure 10.7.

The JSP source used to generate the screen, contained in the file `cart.jsp`, appears in Code Example 10.7 and Code Example 10.8. In this code sample, the first statement sets the `cart` variable to point to an instance of the JavaBeans component `ShoppingCartWebImpl`. This component is used by the shopping cart table.

The include statement towards the middle of the code sample (begins with "<%@ include") causes the page to include the shopping cart table (illustrated in Code Example 10.8). The page also contains a button that accepts a modification to the shopping cart, and a link to a checkout page.

Figure 10.7   Shopping Cart Screen

```
<jsp:useBean
    id="cart"
    class="com.sun.estore.cart.Web.ShoppingCartWebImpl"
    scope="session"
<%
    cart.init(session);
%>
</jsp:useBean>
<p>
<%
  if (cart.getSize() > 0) {
%>

<font size="5" color="black">Shopping Cart:</font>
<p>
  <form action="cart">
  <input type="hidden" name="action" value="updateCart">
  <table bgcolor="white">
    <tr>
      <td>
        <%@ include file="changeable_carttable.jsp" %>
```

```
      </td>
      <td>
        <input type="image" border="0" src="../images/cart-up-
date.gif" name="update">
      </td>
    </tr>
  </table>
  </form>
  <a href="checkout"><img src="../images/button_checkout.gif"
alt="Proceed To Checkout" border="0"></a>

<%
  } else {
  // The cart is empty
%>

  <font size="5" color="red">Shopping Cart is empty.</font>
<% } %>
```

Code Example 10.7 `cart.jsp`

Code Example 10.8 uses JSP scripting capabilities to display all the rows in the shopping cart. The page retrieves shopping cart items from the `cart` component set by the enclosing page `cart.jsp`. The page also includes a button that allows a user to delete an item from the shopping cart.

```
<table bgcolor="#336666">

  <tr background="../images/bkg-topbar.gif" border="0">
  <th><!-- for the remove column --></th>
  <th><font size="3" color="white">Item ID</font></th>
  <th><font size="3" color="white">Product Name</font></th>
  <th><font size="3" color="white">In Stock</font></th>
  <th><font size="3" color="white">Unit Price</font></th>
  <th><font size="3" color="white">Quantity</font></th>
  <th><font size="3" color="white">Total Cost</font></th>
  </tr>
```

```
<%--
% Loop through each item in the shopping cart.  The current item is
% available to the jsp block within the loop as "item"
--%>

<%
  Iterator it = cart.getItems();
  while ((it != null) && it.hasNext()) {
    CartItem item = (CartItem)it.next();
%>

<tr bgcolor="#eeebcc">
<td>
    <a href="cart?action=removeItem&itemId=<%=item.get-
ItemId()%>"><img src="../images/button_remove.gif" border="0"
alt="Remove Item From Shopping Cart">
    </a>
</td>

<td><%= item.getItemId() %></td>
<td>
    <a href="productdetails?item_id=<%=item.getItemId()%>">
    <%=item.getAttribute()%> <%=item.getName()%>
    </a>
</td>

<td><%=(inventory.getInventory(item.getItemId())
    >= item.getQuantity()) ? "yes" : "Back Ordered"%></td>
<td><%=JSPUtil.formatCurrency(item.getUnitCost())%></td>
<td><input name="itemQuantity_<%=item.getItemId()%>"
    type="text"
    size="4"
    value="<%=item.getQuantity()%>">
</td>
<td><%=JSPUtil.formatCurrency(item.getTotalCost())%></td>
</tr>

<% } // end for loop %>
```

```
<tr background="../images/bkg-topbar.gif">
    <td></td>
    <td><font size="3" color="white">Total:</font></td>
    <td></td>
    <td></td>
    <td></td>
    <td></td>
    <td><font size="3" color="white">
        <%=JSPUtil.formatCurrency(cart.getTotalCost())%>
        </font></td>
</tr>
</table>
```

Code Example 10.8 `changeable_carttable.jsp`

10.4   The Model

In this section we focus our attention on the state that needs to be maintained by the application. One can think of the back-end of an application as a collection of state with some rules on how the state changes in response to user interactions. This section explains how the sample application maintains state in the J2EE platform and persistent data in database tables.

10.4.1   State in the J2EE Platform

Typically, the customer will use a number of features of the pet store during a single visit (such as requesting product information and placing items in a shopping cart), resulting in numerous requests during the client session. While the application does not need to store this information in a database, this information must be somehow tracked to maintain a meaningful dialog between the customer and the application.

There is state associated with both the user interface and the business logic. In general, the sample application must maintain the following state:

- The user identity: Typically, the user account module maintains the user identify, which includes the user's login ID and certain security credentials.

- The search cursor and catalog position: The catalog module maintains the cursor's position within the current search and within the catalog hierarchy.

- The items in the shopping cart: The shopping cart module maintains the list of items placed in the customer's shopping cart.

- Order information: When the customer confirms the order, the shopping cart passes this information the order information—billing address, shipping address, and payment method—to the order management module, which eventually stores it to a database.

The J2EE platform provides several choices for storing the application state. An application can store state in the Web tier using the state maintenance capabilities of servlets, which include the HTTPSession and ServletContext objects as well as JavaBeans components. In the EJB tier, state can be maintained using enterprise beans. Also, session state for an application can be divided between these tiers. The decision of where each object representing application state is stored depends on the lifetime and scope of the object. The following sections identify each state component, its lifetime requirements, and discuss why it should be stored using a particular mechanism.

The Web tier maintains state required by JSP pages in JavaBeans components. These JavaBeans components are managed by a class called ModelManager that uses both an HttpSession and a ServletContext to maintain handles to the JavaBeans components. ModelManager is discussed further in Section 10.6.8.1 on page 294. Beans that are specific to a client are maintained by an HTTP session object. Beans that can be shared by all clients are maintained as an attribute of the servlet generated from Main.jsp.

The JavaBeans components contain copies of the state maintained by corresponding model objects which are maintained in the EJB tier. When designing objects in the EJB tier to maintain state, the developer must answer two questions:

- What is the appropriate granularity for the objects? Not every business object should be modelled as an enterprise bean. Since every method call to an enterprise bean is potentially a remote call, the overhead of an inter-component call is likely to be prohibitive for interactions with fine-grained objects. Therefore, the sample application makes extensive use of helper objects, which are non-remote, serializable objects that mirror their respective enterprise beans.

- What type of enterprise bean should I use? An application can use either session beans or entity beans to maintain state. For a non-transactional object, a session bean is the simplest way to maintain session state for a short period of time because it leverages the EJB container's ability to manage session bean state. Using entity beans to maintain state provides transactional support for storing the state data in the database. While there is overhead in making the object transactional, the object reference could persist for as long as needed, even beyond the scope of a single session. For example, an object reference can be stored in a cookie on the browser to be retrieved and used even weeks later. The sample application has examples of using both session and entity beans to store session state.

10.4.1.1 Using Enterprise Beans to Maintain Session State

This section describes how different types of enterprise beans are used to represent objects in the sample application. General guidelines for how to use enterprise beans can be found in Chapter 5.

Stateless Session Beans

A stateless session bean does not contain state for a specific client. However, the instance variables of a stateless session bean can contain state across method calls. Examples of such state include an open database connection and a cache of data retrieved from that connection. Stateless session beans are never written out to secondary storage. As a consequence, stateless beans usually offer better performance than stateful beans.

The sample application uses stateless session beans for objects containing more than one database row. In particular, because stateless session beans provide high performance, stateless session beans are a good choice to provide a fast access to data derived from multiple database rows. In the pet store application, the Catalog stateless session bean functions as a cache that is built up over time.

Stateful Session Beans

A stateful session bean exists during a single client session and can maintain information specific to a client between invocations of methods. The sample application represents the contents of a client's shopping cart with the ShoppingCart stateful session bean.

Entity Beans

The sample application uses entity beans to provide an object view of individual rows in a database. The sample application includes three such beans, Account, Inventory, and Order, to represent individual rows in the corresponding tables.

10.4.1.2   Helper Objects

It is not appropriate to model all objects in the EJB tier as enterprise beans. Therefore, the sample application uses helper objects that are subordinate to their respective enterprise beans for a number of purposes. The different types of helper objects are: data access objects and value objects. The use of helper objects is discussed in detail in Section 5.5 on page 130.

Data Access Objects

A data access object is used to encapsulate access to databases. Data access objects can encapsulate access to more than one database, more than one table within one database, and different types of databases. The sample application uses data access objects for all these purposes.

The sample application uses the abstract data access class `OrderDAO` to access three tables, `order`, `orderstatus`, and `lineitem`, when an order is created, read, or updated. The sample application contains three subclasses, `OrderDAOOracle`, `OrderDAOSybase`, and `OrderDAOCS`, that are used to access Oracle, Sybase, and Cloudscape databases.

Value Objects

A value object is a business object that can be passed by value as a serializable Java object. A business concept should be implemented as a value object when it is fine-grained, dependent, and immutable. The sample application uses two types of value objects: dependent objects and details objects.

An object is a dependent object of another object if its life cycle is completely managed by that object and if it can only be accessed indirectly through that object. Examples of dependent objects in the sample application are `Address` and `CreditCard`.

A value object can also be used to encapsulate an entire remote object. Such objects allow a client to retrieve the value of a remote object in one remote call. The sample application contains details objects for each enterprise bean. Code Example 10.9 illustrates an account entity bean and its corresponding details object. In keeping with its purpose, `AccountModel`'s methods only enable retrieval of the values in the fields of its bean, while `Account` itself provides a method for setting a value and a coarse-grained method (`getDetails`) that returns an `AccountModel`.

```
public interface Account extends EJBObject {
    public AccountModel getDetails() throws RemoteException;
    public void changeContactInformation(ContactInformation info)
        throws RemoteException;
}

public class AccountModel implements java.io.Serializable {
    private String userId;
    private String status;
    private ContactInformation info;
    ...
    public String getUserId() {
        return userId;
    }
    public ContactInformation getContactInformation() {
        return info;
    }
    ...
}
```

Code Example 10.9 Account and AccountModel

10.4.2   Persistent Data

The sample application maintains persistent data in database tables, organized according to the functional areas of the application. Figure 10.8 illustrates the database schema.

The application uses this database schema to maintain accounts and track orders for products. Thus, there are three areas for which data must be maintained: product, account, and order information. The product, category, and item tables represent the business's product catalog. Each item has an associated entry in the inventory table that represents the inventory for that product. The account table maintains customer account information, one record per customer, with information such as customer name, password, and customer address. Finally, there is an orders table with one record per order, for information such as ship-to address, bill-to address, total price of the order, and payment (credit card name, expiration date, type) information. The orders table is linked to lineitem and orderstatus tables. Each item in an order is stored in a separate lineitem record, which contains the quantity ordered and price and a separate `orderstatus` record, which contains a reference to the item and the status of the order.

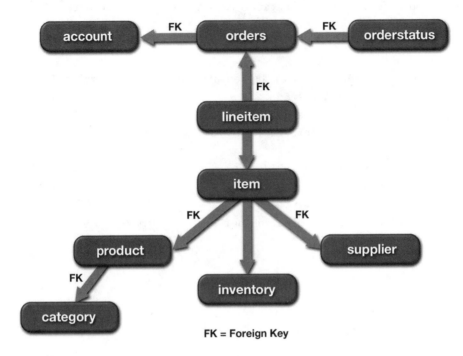

Figure 10.8   Database Tables and Relationships

10.5   Implementation

In the implementation of the view, JSP pages rely on JavaBeans components to mirror model data. These components are named *ESObject*WebImpl (where *ESObject* are the e-store objects Inventory, Account, Cart, and Order). As Code Example 10.10 illustrates, *ESObject*WebImpl extends *ESObject*Model and implements a listener interface so that views can be notified of changes to their corresponding models. For example, when an AccountWebImpl is created, it adds itself to the list of listeners interested in updates to the account model. When an account model changes, the manager of the view objects invokes the performUpdate method on all views that have registered as listeners of the account model. See Section 10.6.8 on page 294 for further discussion of model-view synchronization.

```java
public class AccountWebImpl extends AccountModel
                        implements ModelUpdateListener {
    private ModelManager mm;
    private Account acctEjb;

    public AccountWebImpl(ModelManager mm) {
        super(null, null, null);
        this.mm = mm;
        mm.addListener(JNDINames.ACCOUNT_EJBHOME, this);
    }


    public void performUpdate() {
            if (acctEjb == null) {
            acctEjb = mm.getAccountEJB();
        }
        try {
            if (acctEjb != null) copy(acctEjb.getDetails());
        } catch (RemoteException re) {
            throw new GeneralFailureException(re);
        }
    }
}
```

Code Example 10.10 AccountWebImpl

The model is implemented by enterprise beans named *ESObject*. These beans are supported by data access classes named *ESObject*DAO and details classes named *ESObject*Model. As described in "Value Objects" on page 276, a client can retrieve the contents of an enterprise bean with one remote call that returns a details object.

JavaBeans components and details classes share aspects of their implementation (that is, the *ESObject*Model classes), because the *ESObject*Model classes capture the essential information required to represent e-store business objects in any tier.

The implementation of the catalog does not follow the pattern just described because it implemented in both a Web-centric and EJB-centric fashion. The Web-centric design is used for high performance since the catalog is read-only and the most frequently accessed object in the system. Thus the Web-centric JavaBeans component `CatalogWebImpl` accesses the data access class `CatalogDAO` directly instead of calling an enterprise bean.

Since the shopping cart enterprise bean needs access to the catalog and cannot access the Web-tier catalog it uses a catalog enterprise bean. Note that high performance is not as crucial in this case as compared to the earlier case but access to the catalog is still read-only.

The implementation of the catalog functionality is essentially the same in both cases, so both `CatalogWebImpl` and `CatalogEJB` extend `CatalogImpl` which implements the `CatalogModel` interface.

The relationships between the sample application business objects—view classes in the Web tier, model classes (and their respective helper classes) in the EJB tier, and database tables in the enterprise information system tier—are shown in Figure 10.9.

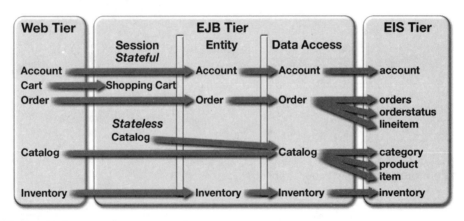

Figure 10.9 Sample Application Business Objects

10.6   The Controller

The sample application must reflect the state of a user's interaction with the application and the current values of persistent data in the user interface. Following the MVC architecture, this functionality is implemented within the controller. In the sample application, the controller is split between the Web tier and the EJB tier. In this section we will discuss the implementation of the controller for the shopping interaction in the sample application.

The controller is responsible for coordinating the model and view. As described in Section 10.2 on page 248, the view depends on the controller for screen selection. The model depends on the controller for making state changes to the model. The controller must accept user gestures from the view, translate them into business events based on the behavior of the application, and process these events. The processing of an event involves invoking methods of the model to cause the desired state changes. Finally, the controller selects the screen shown in response to the request that was processed.

Since the controller must coordinate both the view and the data, it straddles the Web and EJB tiers. Some components of the controller are hosted by the Web tier and facilitate communication with the view, while others are hosted by the EJB tier and control the model.

In the Web tier, the controller consists of several components:

- `Main.jsp` receives and processes HTTP requests. `Main.jsp` calls `ScreenFlow-Manager`, which is responsible for selecting the next screen to be shown to the client after the completion of the current request.

- `RequestProcessor` provides the glue in the Web tier for holding the application components together. It contains logic that needs to be executed for each request. `RequestProcessor` collaborates with two classes:

  - `RequestToEventProcessor` translates HTTP requests into business events that the rest of the application can operate on. Events are represented by the class `eStoreEvent` and its subclasses `CatalogEvent`, `LoginEvent`, `AccountEvent`, `CartEvent`, and `OrderEvent`.

  - `ShoppingClientControllerWebImpl` (SCCWI) provides a Web-tier proxy for `ShoppingClientController`. It delegates all methods to its EJB tier counterpart.

In the EJB tier, the controller is `ShoppingClientController` (SCC), which provides the view with read-only access to the model and handles business events. `ShoppingClientController` collaborates with `StateMachine`, an object that controls the creation and removal of enterprise beans and handles events to modify those objects passed to it by the controller in the Web tier.

Figure 10.10 illustrates the interactions that occur between the collaborating controller objects when an HTTP request is handled. The servlet generated from `Main.jsp` receives all HTTP requests. It passes the request to `RequestProcessor`, which coordinates all handling of the request. `RequestProcessor` uses `RequestToEventTranslator` to translate the HTTP request into a business event. `RequestProcessor` then passes the event to `ShoppingClientControllerWebImpl`, which forwards the event to `ShoppingClientController`, the controller in the EJB tier. `ShoppingClientController` delegates the handling of the business event to `StateMachine`. `StateMachine` changes the state of the model in response to the business event or command and then retrieves a list of model objects that have changed as a result of handling the business event from `ModelUpdateManager` (`MUM`). Finally, `RequestProcessor` notifies all registered views of model changes.

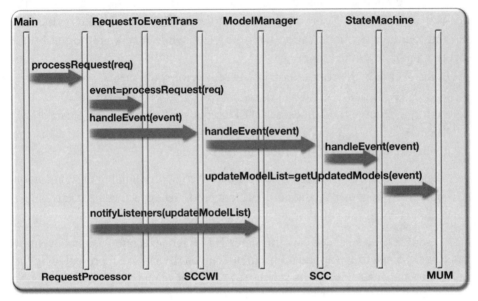

Figure 10.10 Controller Object Interaction Diagram (Part 1)

Figure 10.11 shows what happens after `RequestProcessor.processRequest` returns. `Main.jsp` forwards the initial request to `template.jsp`. The template includes `ScreenDefinitions.jsp`, which uses `ScreenFlowManager` to map the screen to a JSP page.

In the following sections, we will discuss the implementation of each of these components in more detail.

10.6.1   Main

A front component is a component to which all requests for application URLs are delivered. The front component `Main.jsp`, processes these requests and delegates the generation of the response to the template page.

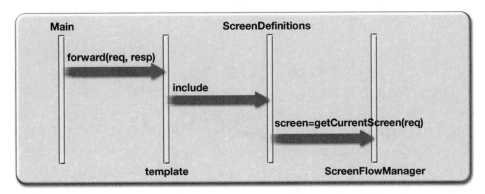

Figure 10.11 Controller Object Interaction Diagram (Part 2)

Code Example 10.11 shows `Main.jsp`. The highlighted lines in the example indicate these two steps. `Main.jsp` delegates all of the request processing tasks to `RequestProcessor`. The response is generated by forwarding to `template.jsp`. An interesting detail to note here is that `Main.jsp` stores references to the request processor and other session-specific beans in the HTTP session object.

```
<jsp:useBean id="modelManager"
    class="com.sun.estore.control.Web.ModelManager"
    scope="session">
    <% modelManager.init(config.getServletContext(), session); %>
</jsp:useBean>

<jsp:useBean id="rp"
    class="com.sun.estore.control.Web.RequestProcessor"
    scope="session">
    <% rp.init(config.getServletContext(), session); %>
</jsp:useBean>

<%
try {
        rp.processRequest(request);
        request.setAttribute("selectedURL" , request.getPathInfo());
    } catch (MissingFormDataException mi){
        request.setAttribute("missingformdata", mi);
        request.setAttribute("selectedURL", "/missingformdata");
```

```
        } catch (DuplicateAccountException du){
            request.setAttribute("selectedURL", "/duplicateaccount");
        }




    getServletConfig().getServletContext()
        .getRequestDispatcher("/template.jsp")
            .forward(request, response);
%>
```

Code Example 10.11 Main.jsp

10.6.2   RequestProcessor

RequestProcessor contains logic that gets executed for each request. For example, when a customer tries to access a feature that requires signin, RequestProcessor checks to detect whether the customer is logged in.

Code Example 10.12 presents an excerpt from RequestProcessor, simplified to illustrate the key aspects of its behavior.

```
public class RequestProcessor {
    private ShoppingClientControllerWebImpl scc;
    private ModelManager mm;
    private ModelUpdateNotifier mun;
    private RequestToEventTranslator eventTranslator;
    private SecurityAdapter securityAdapter;
    public void init(...) {
        mm = (ModelManager)session.getAttribute("modelManager");
        mun = mm;
        scc = new ShoppingClientControllerWebImpl(session);
        eventTranslator =
            new RequestToEventTranslator(this, mm);
        ...
    }
    public void processRequest(HttpServletRequest req) {
        checkForWebServerLogin(req);
        EStoreEvent event = eventTranslator.processRequest(req);
        if (event != null) {
```

```
                    Collection updatedModelList = scc.handleEvent(event);
                    mun.notifyListeners(updatedModelList);
                }
                ...
            }
        }
```

Code Example 10.12 `RequestProcessor`

This excerpt demonstrates the core responsibilities of `RequestProcessor` including:

- Initializing the client session. `RequestProcessor` instantiates an object that implements `ShoppingClientController` and related application objects when a new session is initiated.

- Detecting when the user logs into the server using form-based authentication and generating a login business event when this happens.

- Computing the business event to generate based on the `HttpRequest` that came in, with the help of the `RequestToEventTranslator`.

- Raising a business event by invoking `handleEvent` on the `ShoppingClientController`'s Web implementation.

- Gathering the outcome of the event processing. In particular, `RequestProcessor` passes the business event and its outcome to the `ModelManager` so the model change notifications can be processed by the view components (see Section 10.6.8 on page 294).

10.6.3   RequestToEventTranslator

`RequestToEventTranslator` is responsible for taking an HTTP-specific request and converting it into a business event that is not tied to the specifics of the HTTP protocol.

Application objects that include HTTP-specific functionality are not easy to reuse. By removing HTTP protocol-specific details from the request as early as possible, by turning it into a business event, the sample application ensures that all components that deal with business events would be completely reusable with non-HTTP clients. For example, the `StateMachine` that implements command processing logic for the sample application could be easily used as-is by a stand-alone Java client.

The two standard HTTP requests that can be processed by the translator are GET and POST. It is relatively straightforward to map GET requests to business events. However, POST requests, which represent form submission in the sample application, require the request processor to validate the form data as part of generating the business event. The processor needs to keep track of the values entered in the form so that the presentation screen can show where the error occurred when the form data is invalid. When the form data is valid, the processor must encapsulate the form parameters in an application-specific business event.

Code Example 10.13 presents excerpts from RequestToEventTranslator. The highlighted lines indicate where the translator parses HTTP request parameters and converts them to objects to be used in business events.

```java
public class RequestToEventTranslator {
    private ModelManager mm;
    public EStoreEvent processRequest(HttpServletRequest req)
        throws EStoreEventException,  MissingFormDataException {
        String selectedUrl = req.getPathInfo();
        EStoreEvent event = null;
        if (selectedUrl.equals(ScreenNames.CATALOG_URL)) {
            event = createCatalogEvent(req);
        else if (selectedUrl.equals(ScreenNames.CART_URL)) {
            mm.getCartModel();
            event = createCartEvent(req);
        } else if ...
        return event;
    }


    private EStoreEvent createCatalogEvent(HttpServletRequest req) {
        CatalogEvent event = null;
        String[] category = req.getParameterValues(CATEGORY_ID );
        if (category != null) {
            event = new CatalogEvent(
                CatalogEvent.BROWSING_EVENT, category[0]);
        }
        return event;
    }
```

```
    private CartEvent createCartEvent(HttpServletRequest request) {
        String action = request.getParameter("action");
        if (action.equals("purchaseItem")) {
            return createPurchaseItemEvent(request);
        } else if (action.equals("removeItem")) {
            return createRemoveItemEvent(request);
        } else if (action.equals("updateCart")) {
            return createUpdateCartEvent(request);
        }
    }
}
```

Code Example 10.13 RequestToEventTranslator

10.6.4 ShoppingClientControllerWebImpl

ShoppingClientControllerWebImpl is a proxy object that calls methods on the EJB
tier controller ShoppingClientController. ShoppingClientControllerWebImpl
exposes a read-only interface to the model, so that the view can render the model
as needed. Keeping this interface read-only minimizes dependencies between the
view and the model, to prevent inadvertent modification of the model by the view
outside the scope of the business rules encapsulated in the application.

Code Example 10.14 contains an excerpt from ShoppingClientController-
WebImpl. Notice that all the methods of ShoppingClientController are synchro-
nized so that concurrent requests to ShoppingClientController are serialized.
This is done because an EJB container will throw an exception if a request is made
to a session bean while it is servicing another request.

```
public class ShoppingClientControllerWebImpl
{
    private com....ejb.ShoppingClientController sccEjb;
    private HttpSession session;
    public ShoppingClientControllerWebImpl(HttpSession session) {
        this.session = session;
        ModelManager mm =
            (ModelManager)session.getAttribute("modelManager");
        sccEjb = mm.getSCCEJB();
    }
    public synchronized AccountModel getAccount() {
```

```
        return sccEjb.getAccount().getDetails();
    }
    ...
    public synchronized Collection handleEvent(EStoreEvent ese) {
        return sccEjb.handleEvent(ese);
    }
    public synchronized void remove() {
        sccEjb.remove();
    }
}
```

Code Example 10.14 ShoppingClientControllerWebImpl

10.6.5   ShoppingClientController

ShoppingClientController manages the life cycle of model objects such as the shopping cart and account enterprise beans and processes business events. It delegates the processing of business events in the handleEvent method to StateMachine. ShoppingClientController is also responsible for the life cycle of StateMachine. ShoppingClientController is implemented by ShoppingClientControllerEJB, illustrated in Code Example 10.15.

```
public class ShoppingClientControllerEJB implements SessionBean {
    private StateMachine sm;
    private ShoppingCart cart;
    String userId;
    Account acct;

    public Account getAccount() {
        if (acct == null) {
            createAccountEJB();
        }
        return acct;
    }

    public ShoppingCart getShoppingCart() {
        if (cart == null) {
            try {
                ShoppingCartHome cartHome =
```

```
                    EJBUtil.getShoppingCartHome();
                cart = cartHome.create();
            } catch (CreateException ce) {
                throw new EJBException(ce);
            }
        }
        return cart;
    }
    public void ejbCreate() {
        sm = new StateMachine(this);
    }
    public Collection getOrders() throws FinderException {
        Collection orders = null;
        if (userId != null) {
            OrderHome home = EJBUtil.getOrderHome();
            orders = home.findUserOrders(userId);
        }
        return orders;
    }
    public Collection handleEvent(EStoreEvent ese)
        throws EStoreEventException {
        try {
            return (sm.handleEvent(ese));
        } catch (RemoteException re) {
            throw new EJBException (re);
        }
    }
}
```

Code Example 10.15 `ShoppingClientControllerEJB`

10.6.6   StateMachine

`StateMachine` implements the core command processing business logic of the application. It is responsible for changing the state of the models in response to a business event or command. `StateMachine` consists of methods that handle each of the different business events that the sample application can respond to. One such method is highlighted in Code Example 10.16.

```java
public class StateMachine {
    private ShoppingClientControllerEJB sccejb;
    private ModelUpdateManager mum;
    private HashMap orderTable;
    public StateMachine(ShoppingClientControllerEJB sccejb) {
        this.sccejb = sccejb;
        this.mum = new ModelUpdateManager();
    }
    public Collection handleEvent(EStoreEvent ese)
        throws RemoteException, EStoreEventException {
        if (ese instanceof CartEvent) {
            handleCartEvent((CartEvent)ese);
        } else if (ese instanceof AccountEvent) {
            handleAccountEvent((AccountEvent)ese);
        } else if (ese instanceof OrderEvent) {
            handleOrderEvent((OrderEvent)ese);
        } else if (ese instanceof LoginEvent) {
            login((LoginEvent)ese);
        } else if (ese instanceof LogoutEvent) {
            logout();
        }
        return (mum.getUpdatedModels(ese));
    }
    private void handleCartEvent(CartEvent ce)
        throws RemoteException {
        ShoppingCart cart = sccejb.getShoppingCart();
        switch (ce.getActionType()) {
            ...
            case CartEvent.UPDATE_ITEM :{
                Collection itemIds = ce.getItemIds();
                Iterator it = itemIds.iterator();
                while (it.hasNext()){
                    String itemId = (String)it.next();
                    int quantity = ce.getItemQty(itemId);
                    if (quantity > 0){
                        cart.updateItemQty(itemId, quantity);
                    } else {
                        cart.deleteItem(itemId);
                    }
```

```
                    }
                }
            break;
        }
    }
    ...
}
```

Code Example 10.16 `StateMachine`

`StateMachine` has both read and write access to all of the model objects so that it can coordinate event processing across multiple model objects. For example, when `StateMachine` handles an order event, it interacts with the inventory bean to debit the quantity of the purchased item, the order bean to insert the order details, and the mailer bean to send confirmation email to the user. These functions are performed by the method illustrated in Code Example 10.17. Highlighted lines indicate where enterprise beans are retrieved or created.

```
private Order createOrder(OrderEvent oe) throws RemoteException {
    ShoppingCart cart = sccejb.getShoppingCart();
    Order order = null;
    String userId = sccejb.getAccount().getDetails().getUserId();
    try {
        InventoryHome inventHome = EJBUtil.getInventoryHome();
        Iterator ci = ((ShoppingCartModel)cart.getDetails()).
            getItems();
        ArrayList lineItems = new ArrayList();
        int lineNo = 0;
        double total = 0;
        while (ci.hasNext()) {
            lineNo++;
            CartItem cartItem = (CartItem) ci.next();
            LineItem li = new LineItem(cartItem.getItemId(),
                cartItem.getQuantity(),cartItem.getUnitCost(),
                lineNo);
            lineItems.add(li);
            total += cartItem.getUnitCost() * cartItem.getQuantity();
        }
```

```
            for (Iterator it = lineItems.iterator(); it.hasNext();){
                LineItem LI = (LineItem)it.next();
                Inventory inventRef =
                    inventHome.findByPrimaryKey(LI.getItemNo());
                inventRef.updateQuantity(LI.getQty());
            }

            OrderHome home = EJBUtil.getOrderHome();
                order = home.create(lineItems,
                    oe.getShippingAddress(),
                    oe.getBillingAddress(),
                    ...
                    total);

    // put the requestId and the orderId in a table to match up later
            if (orderTable == null) orderTable = new HashMap();
            orderTable.put(oe.getRequestId() + "",
                order.getDetails().getOrderId() +"");

            // empty shopping cart      .
            cart.empty();

            if (JNDIUtil.sendConfirmationMail()) {
                // send order confirmation mail.
                Mailer mailer = EJBUtil.createMailerEJB();
                mailer.sendOrderConfirmationMail(order.getDetails().
                    getOrderId());
            }
        } catch (DuplicateKeyException dke) {
            ...
        } catch (CreateException ce) {
            throw new EJBException(ce);
        } catch (FinderException fe) {
            throw new EJBException(fe);
        }
```

```
        return order;
    }
```

Code Example 10.17 `StateMachine.createOrder`

10.6.7   ScreenFlowManager

`ScreenFlowManager` is responsible for selecting a screen to present to the user as the outcome of their request. The mapping from a requested URL to a response screen is not one to one. In fact, the response that depends not only on the request itself, but also on the state of the application data model and the outcome of request processing within the application. In other words, the flow manager keeps a state machine that captures the flow of screens in the application. `ScreenFlowManager` looks at the request and the state of the model and computes the screen to be returned.

Code Example 10.18 shows how `ScreenFlowManager` maps many of the request URLs directly into response screens. For some of the requests, such as the `VALIDATE_BILLING_INFO_URL`, the code inspects the model to decide which of two possible screens to present.

```
public class ScreenFlowManager {

    public int getCurrentScreen(HttpServletRequest req)  {
        String selectedUrl =
            (String)req.getAttribute("selectedURL");
        int nextScreen = ScreenNames.DEFAULT_SCREEN;
        if (selectedUrl == null) {
            // do nothing. show the default screen.

        } else if (selectedUrl.equals(ScreenNames.CATALOG_URL)) {
            nextScreen = ScreenNames.CATALOG_SCREEN;

            ...

        } else if (selectedUrl.equals(
                ScreenNames.VALIDATE_BILLING_INFORMATION_URL)) {
            if (req.getSession()
                .getAttribute("shippingAddressRequired") != null) {
                boolean addrReqd = req.getSession()
                    .getAttribute("addrReqd").equals("true");
                if (addrReqd)
```

```
                                nextScreen = ScreenNames.ENTER_SHIPPING_INFO;
                        else
                                nextScreen = ScreenNames.CONFIRM_SHIPPING_INFO;
                }
        }


        return nextScreen;
    }
}
```

Code Example 10.18 ScreenFlowManager

10.6.8   Model-View Synchronization

Following the MVC architecture, views implemented by JSP pages and JavaBeans components present data owned by their associated models implemented as enterprise beans. In the sample application, each Web-tier JavaBeans component serves as the view, with corresponding EJB-tier classes representing the model. Whenever a model changes, it notifies interested views so that the views can update its presentation of the model.

In the sample application, the notification process is managed by ModelUpdateManager and ModelManager. ModelUpdateManager is responsible for converting a business event, such as AccountEvent, to a list of names of models that have changed due to this event. ModelManager uses this list to notify all views that have registered interest in the changed models to fetch the models' data.

The functions of ModelManager and ModelUpdateManager and their interactions with controller objects are described in the following sections.

10.6.8.1   Model Manager

ModelManager extends ModelUpdateNotifier, which provides methods for adding listeners of model change events and causing listeners (that is, views) to perform an update when a change event is received. ModelManager adds methods that create and return instances of view classes.

Code Example 10.19 presents excerpts from ModelManager. Note that Model-Manager maintains references to both a ServletContext and an HttpSession. These objects in turn contain references to view objects (highlighted in the example). View objects specific to a client (for example, AccountModel) are maintained by an HTTP session object. View objects that can be shared by all clients (for example, CatalogModel) are maintained as an attribute of the servlet generated from Main.jsp.

```
public class ModelManager extends ModelUpdateNotifier {
    private ServletContext context;
    private HttpSession session;
    private ShoppingClientController sccEjb = null;
    private ShoppingCart cartEjb = null;
    private Account acctEjb = null;

    public void init(ServletContext context,
        HttpSession session) {
        this.session = session;
        this.context = context;
        getAccountModel();
    }

    public CatalogModel getCatalogModel() {
        CatalogModel catalog = (CatalogModel)
            context.getAttribute(WebKeys.CatalogModelKey);
        if (catalog == null) {
            catalog = new CatalogWebImpl();
            context.setAttribute(WebKeys.CatalogModelKey, catalog);
        }
        return catalog;
    }

    public AccountModel getAccountModel() {
        AccountModel acct = (AccountModel)
            session.getAttribute(WebKeys.AccountModelKey);
        if (acct == null) {
            acct = new AccountWebImpl(this);
            session.setAttribute(WebKeys.AccountModelKey, acct);
        }
        return acct;
    }
```

```
        ...
    }
```

Code Example 10.19 `ModelManager`

10.6.8.2   ModelUpdateManager

`ModelUpdateManager` is responsible for converting an `EStore` event to a list of names of models that have changed due to this event. Code Example 10.20 presents excerpts from `ModelUpdateManager`.

```java
public class ModelUpdateManager {
    ...
    public Collection getUpdatedModels(EStoreEvent ese)
        throws RemoteException {
        ArrayList modelList = new ArrayList();

        if (ese instanceof CartEvent) {
            modelList.add(JNDINames.CART_EJBHOME);
        } else if (ese instanceof AccountEvent) {
            modelList.add(JNDINames.ACCOUNT_EJBHOME);
        } else if (ese instanceof OrderEvent) {
            modelList.add(JNDINames.ORDER_EJBHOME);
            modelList.add(JNDINames.INVENTORY_EJBHOME);
            modelList.add(JNDINames.CART_EJBHOME);
        } else if (ese instanceof LoginEvent) {
            modelList.add(JNDINames.ACCOUNT_EJBHOME);
        }
        return modelList;
    }
}
```

Code Example 10.20 `ModelUpdateManager`

10.7   MVC Summary

Figure 10.12 summarizes the references between the view, model, and controller classes.

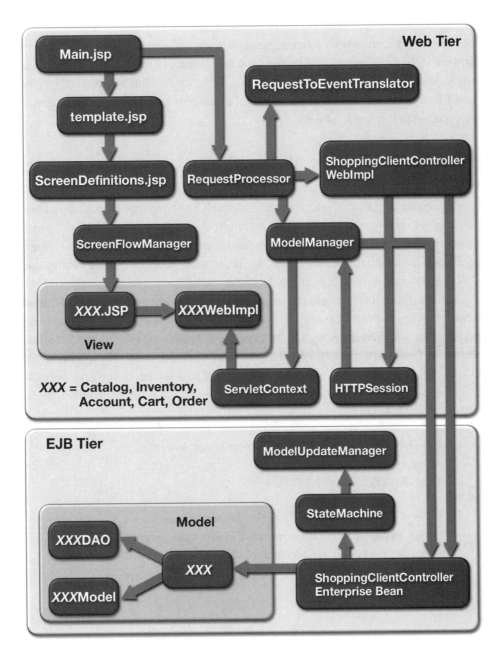

Figure 10.12 Object Reference Diagram

10.8   Stateless Services

The sample application uses stateless session beans for shared service objects. For example, in an e-commerce application, you might want to send order confirmation mail to customers on successful completion of an order. Such a service can be shared by all clients of the application. The sample application `Mailer` service objects are stateless session beans.

10.8.1   Example: A Mailer Bean

When a client places an order, an order event is passed to `ShoppingClientControl-ler`. Although the `handleEvent` method is defined by `ShoppingClientController`, `ShoppingClientController` delegates its implementation to a helper class named `StateMachine`. `StateMachine` interacts with `Inventory`, `Order`, and `Mailer` enterprise beans to debit the quantity of the purchased item, insert the order details, and finally send the confirmation email to the client.

The last thing that `StateMachine` does in the `createOrder` method is to send an order confirmation message. It does this by first creating `Mailer` stateless session bean and then invoking the `Mailer.sendOrderConfirmationMail` method (shown in Code Example 10.21). This `method` uses the order ID to obtain the information needed for the confirmation message from the `Order` and `Account` entity beans. The `Mailer` then invokes the `createAndSendMail` method of its helper class `MailHelper`.

```
public void sendOrderConfirmationMail(int orderId)
    throws RemoteException {
    OrderDetails orderDetails = null;
    try {
    OrderHome orderHome = EJBUtil.getOrderHome();
    Order order = orderHome.findByPrimaryKey(orderId);
    orderDetails = order.getOrderDetails();
    } catch (FinderException fe) {
        ...
        return;
    }
    String userId = orderDetails.getUserId();
    AccountDetails acctDetails = null;
    try {
        AccountHome acctHome = EJBUtil.getAccountHome();
```

```
        Account acct = acctHome.findByPrimaryKey(userId);
        acctDetails = acct.getAccountDetails();
    } catch (FinderException fe) {
        ...
    }
    String subject = "Your order# "+orderId;
    String HTML Contents =
        "This message is a confirmation of your order# "
        + orderId + ". Please save it for your records.";
    getMailHelper().createAndSendMail(acctDetails.
        getEmail(), subject, HTML Contents);
}
```

Code Example 10.21 `Mailer.sendOrderConfirmationMail`

Code Example 10.22 illustrates the `createAndSendMail` method of `Mail-Helper`. This method looks up a mail session in the JNDI namespace, creates a MIME message, sets the mail headers, collects the contents of the message into a string, and then sends the message.

```
public void createAndSendMail(String to,
    String subject, String HTML Contents) {

    try {
        InitialContext ic = new InitialContext();
        Session session = (Session) ic.
            lookup(JNDI Names.MAIL_SESSION);

        // construct the message
        Message msg = new MimeMessage(session);
        msg.setFrom();
        msg.setRecipients(Message.RecipientType.TO,
                            InternetAddress.parse(to, false));
        msg.setSubject(subject);
        collect(subject, htmlContents, msg);
        msg.setHeader("X-Mailer", "JavaMailer");
        msg.setSentDate(new Date());
        // send the message
        Transport.send(msg);
```

```
        } catch (Exception e) {
                ...
        }
    }
```

Code Example 10.22 `MailHelper.createAndSendMail`

10.9   Deployment

Much of the behavior of the sample application is determined by information specified in its deployment descriptors: `estore_ejb.xml`, `estore_ejbruntime.xml`, `estore_war.xml`, and `estore_warruntime.xml`. Elements specified in these deployment descriptors are discussed in detail in Section 7.1 on page 165 and Section 7.3 on page 174.

10.10   Transactions

The sample application's persistent data is stored in two databases: `eStoreDataSource` and `InventoryDataSource`. The `eStoreDataSource` database holds information about accounts and orders. The `InventoryDataSource` database holds information about products, product categories, and the inventory of each product. When an order is placed, `ShoppingClientController` must access both databases. The sample application uses J2EE SDK support for distributed transactions to reduce the inventory of ordered products and add a new entry to the order table in an atomic operation. Note that a J2EE product is not required to support access to multiple JDBC databases within a single transaction. However, some J2EE products might choose to provide these extra transactional capabilities.

Recall that `ShoppingClientController` delegates the implementation of order processing to a helper class named `StateMachine`. `StateMachine` is responsible for maintaining consistency among the database tables represented by the enterprise beans that it calls. When `StateMachine` handles an order event it invokes the method `createOrder` illustrated in Code Example 10.17. For each bean, `StateMachine` gets a reference to the home interface and then creates an instance of the bean. `StateMachine` loops through the list of items in the order, finds the appropriate inventory item, and updates the `inventory` table for that item. Simply creating an instance of the `Order` bean causes an entry to be added to the `order`, `lineitem`, and `orderstatus` tables.

Note that neither the `StateMachine.createOrder` nor individual bean operations explicitly invoke transactions, because `ShoppingClientController` uses container-managed transactions. As a result, all database operations invoked by `ShoppingClientController` are automatically wrapped in a transaction by the container. The transaction context is automatically propagated to any enterprise beans that `ShoppingClientController` invokes (in this case `Inventory` and `Order`).

10.11 Security

This section describes the sample application's security requirements and discusses the ways these requirements are addressed using the J2EE security framework.

10.11.1 Requirements

The pet store application is designed to be deployed on the Internet. Like many Web-based e-commerce applications, it allows anyone to interact with and use the application. Any user, regardless of whether they're a registered customer, can point a browser at the start URL of the application and browse through the catalog, viewing items, prices, inventory status, and so on. We call this *tire kicking*, and this class of users *tirekickers*.

A new customer can *sign up* using a form presented by the application. Once a customer has signed up, the customer can *sign in*, by providing a user name and password to the application. Only customers who have signed in are allowed to place orders and view order status. When an order is placed, the payment details, including the credit card number, must be transmitted in a secure manner.

Some users of the pet store application may receive special treatment. For example, a frequent shopper may a *preferred customer*, able to receive discounts or awards not available to normal customer. Another class of special user might be system administrators, with unlimited access to information on the site. For example, they might be able to fetch a list of all orders placed after a certain date.

These high-level functional requirements translate into the following security requirements:

- **User Authentication**

    Users of the pet store application can be either authenticated or unauthenticated. The user must be authenticated to access a protected resource. The application should be able to identify, differentiate, and be able to make access control decisions based on this distinction.

    There should be a way to associate each authenticated user with one or more categories. For example, user A could be recognized as a customer, while user B could be recognized as a preferred customer.

- **Authorization**

    The application associates permissions with resources such as Web pages or enterprise bean methods. Examples of the kind of authorization constraints the application should allow:

    - Anyone (authenticated or not), to see the URL /control/product, or invoke the getProducts method of Catalog

    - All authenticated users to see the URL /control/placeorder

    - Only preferred users to see the URL /control/discounts

- **Confidentiality**

    Some user information, such as a credit card number, must be transmitted confidentially to the application.

- **User Administration**

    The sample application has its own set of users. This set of users grows when new users add themselves using a Web-based interface. Note that other applications, such as those developed for in-house use within an enterprise assume and use the set of users defined in the operational environment. The sample application does not depend on the operational environment to get its set of users.

10.11.2 Implementation

The pet store application uses many features of the J2EE platform to address its security requirements in a simple and transparent manner. By design, security in the J2EE platform is mostly declarative. In some places however, we make security decisions in our components programmatically, because we needed to make authorization decisions based on the content or state of the object.

10.11.2.1 User Authentication

A J2EE application must be capable of authenticating users that access the application from a variety of clients. This section describes how the pet store application authenticates users of the shopping interaction Web client, how it could authenticate users of an administration application client, and how it handles unauthenticated users.

Web Client Authentication

Most of the interactions with the sample application occur through the Web-based interface. Form-based authentication, one of the standard authentication mechanisms in the J2EE architecture, is used to authenticate these interactions.

In form-based authentication, a Web container designates an application-specific page containing an HTML form for logging in. The sample application uses the page `login.jsp` as this page. This page contains an HTML form that prompts for a user name and password and is displayed when the user tries to access a resource that has been designated as being protected. The sample application also uses form-based authentication to enable:

- Explicit signin

  The sample application allows users to explicitly sign in by clicking the sign-in link in the user interface. The sign-in link points to `/signin` which is a dummy URL that is inaccessible to unauthenticated users.

  When the user clicks sign-in, the application attempts to take them to the `signin.jsp` page, which is denied since the page is protected. As a result, the `login.jsp` form is shown instead.

  Note that we cannot simply make the sign-in link point to `login.jsp` because an authorization failure must occur for the form-based authentication mechanism to be activated.

- Informing the user about failed authentication

   The sample application retries the protected resource after authentication through form-based authentication irrespective of the outcome of authentication. If authentication failed, the login.jsp form will be shown to the user again. At this point, it is desirable to do two things: first, make sure that the form comes back already filled with the values that were posted in the last try, and second, inform the user somewhere in the form that authentication failed the first time.

   Form-based authentication does not provide a portable way to return the form to the user with the values posted in the failed try. The POST to the form is handled by the Web container, and never returned to the form.

   Informing the user that signon failed is easier to accomplish. To do so, the login.jsp page uses a session-scoped bean (see Code Example 10.23) stored each time the form is accessed. If this time is *close* to the current time, and the current request is unauthenticated, then the sample application prints a message indicating that the login failed earlier. A request to login.jsp would always be unauthenticated, unless there is an application programming error. The only situation where login.jsp is shown should be when the request is unauthenticated. Using a similar mechanism, it is also possible to go to an error page after a fixed number of retries.

```
<jsp:useBean id="last_login" class="...">
<% if (last_login.getTime() - currentTime < ... { %>
<font color="red">Login failed, try again<p></font>
<% } %>
```
Code Example 10.23 login.jsp

- Abandoning signin

   Sometimes the login.jsp page comes up because the user tried to access a protected resource. If the user does not have an account and needs to create one, the application should abandon the login process and start user signup instead.

   The pet store application's login.jsp page has an additional button called New User, to let new users sign up before they attempt to sign in.

   The J2EE platform maintains information about the state of the signin in the HttpSession and times it out when the login attempt is abandoned.

- Treating newly created users as signed in

  When a new user *signs up* they should be treated as *signed in* for the duration of that session. This is the case for the sample application, which manages its own set of users. However, in the J2EE architecture, this is not the case. The only way users can sign in is through form-based authentication. Since form-based authentication is not invoked when a user signs up, they still need to explicitly sign in in order to be treated as an authenticated user.

  The sample application uses a non-portable, private API provided by the J2EE SDK to achieve the desired results.

- Detecting user login

  The form-based authentication mechanism is designed to be transparent. However there are cases where we want to be aware of the *first* request that the user makes after they have signed in. For example, in the sample application, the fetching and caching of user profile information is triggered when the user logs in.

  Since the POST to the login form is processed by the platform, there is no direct way of doing this. We use the code shown in Code Example 10.24. RequestProcessor detects when the user logs in and fires a LoginEvent which can then be handled to get the desired effect.

```
private void checkForWebServerLogin(HttpServletRequest req) {
    if ((req.getUserPrincipal() != null) &&
        !req.getUserPrincipal().getName().equals("guest") &&
        !mm.getAccountModel().isLoggedIn()) {
            EStoreEvent loginEvent = null;
            loginEvent = eventTranslator.createLoginEvent(req);
    ...
```

Code Example 10.24 Triggering the Login Event

Let's look at the condition being tested. We first check if the principal is set on the current call. If it is, it means that some user is currently logged in. Next we check if our account bean knows about it. If accountBean.isLoggedIn returns false, it means that the account bean is not aware of the login yet. This is exactly the condition when we want to trigger the login event. Once the login event is processed, `account.isLoggedIn` would return true.

Application Client Authentication

In the J2EE platform, stand-alone clients are authenticated by an application client container. The application client may authenticate its user in a number of ways. The techniques used are platform-dependent and not under control of the application client. The application client container may integrate with the platform's authentication system, providing a single signon capability. The application client container may authenticate the user when the application is started. The application client container may use lazy authentication, only authenticating the user when it needs to access a protected resource. The J2EE specification does not describe the technique used to authenticate the user.

The J2EE SDK generates a client JAR file[1] when enterprise beans are deployed. This library contains stub classes for accessing enterprise beans as well as a mechanism provided by the J2EE SDK for handling authentication to an EJB server.

Handling Unauthenticated Users

The sample application allows for anonymous, unauthenticated users to access the application and browse selected features of the pet store. Even in such cases, calls to the EJB tier must specify a valid principal; the EJB container rejects all calls without a security principal. That is, if the user invokes a feature that tries to call the EJB tier without authentication, the EJB container will not let the call go through.

However, since the Web interface needs to support anonymous, unauthenticated users, the J2EE platform defines a mechanism to do so. The responsibility for ensuring that unauthenticated calls are made using some principal is delegated to the EJB *client* container. In the sample application, the Web container performs this role by:

- Associating the credentials of a *special* user called guest[2] to an unauthenticat-

---

[1]   This is specific to the J2EE SDK. Other J2EE products may provide other mechanisms to create client JAR files.

[2]   We call it guest here. It may be called different things in different implementations. The important thing to note however is that it is different from any valid user of the system and is treated specially at deployment.

ed user when an EJB method is invoked.

- Treating unauthenticated users as follows:

  - The `getUserPrincipal` method of the servlet API returns `null` for such users.

  - The form-based or other authentication mechanism will be activated when a protected Web resource is accessed.

10.11.2.2 Authorization

Sample application security is specified in terms of the security roles `customer` and `gold_customer`.

- A `customer` is a registered user of the application. Users in the `customer` role can place orders and complete purchases. In the current release of the sample application, the default user `j2ee` is in the `customer` role.

- A `gold_customer` is a customer with special privileges. Additional awards are available to them. In the current release of the sample application, all users that sign up are assigned to the `gold_customer` role.

By default, the J2EE SDK assigns the `ANYONE` role to an enterprise bean method. The `guest` user, which is anonymous and unauthenticated, is assigned to the `ANYONE` role.

In the sample application, access to the URLs `/control/signin` (described in Section 10.11.2.1 on page 303) and `/control/placeorder` is restricted to the roles `customer` and `gold_customer`. The `security-constraint` declaration for `/control/signin` is shown in Code Example 10.25.

```
<security-constraint>
    <web-resource-collection>
        ...
        <url-pattern>/control/signin</url-pattern>
        <http-method>POST</http-method>
        <http-method>GET</http-method>
    </web-resource-collection>
    <auth-constraint>
        <description>no description</description>
        <role-name>gold_customer</role-name>
```

```
        <role-name>customer</role-name>
    </auth-constraint>
    ...
</security-constraint>
```

Code Example 10.25 Security Constraint Declaration

In the current release, the sample application does not limit enterprise bean method invocation to specific security roles.

10.11.2.3 Confidentiality

Confidentiality constraints are specified at deployment time by setting the `transport-guarantee` element in the Web component's deployment descriptor to `CONFIDENTIAL`. In the current release, the sample application doesn't demonstrate confidentiality mechanisms.

10.11.2.4 User Administration

Many applications will need to perform two tasks that aren't handled by the J2EE platform: managing user profile information (other than security credentials and attributes) and adding new users to the system dynamically.

Maintaining User Profiles

In addition to keeping security credentials, the sample application needs other information about the user's preferences and personalization. The J2EE security framework will keep the security credentials, such as the user name and password, as well as attributes such as the set of roles that the user belongs to. The sample application needs another mechanism to maintain additional information for a user.

To do so, it maintains a separate relational table for user profile information. This table is called the `accounts` table, and is accessed through the `Account` enterprise bean. The user name is unique for each sample customer, and we use it as a key to the accounts database. Code Example 10.26 shows how the `getCallerPrincipal` method is used to retrieve the `userId` of the user making the current enterprise bean method call. The value returned from this method is used as a key to retrieve profile information for the user.

```
public Account getAccount() {
    if (acct == null) {
        try {
            String userId = sc.getCallerPrincipal().getName();
            AccountHome home = EJBUtil.getAccountHome();
            acct = home.findByPrimaryKey(userId);
        } catch (FinderException fe) {
            ...
        } catch (RemoteException re) {
            throw new EJBException (re);
        }
    }
    return acct;
}
```

Code Example 10.26 ShoppingClientControllerEJB.getAccount

Adding New Users

The J2EE platform does not standardize a mechanism to add users dynamically to applications. Any application that requires this feature needs to do so in a non-portable, container-specific manner.

In such a situation, it makes sense to isolate all the non-portable code in one place. This small piece of platform-specific code can later be replaced if the application needs to be ported to a different container implementation.

The J2EE SDK provides a container-specific API for managing users based on the concept of realms. A realm is a collection of users under the same authentication policy. An application can provide its own realm and plug it into the J2EE SDK for the container to use for authentication, or it can use realm API methods such addUser, on the existing default J2EE realm.

The sample application uses the default J2EE realm. It uses the addUser method of the realm to add new users while processing the signup.jsp form.

In addition to specifying the user name and password of the user being added, we also need to specify the roles that this new user can assume. This is achieved through the addUser method, which takes an array of roles as an argument.

10.11.2.5 Programmatic Security

The J2EE platform encourages the use of declarative security. However there are places where one needs to make access control decisions based on the current state of the system. Such decisions must be made by programmatically encoding their rules in the application.

The J2EE platform allows the application to identify the principal making the call as well as the role that the caller is in, in both the Web and EJB tiers. The sample application uses these facilities as follows.

Web Tier

In the Web tier, the sample application uses the `getUserPrincipal` and the `isUserInRole` methods as follows:

- `getUserPrincipal`: This method is used to get the ID of the user that connects to the application. This user ID could be used in the template to print the user ID in the banner as part of a welcome message. Another way that the sample application uses this information is to determine if a user is logged in. Code Example 10.24 illustrates this use.

- `isUserInRole`: In the current release, the sample application doesn't use this method. This method could be used in the template in order to show a different icon based on whether the user is a preferred or a regular customer. Additionally, there might be special items that we only show to preferred customers. Thus the catalog can be filtered based on the result returned from calling this method with the `gold_customer` role.

EJB Tier

In the EJB tier, the sample application uses `getCallerPrincipal` and `isCallerInRole` methods as follows:

- `getCallerPrincipal`: This method is used to get the caller key to be able to access profile information associated with the principal associated with the call.

- `isCallerInRole`: This method is used by the order processing module to enforce award rules based on whether the customer is a preferred customer. Code Example 10.27 illustrates the use of `isCallerInRole`.

```
private int getBonusMiles() {
    int miles = (totalPrice >= 100) ? 1000 : 500;
    if (context.isCallerInRole("GOLD_CUSTOMER"))
        miles += 1000;
    return miles;
}
```

Code Example 10.27 `OrderEJB.getBonusMiles`

Notice the use of the embedded role name GOLD_CUSTOMER. When role names
are embedded in the code, the Application Component Provider needs to identify
these roles in a deployment descriptor so that the Deployer can ensure that they
are mapped correctly when the application is deployed. Code Example 10.28
shows the portions of the sample application deployment descriptor where this
happens.

```
<security-role-ref>
    <role-name>GOLD_CUSTOMER</role-name>
    <role-link>gold_customer</role-link>
</security-role-ref>
...
<assembly-descriptor>
    <security-role>
        <role-name>gold_customer</role-name>
    </security-role>
    ...
</assembly-descriptor>
```

Code Example 10.28 Deployment Descriptor Element for Embedded Roles

In this excerpt from the deployment descriptor, the Application Component
Provider declares the use of GOLD_CUSTOMER in the application using the security-
role-ref element. The Deployer must ensure that this role is linked to the
gold_customer security role.

10.12 Summary

This chapter illustrates the J2EE programming model in the context of an in-depth description of a multitier Web application: the pet store e-commerce application.

The functionality of the sample application was determined using a scenario-driven approach. Walks through scenarios illustrated the requirements for the user interaction as well as the interactions that happen *within* the system. Analysis of the sample application identified three very different kinds of interactions: a shopping interface that allows shoppers to buy items online, an administration interface for carrying out store administration activities, and a business-to-business interface through which the store can interact with suppliers. The discussions in this chapter focused mainly on the shopping interactions.

The architecture of the sample application partitions its functionality into modules, assigns functionality to tiers, and decomposes the modules into specific objects to represent the behavior and data of the application. The principles guiding the architecture include reuse of software designs and code, separation of stable from volatile code, object decomposition along skill lines, and ease of migration from a Web-centric to EJB-centric model.

The sample application adapts the Model-View-Controller architecture to the domain of enterprise applications. The model represents the application data and the business rules that govern access and modification of this data. The view renders the contents of a model. It accesses data from the model and specifies how that data should be presented. The controller defines application behavior; it interprets user gestures and maps them into actions to be performed by the model. In a stand-alone GUI client, these user gestures could be button clicks or menu selections. In a Web application, they appear as GET and POST HTTP requests to the Web tier. Based on the user gesture and the outcome of the model commands, the controller selects a view to be rendered as part of the response to this user request.

The J2EE platform provides system services that simplify the work that application objects need to perform. The sample application uses the Java 2 SDK, Enterprise Edition support for distributed transactions across multiple JDBC databases. In addition, it uses deployment and security capabilities of the J2EE platform to support customers with different profiles.

Afterword

THIS book has presented an overview of application design and development with the Java 2 Platform, Enterprise Edition. It's goal has been to introduce enterprise developers to the concepts and technology used in designing applications for the J2EE platform, and to give a practical example of a typical enterprise application.

While this book explores many of the key decisions to be made in the application development process, it is necessarily limited in scope. The J2EE Blueprints program is intended to expand on this effort. Its goal is to provide developers using the J2EE platform with ongoing help in designing applications that best use the architecture and features of the platform.

The J2EE Blueprints program will include a Web site, additional publications in various venues, and ultimately, additional books in the Addison-Wesley Java Series. For the latest information on designing enterprise applications with the Java 2 Platform, Enterprise Edition, be sure to regularly check the J2EE Blueprints Web site at `http://java.sun.com/j2ee/blueprints`.

Your comments on this book and your requests for coverage of additional topics are important to the success of the J2EE Blueprints program. Please send your feedback to `j2eeblueprints-feedback@sun.com`.

Glossary

access control The methods by which interactions with resources are limited to collections of users or programs for the purpose of enforcing integrity, confidentiality, or availability constraints.

ACID The acronym for the four properties guaranteed by transactions: atomicity, consistency, isolation, and durability.

activation The process of transferring an enterprise bean from secondary storage to memory. (See **passivation**.)

applet A component that typically executes in a Web browser, but can execute in a variety of other applications or devices that support the applet programming model.

applet container A container that includes support for the applet programming model.

Application Component Provider A vendor that provides the Java classes that implement components' methods, JSP page definitions, and any required deployment descriptors.

Application Assembler A person that combines components and modules into deployable application units.

application client A first-tier client component that executes in its own Java virtual machine. Application clients have access to some (JNDI, JDBC, RMI-IIOP, JMS) J2EE platform APIs.

application client container A container that supports application client components.

application client module A software unit that consists of one or more classes and an application client deployment descriptor.

authentication The process by which an entity proves to another entity that it is acting on behalf of a specific identity. The J2EE platform requires three types of authentication: basic, form-based, and mutual, and supports digest authentication.

authorization See **access control**.

authorization constraint An authorization rule that determines who is permitted to access a Web resource collection.

basic authentication An authentication mechanism in which a Web server authenticates an entity with a user name and password obtained using the Web client's built-in authentication mechanism.

bean-managed persistence When the transfer of data between an entity bean instance's variables and the underlying resource manager is managed by the entity bean.

bean-managed transaction When an enterprise bean defines the boundaries of the transaction.

business logic The code that implements the functionality of an application. In the Enterprise JavaBeans model, this logic is implemented by the methods of an enterprise bean.

business method A method of an enterprise bean that implements the business logic or rules of an application.

callback methods Methods in a component called by the container to notify the component of important events in its life cycle.

caller Same as **caller principal**.

caller principal The principal that identifies the invoker of the enterprise bean method.

client certificate authentication An authentication mechanism in which a client uses a X.509 certificate to establish its identity.

commit The point in a transaction when all updates to any resources involved in the transaction are made permanent.

component An application-level software unit supported by a container. Components are configurable at deployment time. The J2EE platform defines four types of components: enterprise beans, Web components, applets, and application clients.

component contract The contract between a component and its container. The contract includes: life cycle management of the component, a context interface that the instance uses to obtain various information and services from its container, and a list of services that every container must provide for its components.

connection See **resource manager connection**.

connection factory See **resource manager connection factory**.

connector A standard extension mechanism for containers to provide connectivity to enterprise information systems. A connector is specific to an enterprise information system and consists of a resource adapter and application development tools for enterprise information system connectivity. The resource adapter is plugged in to a container through its support for system-level contracts defined in the connector architecture.

Connector architecture An architecture for integration of J2EE products with enterprise information systems. There are two parts to this architecture: a resource adapter provided by an enterprise information system vendor and the J2EE product that allows this resource adapter to plug in. This architecture defines a set of contracts that a resource adapter has to support to plug in to a J2EE product, for example, transactions, security, and resource management.

container An entity that provides life cycle management, security, deployment, and runtime services to components. Each type of container (EJB, Web, JSP, servlet, applet, and application client) also provides component-specific services.

container-managed persistence When transfer of data between an entity bean's variables and the underlying resource manager is managed by the enterprise bean's container.

container-managed transaction When an EJB container defines the boundaries of a transaction. An entity bean must use container-managed transactions.

context attribute An object bound into the context associated with a servlet.

conversational state The field values of a session bean plus the transitive closure of the objects reachable from the bean's fields. The transitive closure of a bean is defined in terms of the serialization protocol for the Java programming language, that is, the fields that would be stored by serializing the bean instance.

CORBA Common Object Request Broker Architecture. A language independent, distributed object model specified by the Object Management Group.

create method A method defined in the home interface and invoked by a client to create an enterprise bean.

credentials The information describing the security attributes of a principal.

CTS Compatibility Test Suite. A suite of compatibility tests for verifying that a J2EE product complies with the J2EE platform specification.

delegation An act whereby one principal authorizes another principal to use its identity or privileges with some restrictions.

Deployer A person who installs modules and J2EE applications into an operational environment.

deployment The process whereby software is installed into an operational environment.

deployment descriptor An XML file provided with each module and application that describes how they should be deployed. The deployment descriptor directs a deployment tool to deploy a module or application with specific container options and describes specific configuration requirements that a Deployer must resolve.

digest authentication An authentication mechanism in which a Web client authenticates to a Web server by sending the server a message digest along its HTTP request message. The digest is computed by employing a one-way hash algorithm to a concatenation of the HTTP request message and the client's password. The digest is typically much smaller than the HTTP request, and doesn't contain the password.

distributed application An application made up of distinct components running in separate runtime environments, usually on different platforms connected via a network. Typical distributed applications are two-tier (client-server), three-tier (client-middleware-server), and multitier (client-multiple middleware-multiple servers).

DOM Document Object Model. A tree of objects with interfaces for traversing the tree and writing an XML version of it, as defined by the W3C specification.

DTD Document Type Definition. A description of the structure and properties of a class of XML files.

EAR file A JAR archive that contains a J2EE application.

EJB™ See **Enterprise JavaBeans**.

EJB container A container that implements the EJB component contract of the J2EE architecture. This contract specifies a runtime environment for enterprise beans that includes security, concurrency, life cycle management, transaction, deployment, naming, and other services. An EJB container is provided by an EJB or J2EE server.

EJB Container Provider A vendor that supplies an EJB container.

EJB context An object that allows an enterprise bean to invoke services provided by the container and to obtain the information about the caller of a client-invoked method.

EJB home object An object that provides the life cycle operations (create, remove, find) for an enterprise bean. The class for the EJB home object is generated by the container's deployment tools. The EJB home object implements the enterprise bean's home interface. The client references an EJB home object to perform life cycle operations on an EJB object. The client uses JNDI to locate an EJB home object.

EJB JAR file A JAR archive that contains an EJB module.

EJB module A software unit that consists of one or more enterprise beans and an EJB deployment descriptor.

EJB object An object whose class implements the enterprise bean's remote interface. A client never references an enterprise bean instance directly; a client always references an EJB object. The class of an EJB object is generated by the container's deployment tools.

EJB server Software provides services to an EJB container. For example, an EJB container typically relies on a transaction manager that is part of the EJB server to perform the two-phase commit across all the participating resource managers. The J2EE architecture assumes that an EJB container is hosted by an EJB server from the same vendor, so does not specify the contract between these two entities. An EJB server may host one or more EJB containers.

EJB Server Provider A vendor that supplies an EJB server.

enterprise bean A component that implements a business task or business entity and resides in an EJB container; either an entity bean or a session bean.

enterprise information system The applications that comprise an enterprise's existing system for handling company-wide information. These applications provide an information infrastructure for an enterprise. An enterprise information system offers a well defined set of services to its clients. These services are exposed to clients as local and/or remote interfaces. Examples of enterprise information systems include: enterprise resource planning systems, mainframe transaction processing systems, and legacy database systems.

enterprise information system resource An entity that provides enterprise information system-specific functionality to its clients. Examples are: a record or set of records in a database system, a business object in an enterprise resource planning system, and a transaction program in a transaction processing system.

Enterprise Bean Provider An application programmer who produces enterprise bean classes, remote and home interfaces, and deployment descriptor files, and packages them in an EJB .jar file.

Enterprise JavaBeans™ (EJB™) A component architecture for the development and deployment of object-oriented, distributed, enterprise-level applications. Applications written using the Enterprise JavaBeans architecture are scalable, transactional, and secure.

entity bean An enterprise bean that represents persistent data maintained in a database. An entity bean can manage its own persistence or it can delegate this function to its container. An entity bean is identified by a primary key. If the container in which an entity bean is hosted crashes, the entity bean, its primary key, and any remote references survive the crash.

finder method A method defined in the home interface and invoked by a client to locate an entity bean.

form-based authentication An authentication mechanism in which a Web container provides an application-specific form for logging in.

group A collection of principals within a given security policy domain.

handle An object that identifies an enterprise bean. A client may serialize the handle, and then later deserialize it to obtain a reference to the enterprise bean.

home interface One of two interfaces for an enterprise bean. The home interface defines zero or more methods for creating and removing an enterprise bean. For session beans, the home interface defines create and remove methods, while for entity beans, the home interface defines create, finder, and remove methods.

home handle An object that can be used to obtain a reference of the home interface. A home handle can be serialized and written to stable storage and deserialized to obtain the reference.

HTML Hypertext Markup Language. A markup language for hypertext documents on the Internet. HTML enables the embedding of images, sounds, video streams, form fields, references to other objects with URLs and basic text formatting.

HTTP Hypertext Transfer Protocol. The Internet protocol used to fetch hypertext objects from remote hosts. HTTP messages consist of requests from client to server and responses from server to client.

HTTPS HTTP layered over the SSL protocol.

impersonation An act whereby one entity assumes the identity and privileges of another entity without restrictions and without any indication visible to the recipients of the impersonator's calls that delegation has taken place. Impersonation is a case of simple delegation.

IDL Interface Definition Language. A language used to define interfaces to remote CORBA objects. The interfaces are independent of operating systems and programming languages.

IIOP Internet Inter-ORB Protocol. A protocol used for communication between CORBA object request brokers.

initialization parameter A parameter that initializes the context associated with a servlet.

ISV Independent Software Vendor.

J2EE™ Java 2, Enterprise Edition.

J2ME™ Java 2, Micro Edition.

J2SE™ Java 2, Standard Edition.

J2EE application Any deployable unit of J2EE functionality. This can be a single module or a group of modules packaged into an .ear file with a J2EE application deployment descriptor. J2EE applications are typically engineered to be distributed across multiple computing tiers.

J2EE product An implementation that conforms to the J2EE platform specification.

J2EE Product Provider A vendor that supplies a J2EE product.

J2EE server The runtime portion of a J2EE product. A J2EE server provides Web and/or EJB containers.

JAR Java ARchive A platform-independent file format that permits many files to be aggregated into one file.

Java™ 2 Platform, Standard Edition (J2SE platform) The core Java technology platform.

Java™ 2 Platform, Enterprise Edition (J2EE platform) An environment for developing and deploying enterprise applications. The J2EE platform consists of a set of services, application programming interfaces (APIs), and protocols that provide the functionality for developing multitiered, Web-based applications.

Java™ 2 SDK, Enterprise Edition (J2EE SDK) Sun's implementation of the J2EE platform. This implementation provides an operational definition of the J2EE platform.

Java™ Message Service (JMS) An API for using enterprise messaging systems such as IBM MQ Series, TIBCO Rendezvous, and so on.

Java Naming and Directory Interface™ (JNDI) An API that provides naming and directory functionality.

Java™ Transaction API (JTA) An API that allows applications and J2EE servers to access transactions.

Java™ Transaction Service (JTS) Specifies the implementation of a transaction manager which supports JTA and implements the Java mapping of the OMG Object Transaction Service (OTS) 1.1 specification at the level below the API.

JavaBeans™ component A Java class that can be manipulated in a visual builder tool and composed into applications. A JavaBeans component must adhere to certain property and event interface conventions.

Java IDL A technology that provides CORBA interoperability and connectivity capabilities for the J2EE platform. These capabilities enable J2EE applications to invoke operations on remote network services using the OMG IDL and IIOP.

JavaMail™ An API for sending and receiving email.

JavaServer Pages™ (JSP) An extensible Web technology that uses template data, custom elements, scripting languages, and server-side Java objects to return dynamic content to a client. Typically the template data is HTML or XML elements, and in many cases the client is a Web browser.

JDBC™ An API for database-independent connectivity between the J2EE platform and a wide range of data sources.

JMS See **Java Message Service**.

JNDI See **Java Naming and Directory Interface**.

JSP See **JavaServer Pages**.

JSP action A JSP element that can act on implicit objects and other server-side objects or can define new scripting variables. Actions follow the XML syntax for elements with a start tag, a body and an end tag; if the body is empty it can also use the empty tag syntax. The tag must use a prefix.

JSP action, custom An action described in a portable manner by a tag library descriptor and a collection of Java classes and imported into a JSP page by a `taglib` directive. A custom action is invoked when a JSP page uses a *custom tag*.

JSP action, standard An action that is defined in the JSP specification and is always available to a JSP file without being imported.

JSP application A stand-alone Web application, written using the JavaServer Pages technology, that can contain JSP pages, servlets, HTML files, images, applets, and JavaBeans components.

JSP container A container that provides the same services as a servlet container and an engine that interprets and processes JSP pages into a servlet.

JSP container, distributed A JSP container that can run a Web application that is tagged as distributable and is spread across multiple Java virtual machines that might be running on different hosts.

JSP declaration A JSP scripting element that declares methods, variables, or both in a JSP file.

JSP directive A JSP element that gives an instruction to the JSP container and is interpreted at translation time.

JSP element A portion of a JSP page that is recognized by a JSP translator. An element can be a directive, an action, or a scripting element.

JSP expression A scripting element that contains a valid scripting language expression that is evaluated, converted to a String, and placed into the implicit out object.

JSP file A file that contains a JSP page. In the Servlet 2.2 specification, a JSP file must have a .jsp extension.

JSP page A text-based document using fixed template data and JSP elements that describes how to process a request to create a response.

JSP scripting element A JSP declaration, scriptlet, or expression, whose tag syntax is defined by the JSP specification, and whose content is written according to the scripting language used in the JSP page. The JSP specification describes the syntax and semantics for the case where the language page attribute is "java".

JSP scriptlet A JSP scripting element containing any code fragment that is valid in the scripting language used in the JSP page. The JSP specification describes what is a valid scriptlet for the case where the language page attribute is "java".

JSP tag A piece of text between a left angle bracket and a right angle bracket that is used in a JSP file as part of a JSP element. The tag is distinguishable as markup, as opposed to data, because it is surrounded by angle brackets.

JSP tag library A collection of custom tags identifying custom actions described via a tag library descriptor and Java classes.

JTA See **Java Transaction API**.

JTS See **Java Transaction Service**.

method permission An authorization rule that determines who is permitted to execute one or more enterprise bean methods.

module A software unit that consists of one or more J2EE components of the same container type and one deployment descriptor of that type. There are three types of modules: EJB, Web, and application client. Modules can be deployed as stand-alone units or assembled into an application.

mutual authentication An authentication mechanism employed by two parties for the purpose of proving each other's identity to one another.

ORB Object Request Broker. A library than enables CORBA objects to locate and communicate with one another.

OS principal A principal native to the operating system on which the J2EE platform is executing.

OTS Object Transaction Service. A definition of the interfaces that permit CORBA objects to participate in transactions.

naming context A set of associations between distinct, atomic people-friendly identifiers and objects.

naming environment A mechanism that allows a component to be customized without the need to access or change the component's source code. A container implements the component's naming environment, and provides it to the component as a JNDI naming context. Each component names and accesses its environment entries using the `java:comp/env` JNDI context. The environment entries are declaratively specified in the component's deployment descriptor.

passivation The process of transferring an enterprise bean from memory to secondary storage. (See **activation**.)

persistence The protocol for transferring the state of an entity bean between its instance variables and an underlying database.

POA Portable Object Adapter. A CORBA standard for building server-side applications that are portable across heterogeneous ORBs.

principal The identity assigned to an user as a result of authentication.

privilege A security attribute that does not have the property of uniqueness and that may be shared by many principals.

primary key An object that uniquely identifies an entity bean within a home.

realm See **security policy domain**. Also, a string, passed as part of an HTTP request during basic authentication, that defines a protection space. The protected resources on a server can be partitioned into a set of protection spaces, each with its own authentication scheme and/or authorization database.

re-entrant entity bean An entity bean that can handle multiple simultaneous, interleaved, or nested invocations which will not interfere with each other.

Reference Implementation See **Java 2 SDK, Enterprise Edition**.

remote interface One of two interfaces for an enterprise bean. The remote interface defines the business methods callable by a client.

remove method Method defined in the home interface and invoked by a client to destroy an enterprise bean.

resource adapter A system-level software driver that is used by an EJB container or an application client to connect to an enterprise information system. A resource adapter is typically specific to an enterprise information system. It is available as a library and is used within the address space of the server or client using it. A resource adapter plugs in to a container. The application components deployed on the container then use the client API (exposed by adapter) or tool generated high-level abstractions to access the underlying enterprise information system. The resource adapter and EJB container collaborate to provide the underlying mechanisms—transactions, security, and connection pooling—for connectivity to the enterprise information system.

resource manager Provides access to a set of shared resources. A resource manager participates in transactions that are externally controlled and coordinated by a transaction manager. A resource manager is typically in different address space or on a different machine from the clients that access it. Note: An enterprise information system is referred to as resource manager when it is mentioned in the context of resource and transaction management.

resource manager connection An object that represents a session with a resource manager.

resource manager connection factory An object used for creating a resource manager connection.

RMI Remote Method Invocation. A technology that allows an object running in one Java virtual machine to invoke methods on an object running in a different Java virtual machine.

RMI-IIOP A version of RMI implemented to use the CORBA IIOP protocol. RMI over IIOP provides interoperability with CORBA objects implemented in any language if all the remote interfaces are originally defined as RMI interfaces.

role (development) The function performed by a party in the development and deployment phases of an application developed using J2EE technology. The roles are: Application Component Provider, Application Assembler, Deployer, J2EE Product Provider, EJB Container Provider, EJB Server Provider, Web Container Provider, Web Server Provider, Tool Provider, and System Administrator.

role (security) An abstract logical grouping of users that is defined by the Application Assembler. When an application is deployed, the roles are mapped to security identities, such as principals or groups, in the operational environment.

role mapping The process of associating the groups and/or principals recognized by the container to security roles specified in the deployment descriptor. Security roles have to be mapped by the Deployer before the component is installed in the server.

rollback The point in a transaction when all updates to any resources involved in the transaction are reversed.

SAX Simple API for XML. An event-driven, serial-access mechanism for accessing XML documents.

security attributes A set of properties associated with a principal. Security attributes can be associated with a principal by an authentication protocol and/or by a J2EE Product Provider.

security constraint A declarative way to annotate the intended protection of Web content. A security constraint consists of a Web resource collection, an authorization constraint, and a user data constraint.

security context An object that encapsulates the shared state information regarding security between two entities.

security permission A mechanism, defined by J2SE, used by the J2EE platform to express the programming restrictions imposed on Application Component Providers.

security permission set The minimum set of security permissions that a J2EE Product Provider must provide for the execution of each component type.

security policy domain A scope over which security policies are defined and enforced by a security administrator. A security policy domain has a collection of users (or principals), uses a well defined authentication protocol(s) for authenticating users (or principals), and may have groups to simplify setting of security policies.

security role See **role (security)**.

security technology domain A scope over which the same security mechanism is used to enforce a security policy. Multiple security policy domains can exist within a single technology domain.

security view The set of security roles defined by the Application Assembler.

server principal The OS principal that the server is executing as.

servlet A Java program that extends the functionality of a Web server, generating dynamic content and interacting with Web clients using a request-response paradigm.

servlet container A container that provides the network services over which requests and responses are sent, decodes requests, and formats responses. All servlet containers must support HTTP as a protocol for requests and responses, but may also support additional request-response protocols such as HTTPS.

servlet container, distributed A servlet container that can run a Web application that is tagged as distributable and that executes across multiple Java virtual machines running on the same host or on different hosts.

servlet context An object that contains a servlet's view of the Web application within which the servlet is running. Using the context, a servlet can log events, obtain URL references to resources, and set and store attributes that other servlets in the context can use.

servlet mapping Defines an association between a URL pattern and a servlet. The mapping is used to map requests to servlets.

session An object used by a servlet to track a user's interaction with a Web application across multiple HTTP requests.

session bean An enterprise bean that is created by a client and that usually exists only for the duration of a single client-server session. A session bean performs operations, such as calculations or accessing a database, for the client. While a session bean may be transactional, it is not recoverable should a system crash occur. Session bean objects can be either stateless or they can maintain conversational state across methods and transactions. If a session bean maintains state, then the EJB container manages this state if the object must be removed from memory. However, the session bean object itself must manage its own persistent data.

SSL Secure Socket Layer. A security protocol that provides privacy over the Internet. The protocol allows client-server applications to communicate in a way that cannot be eavesdropped or tampered with. Servers are always authenticated and clients are optionally authenticated.

SQL Structured Query Language. The standardized relational database language for defining database objects and manipulating data.

SQL/J A set of standards that includes specifications for embedding SQL statements in methods in the Java programming language and specifications for calling Java static methods as SQL stored procedures and user-defined functions. An SQL checker can detects errors in static SQL statements at program development time, rather than at execution time as with a JDBC driver.

stateful session bean A session bean with a conversational state.

stateless session bean A session bean with no conversational state. All instances of a stateless session bean are identical.

System Administrator The person responsible for configuring and administering the enterprise's computers, networks, and software systems.

transaction An atomic unit of work that modifies data. A transaction encloses one or more program statements, all of which either complete or roll back. Transactions enable multiple users to access the same data concurrently.

transaction attribute A value specified in an enterprise bean's deployment descriptor that is used by the EJB container to control the transaction scope when the enterprise bean's methods are invoked. A transaction attribute can have the following values: `Required`, `RequiresNew`, `Supports`, `NotSupported`, `Mandatory`, `Never`.

transaction isolation level The degree to which the intermediate state of the data being modified by a transaction is visible to other concurrent transactions and data being modified by other transactions is visible to it.

transaction manager Provides the services and management functions required to support transaction demarcation, transactional resource management, synchronization, and transaction context propagation.

Tool Provider An organization or software vendor that provides tools used for the development, packaging, and deployment of J2EE applications.

URI Uniform Resource Identifier. A compact string of characters for identifying an abstract or physical resource. A URI is either a URL or a URN. URLs and URNs are concrete entities that actually exist; A URI is an abstract superclass.

URL Uniform Resource Locator. A standard for writing a textual reference to an arbitrary piece of data in the World Wide Web. A URL looks like "protocol:// host/localinfo" where "protocol" specifies a protocol for fetching the object (such as HTTP or FTP), "host" specifies the Internet name of the targeted host, and "localinfo" is a string (often a file name) passed to the protocol handler on the remote host.

URL path The URL passed by a HTTP request to invoke a servlet. The URL consists of the Context Path + Servlet Path + PathInfo, where Context Path is the path prefix associated with a servlet context that this servlet is a part of. If this context is the default context rooted at the base of the Web server's URL namespace, the path prefix will be an empty string. Otherwise, the path prefix starts with a / character but does not end with a / character. Servlet Path is the path section that directly corresponds to the mapping which activated this request. This path starts with a / character. PathInfo is the part of the request path that is not part of the Context Path or the Servlet Path.

URN Uniform Resource Name. A unique identifier that identifies an entity, but doesn't tell where it is located. A system can use a URN to look up an entity locally before trying to find it on the Web. It also allows the Web location to change, while still allowing the entity to be found.

user data constraint Indicates how data between a client and a Web container should be protected. The protection can be the prevention of tampering with the data or prevention of eavesdropping on the data.

WAR file A JAR archive that contains a Web module.

Web application An application written for the Internet, including those built with Java technologies such as JavaServer Pages and servlets, as well as those built with non-Java technologies such as CGI and Perl.

Web application, distributable A Web application that uses J2EE technology written so that it can be deployed in a Web container distributed across multiple Java virtual machines running on the same host or different hosts. The deployment descriptor for such an application uses the `distributable` element.

Web component A component that provides services in response to requests; either a servlet or a JSP page.

Web container An entity that implements the Web component contract of the J2EE architecture. This contract specifies a runtime environment for Web components that includes security, concurrency, life cycle management, transaction, deployment, and other services. A Web container provides the same services as a JSP container and a federated view of the J2EE platform APIs. A Web container is provided by a Web or J2EE server.

Web container, distributed A Web container that can run a Web application that is tagged as distributable and that executes across multiple Java virtual machines running on the same host or on different hosts.

Web Container Provider A vendor that supplies a Web container.

Web module A unit that consists of one or more Web components and a Web deployment descriptor.

Web resource collection A list of URL patterns and HTTP methods that describe a set of resources to be protected.

Web server Software that provides services to access the Internet, an intranet, or an extranet. A Web server hosts Web sites, provides support for HTTP and other protocols, and executes server-side programs (such as CGI scripts or servlets) that perform certain functions. In the J2EE architecture, a Web server provides services to a Web container. For example, a Web container typically relies on a Web server to provide HTTP message handling. The J2EE architecture assumes that a Web container is hosted by a Web server from the same vendor, so does not specify the contract between these two entities. A Web server may host one or more Web containers.

Web Server Provider A vendor that supplies a Web server.

XML eXtensible Markup Language. A markup language that allows you to define the tags (markup) needed to identify the data and text in XML documents. J2EE deployment descriptors are expressed in XML.

Index

The Java™ Series

The Java™ Programming Language
Third Edition

The Java Series

ISBN 0-201-70433-1

The Real-Time Specification for Java™

The Java Series

ISBN 0-201-70323-8

The Java™ Tutorial, Third Edition
A Short Course on the Basics

The Java Series

ISBN 0-201-70393-9

The Java™ Tutorial Continued
The Rest of the JDK™

The Java Series

ISBN 0-201-48558-3

The Java™ Developers ALMANAC 2000

The Java Series

ISBN 0-201-43299-4

ISBN 0-201-43297-8

The Java™ Class Libraries Second Edition, Volume 1
java.io java.lang java.math
java.net java.text java.util

The Java Series

ISBN 0-201-31002-3

The Java™ Class Libraries Second Edition, Volume 2
java.applet java.awt java.beans

The Java Series

ISBN 0-201-31003-1

The Java™ Class Libraries Second Edition, Volume 1
Supplement for the Java 2 Platform Standard Edition, v1.2

The Java Series

ISBN 0-201-48552-4

Java Card™ Technology for Smart Cards
Architecture and Programmer's Guide

The Java Series

ISBN 0-201-70329-7

Inside Java™ 2 Platform Security
Architecture, API Design, and Implementation

The Java Series

ISBN 0-201-31000-7

The Java™ Language Specification, Second Edition

The Java Series

ISBN 0-201-31008-2

The Java™ Application Programming Interface, Volume 1
Core Packages

The Java Series

ISBN 0-201-63453-8

The Java™ Application Programming Interface, Volume 2
Window Toolkit and Applets

The Java Series

ISBN 0-201-63459-7

The Java™ FAQ

ISBN 0-201-63456-2

Designing Enterprise Applications with the Java™ 2 Platform, Enterprise Edition

The Java Series, Enterprise Edition

ISBN 0-201-70277-0

Concurrent Programming in Java™ Second Edition
Design Principles and Patterns

The Java Series

ISBN 0-201-31009-0

JNDI API Tutorial and Reference
Building Directory-Enabled Java™ Applications

The Java Series

ISBN 0-201-70502-8

The Java™ Native Interface
Programmer's Guide and Specification

The Java Series

ISBN 0-201-32577-2

The Java™ Virtual Machine Specification Second Edition

The Java Series

ISBN 0-201-43294-3

Applying Enterprise JavaBeans
Component-Based Development for the J2EE Platform

The Java Series, Enterprise Edition

ISBN 0-201-702-673

Java™ 2 Platform, Enterprise Edition
Platform and Component Specifications

The Java Series, Enterprise Edition

ISBN 0-201-70456-0

The Java 3D™ API Specification, Second Edition

The Java Series

ISBN 0-201-71041-2

The JFC Swing Tutorial
A Guide to Constructing GUIs

The Java Series

ISBN 0-201-43321-4

JDBC™ API Tutorial and Reference, Second Edition
Universal Data Access for the Java™ 2 Platform

The Java Series

ISBN 0-201-43328-1

Java™ Platform Performance
Strategies and Tactics

The Java Series

ISBN 0-201-70969-4

Please see our web site (http://www.awl.com/cseng/javaseries)
for more information on these titles.

Register Your Book

at www.aw.com/cseng/register

You may be eligible to receive:

- Advance notice of forthcoming editions of the book
- Related book recommendations
- Chapter excerpts and supplements of forthcoming titles
- Information about special contests and promotions throughout the year
- Notices and reminders about author appearances, tradeshows, and online chats with special guests

Contact us

If you are interested in writing a book or reviewing manuscripts prior to publication, please write to us at:

Editorial Department
Addison-Wesley Professional
75 Arlington Street, Suite 300
Boston, MA 02116 USA
Email: AWPro@aw.com

Addison-Wesley

Visit us on the Web: http://www.aw.com/cseng